MR. HORNADAY'S WAR

Mr. Hornaday's War

*How a Peculiar Victorian Zookeeper
Waged a Lonely Crusade for Wildlife
That Changed the World*

Stefan Bechtel

BEACON PRESS, BOSTON

Beacon Press
25 Beacon Street
Boston, Massachusetts 02108-2892
www.beacon.org

Beacon Press books
are published under the auspices of
the Unitarian Universalist Association of Congregations.

15   14   13   12   8   7   6   5   4   3   2   1

This book is printed on acid-free paper that meets the uncoated paper
ANSI/NISO specifications for permanence as revised in 1992.

Text design and composition by Wilsted & Taylor Publishing Services

FRONTISPIECE: W. T. Hornaday in his office at New York Zoological Park, 1910.
Photo courtesy of the Library of Congress.

Library of Congress Cataloging-in-Publication Data
Bechtel, Stefan.
Mr. Hornaday's war : how a peculiar Victorian zookeeper waged a lonely
crusade for wildlife that changed the world / Stefan Bechtel.
    p. cm.
Includes bibliographical references and index.
ISBN 978-0-8070-0635-1 (acid-free paper) 1. Hornaday, William T.
(William Temple), 1854–1937. 2. Hornaday, William T. (William Temple),
1854–1937—Political and social views. 3. Wildlife conservationists—
United States—Biography. 4. Zoo keepers—United States—Biography.
5. Zoologists—United States—Biography. 6. Taxidermists—United States—
Biography. 7. Wildlife conservation—United States—History. 8. Wildlife
conservation—History. 9. Game protection—United States—History.
10. Game protection—History. I. Title. II. Title: Mister Hornaday's war.
QL31.H67B43 2012
590.92—dc23 [B]   2011048450

For my grandfather,

Earl S. Krom,

who taught me to love the woods.

CONTENTS

NOTE TO READER

This is a work of nonfiction. So far as possible, all assertions of fact in this book are supported by original source material, including William Temple Hornaday's private letters and papers, books (both published and unpublished), news clippings, and official documents. Dialogue that appears in direct quotations is taken from an account of the conversation by someone who was present (usually Hornaday). Dialogue that appears in italics is a reasonable reconstruction of conversations whose substance was described by someone who was there (for instance, Hornaday's description of his first meeting with Theodore Roosevelt). All errors of fact or inference, of course, are mine.

the dark river, she'd relented. That was his manner: blunt, aggressive, acquisitive. If he saw something or someone he liked, he just put his head down and went for it, like a country boy tackling a calf. Life was short, and those who hesitated lost.

His audacity, as well as his boundless love of the natural world, eventually carried him to some of the remotest places on the planet. He'd been one of the first white men to penetrate the interior of Borneo, voyaged up the Malay Archipelago not long after the young naturalist Alfred Russel Wallace had been so astounded by the profusion of life there that it had led to the theory of evolution he cofounded with Darwin, and hunted big game on the Indian sub-continent, the Amazon basin, Trinidad, the Everglades, the Canadian Rockies, and the Montana Territory. In the Everglades, he'd tried to grab an immense alligator by the tail. He'd stalked man-eating tigers on foot, nearly drowned, starved, perished of tropical fever, or other-wise died on multiple occasions, and told people he'd always felt more at home in a remote hunting camp than in any of the finest salons of New York.

Pugnacious, intrepid, and blessed with amazing physicial stamina, he had survived all manner of escapades and adventures, but now—and he found this difficult to admit—his long life had begun to catch up with him at last. Both his feet were crippled by a mysterious form of neuritis, which his doctors were struggling to overcome but which left him virtually unable to get around except with a walker. Now the old adventurer and naturalist spent a good deal of time in bed or in his chair, with a blanket over his lap. The pain was continuous, like a grinding noise.

"Tonight as I sit in the glow of my library fire,"[1] William Temple Hornaday began, "with a perfectly clear mind, and a memory for these events almost as good as new, I see the main features of the past years more sharply than contours of terrain are seen from an airplane." From these heights, his life looked like a Civil War battlefield, with smoking battlements, the clash of advancing infantry lines, strategic retreats, desperate regrouping, and dauntless charges against impos-sible odds.

Glaring down the corridors of history at his many critics, living, dead, and yet unborn, Hornaday spat in their eyes: "I now give notice that in writing the stories of my own campaigns I am perfectly indif-ferent to all the scoffs and charges of 'egotism' that my enemies can

The Fear

Long after the early dark had fallen on the evening of December 1, 1934, an old man with a neatly trimmed gray beard and fierce, slightly accusatory eyes sat down in the library of the rambling, comfortable home he called "The Anchorage," in Stamford, Connecticut, rolled a sheet of blank paper into a typewriter, and began to write the story of his life.

It was his eightieth birthday. Earlier in the day, there had been a small celebration attended by a few of his colleagues from the wars and, of course, by his sweet and long-suffering wife, Josephine, the one he liked to call "the Empress Josephine" because of her grand, high-born manner and discerning intelligence, and because, quite simply, he adored her. She'd been by his side for nearly six decades, since a long-ago dinner party in Battle Creek, Michigan, when both of them had been twenty-one. She'd been a comely young schoolteacher wearing her best black silk dress; he, a naturalist and adventurer preparing to depart on a collecting expedition into the dark and fateful Orinoco River delta in Venezuela. Hoping to win her sympathy, he'd regaled her with the dangers that he would soon face on the Orinoco, with its flesh-eating fish, giant electric eels, and forty-foot snakes. He'd gazed directly into her eyes. He'd reached out and lightly touched her arm. In the corseted Victorian age, his boldness and presumption, verging on rudeness, was shocking. At one point, he'd even corrected her grammar. She had been taken aback, but when he pressed for her address, so he might perhaps write to her from some lonely outpost on

1896–1926 Serves as director of the New York Zoological Park (the Bronx Zoo).

1900 Lacey Law, the first federal law protecting wild birds, game, and plants from illegal trafficking, passed; repeatedly amended, it remains in effect today.

1906 Ota Benga incident at the Bronx Zoo.

1907–10 Serves as president of the American Bison Society.

1907 First bison sent to Wichita National Forest and Game Reserve, in Oklahoma. By 1919, Hornaday and the American Bison Society have established nine herds across the West.

1911 Hay-Elliot Fur Seal Treaty, which saves the Alaskan fur seal from extinction.

1913 Hornaday creates the Permanent Wildlife Protection Fund, which he uses to finance his "crusade for wildlife" until his death. Publication of *Our Vanishing Wild Life*.

1937 Dies in Stamford, Connecticut, at age eighty-two.

WILLIAM TEMPLE HORNADAY

A Life in Brief

1854 Born on a farm near Plainfield, Indiana.

1871 Attends Okaloosa College and the Iowa State Agricultural College (now Iowa State).

1873 Hired by Ward's Natural Science Establishment of Rochester, New York.

1874 First collecting expedition to Florida, Cuba, and the Bahamas. First zoo in the United States opens in Philadelphia.

1875 Meets Josephine Chamberlain at a dinner party. Collecting expedition to the Orinoco River delta, Venezuela.

1876–77 Two-year collecting expedition to India, Ceylon, Malaya, and Borneo.

1879 Marries Josephine in Battle Creek, Michigan. The marriage lasts fifty-eight years, until his death.

1882–90 Appointed chief taxidermist at the U.S. National Museum (the Smithsonian).

1885 *Two Years in the Jungle* published.

1886 *The Last Buffalo Hunt* published.

1889 Becomes founder and first director of the National Museum in Washington. Publication of *The Extermination of the American Bison.*

or will make. I do not propose to write misshapen history under any handicaps of false modesty."[2]

Yet, at the same time, with this declaration of war against his detractors and implied promise of ruthless truth-telling, there was one enormous thing in particular that he would fail to mention at all. The document that he was now writing, which would grow into a full-blown, three-hundred-page autobiography called *Eighty Fascinating Years* (and would never be published), would not breathe a word about it. The archive of his papers at the Library of Congress alone, one of several such historical data banks, would run to 39,000 items but with no more than a single sentence referring to it. Squarely at the center of the life of a man who could rightly be considered one of the greatest environmental heroes of the nineteenth and early twentieth centuries was a crime against humanity, yet he did not address the charges against him either in his public or his private writings. The man who would later be credited with saving at least two species—the American bison and the Alaskan fur seal—from extinction, a man whose greatest contribution to the environmental battles of the twenty-first century would be a sense of *moral responsibility* and *moral outrage* concerning the natural world, this man would be the central player in one of the most morally repellent incidents of his day. Yet nowhere in the voluminous written record of his life did he directly address the incident for which he would still be remembered seventy-five years after his death. (In fact, he would no doubt be aghast to learn, it would be almost the *only* thing he would be remembered for, if he were remembered at all.) He was the man who, in 1906, displayed a human being—a black pygmy from the Congo—in a cage at the Bronx Zoo.

Instead, Hornaday preferred to view his life as a war, with himself in the thick of the fight. "With the exception of the period from 1890 to 1896"[3]—when he'd made an ill-fated attempt to leave the battle behind and become a businessman—"I have been continuously on this wild-life job. The total period of my really MILITANT activity in this field is now (at the close of 1934) about 40 years." The past four decades of his life had been one of more-or-less continuous war—what he called his "war for wildlife," which to his mind was undoubtedly the greatest and most important armed conflict in human history. The Civil War had quite literally ripped the nation asunder, but at least it eventually came to an end; but the slaughter of birds and wildlife, if they were driven to the desolate terminus of extinction, would leave a wound that would last forever.

Hornaday did not shrink from combat—in fact, there was nothing he loved more than a good fight, for good reason. But what had pained and surprised him almost more than anything else was that so many of his battles were against people who were allegedly on the same side. When the avowed lovers of birds and game turned on him, betrayed him, double-crossed him, made secret deals with the enemy—*that* was what had made him feel mortally wounded and unutterably alone. He needed all the friends he could find in the battle against the destroyers of wildlife because, over the past seventy years, the history of game protection had been "a bad and bitter chronicle of the folly and greed of civilized man—of amazing wastefulness, duties horribly ignored, and a thousand lost opportunities."[4] Of the story of the greedy and senseless war *against* wildlife, he wrote, "there are enough facts to make half a dozen volumes; but what is the use?"

As the years went by, Hornaday's life led him to ever-higher pinnacles of public achievement. He was the founder and first director of the National Zoo in Washington, D.C. (until a nasty fight with Samuel Langley, the secretary of the Smithsonian, "a man of lonely habits and all the congeniality of an iceberg,"[5] and Hornaday had quit in disgust); had served for thirty years as director of the New York Zoological Park (which would become known to the world as the Bronx Zoo); had written almost two dozen books about wildlife and conservation; led the charge in Congress for innumerable game protection laws and the creation of game reserves for birds and mammals; and had fought the gun lobby, the feather lobby, and, always, the great immobile apathy of the American public.

What he cared about most, and what he had cared about throughout his long life, was the attempt to preserve the whole great phantasmagoria of nonhuman life in the United States, and on the planet as a whole. In the fight to save the birds and mammals, he didn't care how many enemies he made—and, to be sure, he made plenty. "Any man who enlists in any great cause for the defense of the rights of wild life and is discovered in the act of promoting a reform that is worthwhile soon finds himself fighting all the enemies of wildlife on whose toes he treads," he wrote. "If he is devoted to peace and harmony at the expense of justice and success, he may just as well quit before he begins. To me, the saving of wild life always was more important than 'harmony' with its destroyers."[6]

Still, despite all the battles he'd won against the destroyers, and all he'd accomplished in his life, he knew very well that in many ways, the war for wildlife was going badly. "In America," he wrote wearily, "the national spirit may truly be expressed in the cry of the crazed Malay: *Amok! Amok!* Kill! Kill!"[7] All over the country, dozens of species of birds and animals had been reduced to tiny remnant populations struggling to survive against the onslaught of "civilization." The destroyers had gained all the high ground and were bitterly determined and heavily armed. In his prophetic poem "The Second Coming," William Butler Yeats was describing the strategic situation facing American conservationists in the late nineteenth century when he howled: "The best lack all conviction, while the worst are full of passionate intensity."

Thinking back now, from the vantage point of eight decades, Hornaday could feel again what he had first felt so long ago—that nauseating stab of fear and sorrow—when he realized just how bad things had gotten and how few people seemed to realize it, or even seemed to care. "Just as a carefree and joyous swimmer for pleasure suddenly is drawn into a whirlpool—in which he can swim but from which he cannot escape—so in 1886 was I drawn into the maelstrom,"[8] he wrote, remembering the shock of what happened during the terrible spring and summer of that year. What he had witnessed in the West that tender May of 1886 had frightened him right down to the smallest cell in his body. He'd seen something that few others on the planet, save scattered hunters and Indians, had noticed. It was the beginning of something so frightful, and so gigantic, that even he did not fully grasp its significance.

More than a hundred years later, biologists would give it a name: The "sixth extinction" or the "Holocene extinction" (in reference to the Holocene epoch in which we live). Almost entirely caused by human activity, it is a wave of species loss so enormous that it has taken its place alongside the five other major extinction events in the past 500 million years of life on Earth. The previous extinction, the "end-Cretaceous event" of 65 million years ago, not only annihilated the dinosaurs but also 75 percent of all species on our home planet, the only planet we have.[9]

Now another dark shadow was slipping down over the world. Everywhere Hornaday looked, he could see it happening: in the disappearance of migratory songbirds all up and down the Eastern seaboard, in the steady loss of wild field, forest, and shore. It was time to raise the alarm, to shout to the everlasting skies, to mobilize for war against the destroyers of wildlife—if it were not already too late.

He was galvanized by rage. But in his heart, all he felt was fear.

The fear: that's where it had all begun.

PART ONE

The Awakening

CHAPTER I

His Name Was Dauntless

On the fair spring morning of May 6, 1886,[1] an intense-looking young gentleman with eyes that burned like meteors and a jet-black beard vaulted up the stairs of a Pennsylvania Railroad westbound train, which was steaming at the platform in Union Station, near downtown Washington, D.C. He was a small man—all of five foot eight in his stocking feet—but lithe, compact, and powerfully built, like a predatory animal. He was wearing a new bowler hat, a slightly uncomfortable-looking tweed suit, and scuffed alpine walking boots. The young man's whole body seemed to follow the forward thrust of his chin as he mounted the stairs into the railway car; trailing along behind him, scarcely able to keep up, were a middle-aged man and an adolescent boy whose face bore a touch of acne and a look of perpetual astonishment.

The bearded young man was in a frightful hurry. He was, in fact, desperately afraid that all his hurrying was in vain, that it was already too late. He hardly dared imagine the possibility: when he got where he was going, a monstrous crime would be a fait accompli, an unspeakable slaughter beyond the reach of redemption.

The young man, whose name was William Temple Hornaday, was thirty-two years old. He'd lived his whole life to date with such breathless velocity that one of the most arresting things about him now was the disconnect between his relative youth and the gravity of his purpose and station in life. Born on a hardscrabble farm in Indiana, without wealth or connections, he'd risen to become chief taxidermist at the U.S. National Museum—later, in 1911, part of the Smithsonian Institution—when he was only twenty-eight years old. He was considered one of the most masterful taxidermists in the country at a time when mounting skins for museums was considered the highest form of "nature art" and the closest most people would ever get to exotic species like a wildebeest or an African lion. (Few people would ever see live animals in a zoo—the first zoo in the country had opened in Philadelphia just a few years earlier, in 1874.[2]) Because of his deft artistic touch, his ingenious method of creating sculpted, clay-covered manikins over which the animal skins were mounted, and most of all because of his intimate acquaintance with living animals in the wild in some of the world's most remote places, Hornaday was able to bring a Bengal tiger or a harpy eagle to life with an almost spooky realism.

Hornaday was in such a hurry now because his immediate superior at the museum, Dr. G. Brown Goode, had asked him a few months earlier to inventory the museum's specimen collection of *Bison americanus*, the American bison, once one of the greatest glories of the continent. But when Hornaday looked into the matter, peering into dim cabinets and specimen drawers, he was appalled to discover that, as he later wrote, "the American people's own official museum was absolutely destitute of good bison specimens of every kind."[3] He could find only a few dusty old skins and skeletons—sad, neglected relics, like discarded overcoats whose owners would never return.

Hornaday had then undertaken a census of the bison in North America, writing to ranchers, hunters, army officers, and zookeepers across the American West and in Canada as far north as the Great Slave Lake in an attempt to come up with some estimate of how many buffalo still might be left alive by 1886. Although no man, white or red, would ever know for certain how many buffalo had once roamed the plains of North America, the estimates ranged up to 60 *million* or more (though more recent estimates have reduced this number to something closer to 30 million). But whatever the actual numbers were, buffalo were the largest herds of quadrupeds ever to walk the face of the earth, including the epic migrations of Africa. But, as the news came back from all these far-flung correspondents, the true story of what had happened to the millions of bison became heartbreakingly apparent.

Based on the best firsthand accounts he could find, Hornaday estimated that as recently as 1867, only about twenty years earlier, the total number of wild bison in the trans-Missouri West was about 15 million. But what had happened to these last representatives of a mighty race during the subsequent two decades was a testament to astounding human greed and short-sightedness, as well as the shiny new efficiencies of capitalism. The same ingenious interlocking mechanisms that mass-produced washing machines, farm implements, and, later, the Model T Ford, and then marketed and distributed them worldwide, had been put to use exterminating the American bison, and with breathtaking haste. The slaughter became mechanized, streamlined, and eerily calm, with armies of hunters (who were paid by the carcass) killing and butchering bison by the tens of thousands and then loading their hides by the bale onto eastbound trains.

The fact that there was, in all of this, a ghost in the machine—an end to it all—went largely unnoticed. Even the hide hunters themselves did not notice what was happening. In retrospect, Hornaday later wrote, it appeared that the last of the great herds disappeared in 1883–84, but the hide hunters prepared for another season nonetheless, laying in Sharps rifles, cases of ammunition, skinning and butchering tools, tents, commissary supplies, tons of feed for the horses, and all the rest of it, not realizing that they were preparing to hunt for ghosts.

Although bison herds had once darkened the earth from horizon to horizon, now they were reduced to a few thin, embattled droves defended by a scattering of bewildered bulls, their great shaggy heads turned outward toward a threat they could not understand. When the magnitude of the crime began to dawn on the young taxidermist, it was as if the world had crashed down on his head. "In March, 1886," Hornaday later wrote in his unpublished autobiography, "I received a severe shock, as if by a blow on the head from a well-directed mallet. I awoke, dazed and stunned, to a sudden realization of the fact that the buffalo-hide hunters of the United States had practically finished their work."[4]

These noble, prehistoric-looking animals, millions of years in the making, with their mountainous forequarters and magnificent heads, were like a candle flame that was one breath away from winking out. And once the gate of extinction clanged shut, the living history of an ancient life form would close forever, never to be reopened.

Hornaday dashed off a letter summarizing his alarming conclusions and hand-delivered it to Dr. Goode at the museum. In the letter, he reported that "by extensive correspondence it was ascertained that in the United States the extermination of all the large herds of buffalo is already an accomplished fact. While it was supposed that at least some thousands remained in the more remote regions of the North-west, it was found that the total number is estimated at less than five hundred."[5] By including all the animals held in captivity by zoos or private individuals, Hornaday estimated that there were now fewer than eight hundred bison left on the face of the earth. It was likely only a matter of a few years—or even months—before all the wild bison on the planet would join the woolly mammoth in the sepulchre of extinction.

Hornaday stood there in Dr. Goode's office, watching, as the kindly superintendent read his terrible letter. The old man's face fell. He seemed momentarily unable to speak. Then he lifted his eyes to Hornaday and said finally, "I'm greatly shocked and disturbed by your letter. . . . I dislike to be the means of killing any of those last bison, but since it is now utterly impossible to prevent their destruction we simply must take a large series of specimens, both for our own mu-seum, and for other museums that sooner or later will want good specimens."[6]

It was the Faustian bargain of science: to save some vestige of a vanishing species for future generations, a few specimens would need to be sacrificed and carefully preserved. "To all of us the idea of killing a score or more of the last survivors of the bison millions was exceed-ingly unpleasant," Hornaday wrote, "but we believed that our refrain-ing from collecting the specimens we imperatively needed would not prolong the existence of the bison species by a single day."

When Hornaday begged Dr. Goode to allow him to mount a small exploratory expedition to the Montana Territory right away, Goode readily agreed. It was still early spring, and the bison—if they could find any—would be shedding their winter coats in great disor-derly bolts; bison hides were not considered "prime" for harvest until November or December. But the young taxidermist felt that he had to go west at the earliest possible moment owing to the ongoing crime he now knew was taking place there.

On this hastily arranged expedition, Hornaday was accompanied by his old hunting pal George Hedley, an experienced outdoorsman and taxidermist from Medina, New York; and a youthful museum assistant named A. H. Forney, who seemed all arms, legs, and Adam's apple but who proved to be both brave and cheerful. Now the three of them made their way through the train to their berths in a Pullman sleeping car, widely marketed as "luxury for the middle class" and replete with heavy, dark green drapes, hanging lamps, and porter service. Each sleeping car had its own porter, each of them black and each known simply as "George."[7] For Hornaday, on his modest government salary, all this unaccustomed luxury—middle class or not—was possible only because the three men had been provided with free train tickets by the museum. A sleeping car would be lovely, though: the rail trip was to last four days and take them all the way to Miles City, in the Montana Territory, a muddy settlement on the Yellowstone River in the flat, wind-whipped grasslands of the northern Great Plains, a place still haunted by the Crow, the Paiute, and the Blackfoot, but no longer by the great herds that these tribes had once hunted and revered.

Once the men stowed their bags in the green lap of their Pullman berths and the train pulled out of the station, they made their way forward to the dining car for a late breakfast. As it happened, they were seated across the table from two young, sunburned Army officers, who told them that, after a visit to Washington, they were returning to their desolate outpost in the Montana Territory. Hornaday brightened at this happy coincidence. He told the officers about the mission of his three-person Smithsonian expedition: to travel west to the territories, and with the assistance of local guides, cowboys, and soldiers garrisoned to Fort Keogh, attempt to locate and procure specimens of the American bison for the museum.

The two officers exchanged quick glances which, it seemed to Hornaday, were filled with wry amusement. Then one of them turned to him and spoke.[8]

The chances of you fellas finding any buffalo, anywhere in the territories—at least, any buffalo that are still alive—are next to nothing.

In fact, he told Hornaday, leaning across the table with a butter knife in one hand and a fork in the other, *I'd be willing to bet you cash money you won't find a single buffalo in the Montana Territory, or anywhere else for that matter.*

It wasn't as if people out East were entirely uninformed about what was happening. As recently as 1869, *Harper's Weekly* magazine had carried an engraving of Western tourists firing from a slow-moving train at a herd of buffalo with Sharps rifles, carbines, pistols—any armament they could lay hands on. "An American scene, certainly,"[9] the editors observed breezily, as if the people were merry picknickers. Did people believe this could go on forever? And boarding the train only an hour earlier, Hornaday had noticed that the station platform was crowded with well-dressed women wearing extravagant Gilded Age hats, nearly all of which were festooned with feathers—feathers plucked from native songbirds and from wading birds of the swamp and shore, feathers stolen from birds of the equatorial jungle. Did people imagine that there was no end to nature's bounty? That they had the right to sacrifice a snowy egret or a lyrebird simply because its feathers were pretty, or a buffalo because its hide was warm? Didn't anybody see what was going on? Was the entire country asleep?

He'd known things were bad out in the Western territories, but seated in the dining car across from the sunburned officers, Hornaday was just beginning to realize *how* bad. In his correspondence with ranchers, hunters, and stockmen across the West, attempting to locate the remnant bison herds, he'd learned that bison sightings had become so rare they were cause for special celebration (and of course, a celebratory hunt). Theodore Roosevelt, in his book *Hunting Trips of a Ranchman*, had written that a rancher who'd traveled a thousand miles across northern Montana told him "he was never out of sight of a dead buffalo, and never in sight of a live one."[10] Now, on the westbound train, Hornaday was seized with the terrible fear that the few remaining herds might reach the vanishing point of extinction before he even got there.

Still, William Temple Hornaday was not a man who was easily daunted by a dismal prophecy about his chances from strangers on a train, or superior firepower, or overwhelming odds of any kind. He was a fighter down to his fingernails. He had all the belligerent pugnacity of a small man with an outsized notion of his importance in the world. A proud, prickly, imperious man with a fierce, almost swordlike nose, ferociously unsettling eyes, and eyebrows so black and overbearing they appeared to have been painted on, he bore a passing resemblance to the young Sigmund Freud. His manner was one of calculated crudeness, his hands were calloused, and even in a fine suit and a high, stiff Victorian "turnover" collar, like two small white wings at the throat, his hair would sometimes be matted with flecks of mud or bits of grass from recreating nature scenes in the taxidermy shop.

Born six years before the beginning of hostilities in the Civil War, Hornaday was too young to have served in the Union army, but he was deeply affected by it nonetheless—his beloved older brother Clark died in a military hospital after being grievously wounded in the war.[11] By the time he was fourteen, both of Hornaday's parents had died, the family farm and everything in it had been auctioned off, and he was sent off to live with distant relatives in Illinois. His brothers and sisters had moved away or were dead, and he was quite alone in the world. So he learned to fight. And the defiant boldness he learned from being thrown on the world so young, without any advantages, became the defining characteristic of his life.

He was still a teenager when he went to work for the famous Ward's Natural Science Establishment of Rochester, New York, a kind of Sears, Roebuck of natural history specimens for museums, universities, and private collectors. He'd worked there all of six months when he decided, at the age of nineteen, to mount a collecting expedition, alone, to the remotest part of Africa. He'd been inspired by the exploits of Paul Du Chaillu, the French-American explorer who was the first man to bring back a great ape from the dark continent and whose 1861 book *Explorations and Adventures in Equatorial Africa* later inspired the movie *King Kong*. Hornaday's uncle Allen had to bribe the boy with $500 to keep him from going (and in Allen's view, saved his life).[12]

As a hunter and tracker, Hornaday was fearless. In India, where more than eight hundred people had been killed and eaten by tigers in the single year 1878, he stalked an immense Bengal tiger into a bamboo thicket, on foot, and shot it at thirty yards with such a small-bore rifle that it was practically a toy. To call him dauntless was to understate the case.

Hornaday was also "obsessive, unbuckling, and stubborn beyond words," writes historian Douglas Brinkley. "His certainty about zoology bordered on arrogance. His daily conversation was filled with such bio-trivia as the flesh preference of wolverines and why hawks were copper-clawed." At the same time, "there was always a mischievous twinkle in his eyes, like a child who had suddenly aged overnight."[13]

Now, staring across the table at the two officers on the westbound train, who had just told him he could not do what he intended to do, all Hornaday felt was a stiffening of his resolve, as if, through sheer willpower, he might be able to conjure a thundering herd of buffalo out of thin air.

The zeitgeist of those days, and a general sense of the enemy's astonishing obliviousness and power, is succinctly summed up by a story which appeared in the *Chicago Tribune* on November 22, 1886. The paper published an account of a sumptuous wild game dinner that was to be held at the Tremont House, a lavish hotel at the corner of Dearborn and Lake Streets. This feast, hosted by the Tremont's proprietor, John B. Drake, would be held just before Thanksgiving, just as it had for thirty-eight consecutive years previously, and would be attended by such notables as Ulysses S. Grant; General Philip Sheridan; Senator Stephen A. Douglas; Mr. and Mrs. Marshall Field, of department store fame; and Mr. and Mrs. George M. Pullman, the eponymous owners of the railcar company. The menu, apparently meant to tantalize the masses with the imagined immoderation of the ruling classes, stands as a mute testament to what was happening to wildlife in the United States in the late nineteenth century—not just to the buffalo, but to every other wild thing that crawled, walked, or flew. It was a saturnalia of blood that invites the modern reader to nothing so much as indigestion:

PROCESSION OF GAME

SOUP
Venison (Hunter style) Game Broth

FISH
Broiled Trout, Shrimp Sauce, Baked Black Bass, Claret Sauce

BOILED
Leg of Mountain Sheep, Ham of Bear, Venison Tongue, Buffalo Tongue

ROAST
Loin of Buffalo, Mountain Sheep, Wild Goose, Quail, Redhead Duck, Jack Rabbit, Blacktail Deer, Coon, Canvasback Duck, English Hare,

Bluewing Teal, Partridge, Widgeon, Brant, Saddle of Venison,
Pheasants, Mallard Duck, Prairie Chicken, Wild Turkey,
Spotted Grouse, Black Bear, Oppossum, Leg of Elk, Wood Duck,
Sandhill Crane, Ruffed Grouse, Cinnamon Bear

BROILED

Bluewing Teal, Jacksnipe, Blackbirds, Reed Birds,
Partridges, Pheasants, Quails, Butterballs, Ducks, English
Snipe, Rice Birds, Red-wing Starling, Marsh Birds, Plover,
Gray Squirrel, Buffalo Steak, Rabbits, Venison Steak

ENTREES

Antelope Steak, Mushroom Sauce; Rabbit Braise,
Cream Sauce; Fillet of Grouse with Truffles; Venison Cutlet,
Jelly Sauce; Ragout of Bear, Hunter Style; Oyster Pie

SALADS

Shrimp, Prairie Chicken, Celery

ORNAMENTAL DISHES

Pyramid of Game en Bellevue, Boned Duck au Naturel,
Pyramid of Wild-Goose Liver in Jelly, The Coon Out at Night,
Boned Quail in Plumage, Red-Wing Starling on Tree,
Partridge in Nest, Prairie Chicken en Socle[14]

Staring out the window of the westbound train, William Temple
Hornaday was consumed with fear and impatience. Unable to sleep,
he watched as the sun rose, flared, set, and rose again and the little
towns with their grain silos and saddle horses went by, a smoky dawn
over some dinky city hall, the oceans of corn. Baltimore, McKeesport,
Pittsburgh, Akron, Goshen, South Bend. Then Gary, Indiana, which
smelled like a dirty nickel, and on to the darkness and steam and
clambor of Chicago, where Hornaday and his companions changed
trains onto the storied Northern Pacific railroad—a new Pullman car,
a new "George"—for the last long leg of the journey west. Only three
years earlier, on September 8, 1883, former president Ulysses S. Grant
had driven the final "golden spike" that joined the eastern and western
Northern Pacific rail lines, linking Chicago with far-off Seattle. Now

the train steamed north along Lake Michigan, through Milwaukee and northwest through the little farm towns and the melancholy blue-black lakes of Wisconsin, into Minnesota, the white birches flashing out of a dark sea of spruce forest, Minneapolis, St. Cloud, Fergus Falls, Fargo.

The old buffalo hunters claimed there was a different, slightly larger species of bison with a more pronounced hump, known as the "wood buffalo," that haunted the green eastern forests in ancient times. But now that the train was entering the northern Great Plains, Hornaday was passing into the ancestral homeland of the western herd bison, whose numbers were so vast they were often said to be "beyond counting." He watched as the near-limitless West of the imagination spread out before him—home to what until quite recently were two vast herds, the larger "southern herd," south of the Platte River which transected the West at Denver, and the "northern herd," which roamed the plains north into Canada. But now all he saw was emptiness, yucca and greasewood growing in the sandy washes, distant cattle, and the occasional pronghorn antelope, like tiny insects at the foot of an immense, unforgiving sky.

How could people be so stupid? How could they be so rapacious? Wasn't there any ethic of *limits* in this country? In some perverse way, the very fact that a thing was rare and endangered made it all the more tempting a prize. "The nearer the species approaches to complete extermination," Hornaday had written, "the more eagerly are the wretched figures pursued to the death wherever found."[15] Moreover, much of this slaughter was for no purpose whatsoever. The vast majority of the meat from the buffalo massacre was simply wasted. The native peoples, by contrast, made use of every scrap—meat for food, hides for clothing, sinew for rope, stomach for carrying sack. Hornaday had once estimated that "probably not more than one-thousandth of the buffalo meat that might have been saved and utilized was saved." Millions of people could have been fed with the meat that was left to rot on the plains.

Hornaday himself was an experienced tracker, hunter, and marksman; he'd killed more than his fair share of game, from Borneo to the Orinoco River delta. But, except for "bush meat" taken to survive in remote jungle camps, these kills were always in the service of science. He forcefully maintained throughout his life that virtually all the specimens he had ever taken were later mounted and displayed in museums, universities, and private collections for the edification of scientists and the public. He insisted that "bringing wildlife to the millions"—allowing people to see, up close, what he was asking them to save—was a key part of his war for wildlife. The moral queasiness that he sometimes felt about killing the animals that appeared in his museum displays was trumped by his absolute conviction that what he was doing was not only right, but urgently important.

He was already envisioning a magnificent habitat grouping of perhaps six or eight mounted bison, a big bull, a couple of cows, several yearlings, and calves, which would enthrall visitors to the Smithsonian for years to come and, more importantly, galvanize them to action when they read about the slaughter of the living bison in Montana or the Dakotas. It grieved him to be westward bound on a mission of death. But all those birds depicted so lovingly by John James Audubon in *Birds of America*—the radiant scripture of the New World— had all been shot first, their feathered corpses tenderly arranged in lifelike poses. Audubon's book was a chronicle of death, a hunting diary, but its ultimate purpose was noble: to awaken the American public to the glories of their country and awaken their hearts to the crying need for preservation.[16]

On the third day out of Washington, in the western Dakota Territory, Hornaday awoke in his nest of temporary dark-green luxury and peered out of the window. "Houses few and far apart, & the country looks dreadfully lonesome,"[17] he confided to his journal. The country was deserted partly because the train was passing through the ancient borderlands of the fierce plains peoples, the people of the buffalo—the Santee and Yankton Sioux, the Hidatsa, Mandan, and Arikara, and the Crow. This country had never been hospitable to humans—too dry, too infertile, too hot in summer, too cold in winter—and the Indians only made white settlers feel more unwelcome.

In all of his dismal correspondence with ranchers and hunters, Hornaday had stumbled across a few reasons to hope that he and his small hunting party might be able to find some buffalo, somewhere. One army doctor named J.C. Merrill, stationed in the windswept northeastern reaches of the Montana Territory, wrote to Hornaday that he felt it still might be possible to find a few scattered buffalo, but only in three places—on the headwaters of the Powder River, in Wyoming; and in the Judith Basin and along the Big Dry Creek, both in Montana.[18]

Along the banks of the Little Missouri River, the train passed through the tiny cow town of Medora. Theodore Roosevelt, then a twenty-eight-year-old New York assemblyman and author who had abandoned his political career temporarily to become a Dakota rancher, had bought a place near here recently. It was still lawless country, plagued by cattle rustlers, and just a month before Hornaday's train passed through Medora, Roosevelt had made the much-celebrated capture of a notorious horse and cattle thief named Mike Finnegan. Roosevelt walked forty-five miles with Finnegan in custody to deliver him to the local jail. At one point, Roosevelt borrowed the rustler's dime Western to read, so he could stay up all night while guarding his prisoner at gunpoint.[19]

The Montana Territory in 1886 was still a raw, wild, and dangerous place. It was only ten years earlier, in June 1876, that a reckless cavalry officer whom the Crow called "Son of the Morning Star" attacked an enormous gathering of Lakota Sioux and Northern Cheyenne warriors under chiefs Crazy Horse and Sitting Bull, camped on the banks of the Little Bighorn River, in the Montana Territory. General George Armstrong Custer, who had graduated dead last in his class at West Point, was slaughtered by the Indians, along with 268 of his men.[20] Elsewhere, rustlers and outlaws were commonplace. In many places, the Northern Pacific Railroad line into the territory was so new that the rails were still shiny as mint dimes.[21] People back East, extravagantly overdressed in their *fin de siecle* hats, crinolines, corsets, frock coats, and twenty-button shoes, were fascinated by this almost unimaginable openness and wildness. A teenage boy from St. Louis named Charles M. Russell became so obsessed with sketching cowboys and Indians that his parents allowed him to go out to the Montana Territory in 1880, at the age of sixteen, where he got work as a cowhand and began sending back a steady stream of drawings and paintings of Western life to the people of New York, Chicago, and Boston. The images of wranglers, rustlers, and feathered braves in war paint were as startling as pictures from another planet.[22]

But there was another story unfolding in the United States at the same time, a story that very few people had heard or seen. It was a story that William Temple Hornaday was determined to shout from the rooftops, even if it made him look like a kook, a crank, or a busybody. It was a story that was not readily apparent to others because few men of his day had spent as much time as Hornaday had in such remote places—from the Orinoco River delta, to Ceylon, the Malay Peninsula, and Borneo. He had been appalled to realize that, even in these wild places, enormous regions had been almost completely "shot out"—where the forest had been emptied of birds, mammals, reptiles, and almost everything else that breathed. Returning from these exotic locales to the United States, he'd been able to see that here too, a virtual war of extinction was in progress, and the war was going very badly indeed.

On two successive winter afternoons in 1886, an ornithologist from the American Museum of Natural History named Frank Chapman took a stroll down Fourteenth Street, in Lower Manhattan. In the course of this ramble through the crossroads of New York fashion, Chapman observed more than 700 extravagant Gilded Age women's hats, bearing the plumage of forty different species of birds, from the white-throated sparrow to the bobolink, the laughing gull to the sanderling. Was anyone paying attention? Was anyone outraged?[23]

There was a bitter, bloody war going on—what Hornaday called a "war for wildlife," but it was more accurately a war *against* wildlife —and very few people seemed to realize how badly outgunned the friends of wildlife were. In fact, according to Hornaday's own calculations, the enemies of wildlife outnumbered the friends by at least *500 to 1*. Worst of all, the enemies included enormously influential people like General William Tecumseh Sherman, Secretary of the Interior Columbus Delano, and even, by his failure to act, the former president of the United States, Ulysses S. Grant.[24]

Meanwhile, gun manufacturers were churning out ever more deadly and efficient weapons, like the new Winchester Autoloader, which could get off five shots in four seconds and was loaded and cocked by its own recoil. These weapons were like machine guns, more suited for war than for sport. At the same time, in states and localities across the United States, the legal system for protecting wildlife was like a defensive perimeter made of sticks and leaves—bag limits, hunting laws, hunting seasons—almost all of them had been dictated by hunters and hunting lobbies to ensure that they could kill as much game as they liked. A man could shoot thirty ducks if it pleased him, then shoot thirty more the next day, and it was perfectly legal. His hunting partner was likely to be the county sheriff.

Now, hurtling westward, Hornaday could think only of the great quest that lay ahead. Were the ranchers and hunters right? Had the "extinction event" already overtaken the few buffalo that were left in the wild? Would this journey turn out to be a requiem? All he knew for sure was that the gauntlet had been thrown down, and he intended to answer the battle call. There was not a moment to be lost.

CHAPTER 2

A Melancholy Insanity

Even in the full dress blues of the Union Army, General William Tecumseh Sherman tended to look dishevelled, as if he'd slept in a tent. The hair on the back of his head was crazed, like a wild dog's; and there was a strange, clenched muscle that crossed his cheek on the diagonal like a scar left by some primitive ritual of war. One soldier recollected that Sherman "generally looked like some old farmer; his hat all slouched down and an old brown overcoat." Another observed that Sherman was "a very nervous man and can't keep still a minute,"[1] forever fidgeting with his hands and feet, glancing about sharply as if someone were after him, which generally was the case.

But it was Sherman's eyes that riveted you. They were a predator's eyes, and once they locked on you, it was clear that you were the prey. They were eyes that had seen things no man should ever have to see, eyes that had peered into the darkness of which men are capable and seen no end to it.

The net effect was one of ferocious intensity and near-derangement, an impression that was augmented by the well-known fact that, after the first Battle of Bull Run in 1861, Sherman had had a nervous breakdown and been temporarily relieved of his command. The papers reported that he'd gone insane. Even his wife, Ellen, had written in a letter to Sherman's brother that Sherman suffered from "that melancholy insanity of which your family is subject."[2]

But although Sherman may have seen the darkness in other men's souls, most Southerners said it was Sherman himself who was the man of bottomless darkness. This was the man who had said, after sacking and burning Atlanta in 1864, then burning and killing his way across Georgia on his way to the sea, "War is cruelty. There's no use trying to reform it. The crueler it is, the sooner it will be over."[3]

When the war finally ended, Grant made Sherman Commanding General of the Army, which meant that he was responsible for the ongoing Indian wars in the West. In some ways, the appointment was a curious choice: Sherman's father had named him after the great Shawnee chief, Tecumseh,[4] who tried unsuccessfully to unify the Indian nations of the Ohio River Valley to fight the white man. Tecumseh (the name means "shooting star") was as fearless as Sherman, forever rallying the tribes to war, even in the face of certain defeat and death:

> *Where today are the Pequot? Where are the Narragansett, the Mo-chican, the Pocanet, and the other powerful tribes of our people? They have vanished before the avarice and oppression of the white man, as snow before the summer sun. . . . Sleep not longer O Choctaws and Chickasaws. . . . Will not the bones of our dead be plowed up, and their graves turned into plowed fields?*[5]

Sherman did not particularly care for the Indian wars, which were a bloody, disorganized business that was not like real war at all. The enemy was absolutely ruthless, scalping and disembowelling those who were captured, then skulking away into the night. It was a kind of guerilla warfare, in which the enemy seemed more like a conspiracy of shadows than a regular uniformed army. Their desecration of bodies was part of their strategy of psychological warfare, meant to horrify and dishearten the white man at the same time it disguised the Indians' smaller numbers. Sherman responded to these grisly tactics with the same methods he'd used to bring the Confederacy to its knees: total war. War not just against an army, but against a whole society. Utter desolation. Blackened earth, bare and without sustenance.

To Sherman, the centerpiece of the fight against the Indian was the buffalo, who supplied the enemy with meat, hides, bones, and a way of life. Both the buffalo and the Indian were enemies of civilization, and both would have to be destroyed if the grand promise of America were to reach all the way to the western sea. Because the Indians not only depended on the buffalo for food, clothing, and shelter, but the animal also was tangled up somehow in that blasphemous "religion" of theirs, to take away the buffalo was to break their spirit as well as their bodies. And breaking the enemy's spirit, he knew as well as anyone, was the key to victory. Sherman had once said to General Philip Sheridan that "it would be wise to invite all the sportsmen of England and America ... for a Grand Buffalo Hunt, and make a grand sweep of them all."[6]

In 1874, Sherman convinced Grant, then president of the United States, to pocket-veto a bill that would have protected buffalo from commercial hunting. He and Grant were old friends from the war, and saw eye to eye on most things. Sherman had said of Grant, "He stood by me when I was crazy, and I stood by him when he was drunk, and now we stand by each other."[7] Sherman argued that commercial hunting of buffalo was actually like a batallion of soldiers doing battle with the enemy, and Grant evidently agreed.

During floor debate in the Texas State Legislature on another bill to protect the buffalo in 1874, Sherman dispatched General Sheridan to the Texas statehouse to spread his message of total war. Sheridan was as fearless as Sherman, having broken the Confederate line at Missionary Ridge and fought at Chickamauga, one of the bloodiest engagements of the war. Sheridan thundered:

> They [the buffalo-hunters] are destroying the Indian's commissary; and it is a well-known fact that an army losing its base of supplies is placed at a great disadvantage. Send them powder and lead, if you will; but for the sake of lasting peace, let them kill, skin, and sell until the buffaloes are exterminated. Then your prairie can be covered with speckled cattle, and the festive cowboy, who follows the hunters as the second forerunner of an advanced civilization.[8]

The Texas legislature, like Grant, agreed. The bill died. The attitudes espoused by Sherman and Sheridan had enormous popular support in the country, especially among sportsmen. One hunter wrote in a large-circulation magazine in 1881: "The buffalo must go with the Red Man. Both are stumbling blocks to the improvement of this country."[9] Even some prominent conservationists began to believe that the extermination of the buffalo was inevitable. "We know now that the extermination [is] a necessary part of the development of the country," admitted George Bird Grinnell.[10] And rather than being shamed or shunned, at least one bison hunter—William "Buffalo Bill" Cody—decked out in buckskins, waxed moustache, and long-barreled six-shooters, became a sort of nineteenth-century rock star, a glamorization of the war against the buffalo.

The Secretary of the Interior himself, a man named Columbus Delano, was in full-throated agreement with the views of Sherman, Sheridan, and the general public. "I would not seriously regret the total disappearance of the buffalo from our western plains, in its effect upon the Indians," Delano wrote in his department's annual report in 1873.[11] Delano, who had been appointed by President Ulysses S. Grant, was a peculiarly apt spokesperson for Western civilization. He had flinty, glittering eyes overshadowed by preposterously huge eyebrows, a lipless mouth set in an inverted *U* of permanent disapproval, and a slab-like beard, similar in size and shape to the tablet of the Ten Commandments.

"In our intercourse with the Indians it must always be borne in mind that we are the most powerful party. . . . We are assuming, and I think with propriety, that our civilization ought to take the place of their barbarous habits," Delano wrote. Later the next year, in testimony before Congress, he repeated these convictions: "I regard the destruction of such game as Indians subsist upon as facilitating the policy of the Government, of destroying their hunting habits, coercing them onto reservations, and compelling them to begin adopting the habits of civilization."

Although he tended to thunder like an Old Testament prophet, Delano was simply giving voice to the will of the commander-in-chief and, by extension, the views of a majority of the nation's God-fearing populace. In truth, the plains peoples of the Western wilderness had provided people like Columbus Delano with plenty of ammunition. Sensing their own impending extinction along with the buffalo's, the Blackfoot, the Sioux, and the Cheyenne were fighting back with such grim savagery that even a glancing description of their atrocities was enough to turn the stomach.

If destroying the buffalo was the final solution to the "problem" of the Indian, so be it. The vast majority of Americans had never even laid eyes on an Indian, a buffalo, or the West, and never would, so there was little they would miss. They got most of their information about what was happening out there from the newspapers, which had come to treat the slaughter of the buffalo as something of a joke. A

June 6, 1874, edition of *Harper's Weekly* featured a cover cartoon of a buffalo removing its own skin and handing it to a white man, with the caption, "Don't shoot, my good fellow! Here, take my robe, save your ammunition, and go in peace."[12]

Even so, not everyone in America was as intent on waging a holy war against the buffalo as Columbus Delano. There were a few angry and despairing voices being raised in the animal's defense, though not nearly enough to constitute a movement. "Conservation," whether of the buffalo or any other natural resource in America, was not a word that had yet come into popular usage.

In the years to come, the loudest, most persistent, and most authoritative voice in opposition to the slaughter of the buffalo would be that of the U.S. National Museum's chief taxidermist, William Temple Hornaday.

There were so many buffalo in the West, of course, that their numbers appeared to be inexhaustible. Stripping the Indian of his food supply would be an enormous, perhaps impossible task. At one time, bison herds had roamed north from northern Mexico across the Great Plains all the way to the shores of the Great Slave Lake, in the Northwest Territories of Canada. They extended west to the Sierra Nevadas, in California, and in the late 1700s, Daniel Boone had found vast herds of buffalo as far east as eastern Tennessee. The herds were so enormous that there were dozens of documented incidents in which trains, brought to a complete standstill by migrating herds, were actually knocked off the tracks. In 1868, a man named William Blackmore reported riding 120 miles from Ellsworth to Sheridan, Wyoming, and passing through an almost unbroken herd of buffalo the entire way. In another case, a herd was reported to take five days to pass a given point.[13]

Fortunately, there were plenty of people hard at work at the task of destroying them for the benefit of civilization. The Indians had started the work in ancient times by forcing herds over cliffs into "buffalo jumps" and killing them by the thousands. One buffalo jump near Sundance, Wyoming, was thought to contain the bones of twenty thousand animals.[14] The whites vastly accelerated the massacre beginning around 1820, and what later came to be called "The Great Slaughter" steadily gained momentum until it peaked around 1880, culminating in one of the greatest animal bloodbaths in history.

A few buffalo were killed to feed settlers' families or provision workers building the Union Pacific railroad line, the first to cross the West. Huge numbers also were killed for their luxurious pelts, used as carriage blankets, fashionable "buffalo robes," or coats. The American market alone absorbed more than 200,000 buffalo robes a year.[15] But many also were killed in a great American extravaganza of waste—hunters killed buffalo simply for their tongues or their humps, which were considered delicacies, leaving the slaughtered bulls, calves, and cows to rot. Even if the hides were harvested (and later sold for about fifty cents apiece), the rest of the animal was left for the vultures, coyotes, and the desert sun. But the herds were so vast that people crossing the Western territories on the Union Pacific line would simply fire their Sharps rifles out the train windows for sport. It wasn't much sport: it would take more skill to miss a buffalo than to hit one. The sport hunters didn't even take the tongue; they simply discarded the entire animal and took only the thrill of the kill.

Still, much work remained if the Indian were to be stripped of all sustenance and exterminated once and for all. When the Union Pacific Railroad was built from Omaha to Cheyenne in 1866 and 1867, it not only opened up the West, it also split the vast buffalo herd into a "southern herd" and a "northern herd."[16] Hunters got to work on the southern herd, and it was destroyed completely within about three years. Then they moved north from Texas to the Montana Territory and started in on the northern herd, which was said to be twenty times larger. At one point, there were said to be 5,000 buffalo hunters and skinners permanently encamped on the plains of the Montana Territory. In 1871, a new process for tanning buffalo hides made it possible to use buffalo leather for industrial uses, such as engine belts, and the speed with which the last herds were disappearing accelerated yet again.

Unfortunately, the Indian wars were not going as well as the war against the buffalo. In the summer of 1876, when word of the massacre of Custer and his men reached the cities of the East, Sherman, Sheridan, and most of the rest of the country were as shocked as they were angry. It seemed impossible that this gallant, well-known officer—and 268 of his men, no less!—could have been destroyed by what was supposed to be a weakened, desperate enemy.

The Indians, and the buffalo, would need to be wiped out once and for all.

CHAPTER 3

The Second Civil War

Hornaday, Hedley, and young Forney arrived in Miles City just after dawn on the morning of May 10, 1886, leaving a small tip for George the porter in the green-velvet Pullman car.[1] When they tumbled out of the train into the awakening town, they were surprised to discover that the little settlement had a few substantial, false-fronted brick buildings, and the shop windows were stocked with fancy goods, including parasols and ladies' gloves, as well as a huge assortment of fine leather saddles, bridles, spurs, and chaps. Although it would be three more years before the Montana Territory became a state, Miles City seemed on its way to becoming a real, bona-fide "city" in more than name only.

The three men found a place to stay in an incongruously well appointed hotel called the Drover House. Miles City was the northern terminus of the Old Western Trail, the longest of the cattle trails out of Texas, and "drovers" were the lean, hard men who drove the great herds of longhorns north—the original cowboys. Men who had not slept in a bed in six months and had just gotten paid came to the Drover House to live in the lap of luxury. To them, it must have seemed like heaven, with its brass spittoons, hanging lamps, and embossed tin ceilings.[2]

Hornaday noted in his journal that as he strolled through the town that first morning, almost every door on the side streets seemed to open into a cheap saloon, and the town was overrun with soldiers, Indian scouts, bullwhackers, cowboys, and idle, underdressed women.

In 1880, a local doctor had boasted of Miles City in the *Yellowstone Journal:* "We have twenty-three saloons in our town and they all do a good business; we are going to have one church soon."[3] The tiny town was tossed about like a fallen speck into the windy immensity of the northern Great Plains, and there seemed to be no place in the town to escape the wind and dust. Proper women sewed small weights into the hems of their long skirts to keep a frisky gust from revealing their ankles.

Miles City, on the Tongue River, was a bustling shipping center for the open-range cattle industry, and the place where beef cattle were loaded onto trains for shipment to the slaughterhouses of Chicago.[4] A huge annual meeting of the Montana Stockmen's Association had just taken place, and young Theodore Roosevelt, a member of the executive committee and a man who seemed to be everywhere, had been in town for the event. Wherever Hornaday walked in town, the smell of cattle manure hung in the air like wood smoke, an ever-present reminder that the cattle industry was rapidly putting an end to the day of the buffalo.

Not wanting to waste a single moment, Hornaday, Hedley, and Forney decided to walk the two miles down the railroad tracks to Fort Keogh in the early afternoon of that first day they arrived in Miles City. Spencer Fullerton Baird, the Smithsonian director, had informed Hornaday that he would contact Secretary of War William C. Endicott about the Smithsonian party expedition. Baird promised that he'd ask the secretary to direct the commander of the post at Fort Keogh to provide a military escort into what might well turn out to be hostile territory. There was good reason to worry: Fort Keogh had been built only ten years earlier, shortly after Custer's massacre on the Little Bighorn, about a hundred miles southwest of Miles City. The fort was now garrisoned by a part of the Fifth Infantry and the Seventh Cavalry, Custer's old regiment.

When Hornaday and his companions arrived at the fort, they found little more than a forlorn collection of rough buildings at the edge of the sagebrush flats and tethered saddle horses, their heads hanging down in the midday heat. When Hornaday and his companions were ushered in to see the commander of the post, Hornaday informed him that they were there on behalf of the Smithsonian Institution, in Washington, D.C., and that their intention was to collect museum specimens of the American bison. The commander could scarcely contain his amusement: *Buffalo? Mister Hornaday, you're joking. You'll never find any around here, and I don't think anybody in this post would disagree.*

Hornaday and his companions walked disconsolately back up the railroad tracks to their hotel, more like downcast boys than members of the vaunted Smithsonian Expedition of 1886. Over the next several days, Hornaday worked the telegraph office, trying to get the Secretary of War in Washington to authorize a military escort out of Fort Keogh. He also began making inquiries among local ranchers, stockmen, and landowners about where (if anywhere) he stood a chance of finding buffalo. Eventually, he began to tire of the inevitable letdown: *There's no buffalo anymore, and you can't get any anywhere.*[5]

Finally, he got some encouraging news. J. C. Merrill, the army doctor whom he'd corresponded with earlier, left a letter for Hornaday at Fort Keogh emphasizing his conviction that buffalo still could be found along Big Dry Creek, a tributary of the Missouri.[6] Merill's opinion was clearly the minority view, however—other people Hornaday spoke with told him, emphatically, that there were no buffalo left on the Big Dry, nor were there any left in the Powder River country of Wyoming, or the Judith Basin in Montana. Apparently, all three of the locations Dr. Merrill had thought likely hiding places for buffalo were "shot out."

The third night after arriving in Miles City, though, Hornaday's fortunes seemed to shift. He happened to fall into conversation with a rancher named Henry Phillips, of the LU-Bar Ranch, who was broad as a barn door but oddly soft-spoken and polite. The LU-Bar was up on Little Dry Creek, about eighty miles northwest of Miles City, Phillips explained. This region, in a desolate triangle formed by the Yellowstone, Missouri, and Musselshell rivers, had once been a favorite of the hide-hunters, where there were rumored to have been as many as a quarter-million buffalo only a few years earlier. In a "quiet but mighty convincing way," Hornaday later said, Phillips told him that he knew there were at least a few buffalo in the rugged badlands west of the LU-Bar Ranch. In fact, one of his men had killed a cow on Sand Creek just a few days earlier. The cowboys said they'd seen about thirty-five head altogether, Phillips told Hornaday. If he hunted up in the Sand Creek area, and stuck to it, he was sure Hornaday would get some in the end.

Hornaday had struck on some more good news. He decided to

take the museum party north, toward the Missouri-Yellowstone Divide, and explore the badlands around the headwaters of the Little Dry Creek, Big Dry Creek, and Sand Creek, the place that had been mentioned by two different people so far as the place the last remaining buffalo in the West might be hiding.

Once the Secretary of War finally made contact with Fort Keogh, the Smithsonian party had been provided by the quartermaster with camp equipment, field transportation, a lumbering wagon pulled by six mules, and a small military escort of five soldiers from the Fifth Infantry.[7] (The very fact that only five soldiers were considered sufficient for a journey through Indian country showed how weakened the tribes had become, their strength and numbers diminishing with the disappearance of the great herds.) Still, it was a measure of safety for a journey through country still shadowed by Sioux, Crow, and Blackfoot, and by outlaws and rustlers.

Hornaday also had arranged to hire a guide through this unfamiliar country—a Cheyenne Indian called White Dog, who showed up wearing, absurdly, a pair of red overalls. White Dog turned out to be not only utterly worthless as a guide, but also a lazy crybaby who would pretend to be sick when there was any work to be done (according to Hornaday's account). Far more helpful were the two rangy cowboys who'd also signed on for the trip. The cowboys were not the picturesque cowpunchers of lore, but polite young men in their twenties, many of whom had come west for adventure. They were not so much the mythological embodiment of the West as young wayfarers who had come in search of it.[8]

Nevertheless, they'd all spent so much time riding the wide stock saddles favored by cowboys that they'd become bowlegged—one cowboy's legs were so wide "he could have thrown a cat between them, with perfect safety—to the cat," Hornaday said. They all wore battered cowboy hats, leather chaps, and high-heeled riding boots, and carried six-chambered .45-caliber revolvers, with ammo belts full of cartridges. They used their guns for only two reasons, Hornaday found out—to shoot game on the range and to shoot out the lights at the local saloon, when they'd been paid a year's wages and were in the process of wasting every bit of it on whiskey, women, and cards.

Even so, he found these young cowboys to be the hardest-working men he'd ever known, and also the most generous, loyal, and sweet-tempered. They were also among the most poorly paid. One of them, a young man who had been working as a store clerk in Chicago making twenty dollars a week, had come West to become a cowboy and was now working "sixteen hours a day in all kinds of weather, and without any of the comforts of life, at thirty dollars a month." This, Hornaday said, was "pitiful," although most of the cowboys seemed happy enough to be living this rough outdoor life under the boundless Montana sky. Still, more than one confided to him, "I'm sick of cowpunchin,' and I'm going to quit it forever this fall."[9]

The party crossed the Yellowstone River just outside Miles City on an old ferry, then began to rumble slowly northward on the Sunday Creek Trail, a famous cattle trail along Sunday Creek known variously as the Texas, Montana, or Northern Trail, and along which generations of cattle were driven north from Texas into the Missouri River country.[10] A couple of the soldiers generally rode the buckboard of the clattering six-mule wagon, which was loaded to the wagon-bows like a floundering ark. Along with Forney, Hedley and Hornaday usually rode their own mounts alongside the wagon. Hornaday, easy in the saddle and often wearing his Norfolk hunting jacket and low-brimmed Western hat, kept a constant eye on the party like a mother hen. White Dog trotted along on his Indian pony, along with the other soldiers and cowpokes, some on horseback, some on foot. Together, this motley museum party made its way into the "Big Dry country" of the badlands.

They reached the big divide between the Yellowstone and the Missouri rivers, a high, bare promontory that allowed them to gaze out across this sunbaked, godforsaken country, with its distant flat-topped buttes, unending sky, and vast canyons. They were searching for buffalo, or perhaps only buffalo ghosts. They scanned the horizon with a glass, but they spotted no life larger than a pronghorn antelope or a kettle of turkey vultures spiralling into the heat-hazy Western sky.

"What a prospect!" Hornaday scribbled in his journal of one of these surveys. "In every direction the view swept over from ten to twenty-five miles of wild, rugged country, composed of buttes, divides, coulies, wash-outs, and rugged ravines and creeks—nothing but badlands. But the view was truly grand, and impressive. We seemed to be looking over the whole of Montana, indeed."

Now, as the lurching wagon, mules, and horses of Hornaday's Smithsonian party crossed the desolate headland of the Missouri-Yellowstone Divide and began descending the north side, they found themselves entering a world that had been dramatically, and tragically, changed since the days when the plains peoples lived and flourished here. Now they were entering a vast sepulchre of death.

There, along the Sunday Creek Trail, sprawled in the prairie grass, lay the skeletonized carcass of an enormous buffalo bull, completely stripped of its hide like a dead chicken. The great head, fierce as a tribal mask with its muddy, lionlike mane and beard, had been left unskinned. The bull lay precisely as it had fallen, its head stretched far forward, as though at full gallop, its legs scattered behind it as though straining to escape. Moments later, Hornaday saw another of these "ghastly monuments of slaughter," as he later described them, then another, and another, until the party found itself passing through a hushed battlefield that stretched to the far distance, where crumpled corpses appeared as little more than dark specks. It was as if, far out of sight of almost everyone in America, a second Civil War had been raging for decades, with such grievous losses, there was nothing left but silence and bones.[11]

Most of the men were wearing scarves over their mouths and noses, like rustlers, to keep the akali dust out of their throats. But the scarves also kept them from speaking in this lonesome place, where words meant nothing. It was a country almost completely bare of trees in every direction except for a few aspen and cottonwoods in the rugged brakes along the creek bottoms. It was also almost emptied of game. During the first two days of travel north of Miles City, in a country that was custom-made for pronghorn antelope, they did not see a single one; the only living creatures they saw were prairie dogs, rabbits, and turkey vultures, wheeling high overhead as if scouting for the last meal in Montana. It was forlorn, abandoned country, a country of great absences, which had once been filled by the dust and noise and dung of one of the planet's greatest zoological spectacles but now was almost completely silent.

This area, they'd been told, was once a famous buffalo range. But now, to Hornaday's infinite sorrow, it was a place whose name was desolation, the place, he wrote later, "where the millions had gone." On either side of the wagon trail lay the bleaching skeletons of a great buffalo slaughter, from huge bull skeletons sprawled close beside the trail to those scattered into the distance like dark stars. Many of the skeletons were not even skinned, with hides baked hard as wood by the desert heat and wind. Sometimes there were forty or fifty skeletons in sight at one time. The killing-ground appeared to be frozen in the moment the animals had fallen, what Hornaday estimated to be about four years earlier, "except that the flesh was no longer upon them."

The emotional burden of these terrible sights, in this terrible place, was something that would change Hornaday's life forever. "It was impossible to look at one without a sigh," he wrote, "and each group of skeletons brought back the old thoughts, 'What a pity!' 'What a pity!'"

The blast furnace of the desert heat and wind had stripped the flesh from the bones, which were bleached white as porcelain. Some of the enormous skeletons were perfectly preserved, the rib cages held together like strung bows with dried bits of ligament, and even the tiny carpal and tarsal bones, the size of hazelnuts, were preserved so fastidiously that it was as if the buffalo had been preserved for some far-off, fairer afterlife, like Egyptian pharaohs.

CHAPTER 4

Souvenir of a Lost World

The Smithsonian museum party, with its rattling six-mule wagon and assortment of Indian ponies and saddle horses, soldiers, hunters, and taxidermists, carefully trundled their way down the dusty switchbacks on the north scarp of the divide, which opened out across a world so vast it appeared to reveal the curvature of the earth. When they reached the bottom, they found Little Dry Creek, a small tributary of the Missouri which, despite its name, had a faint ribbon of muddy water coursing through it. The water was foul-tasting and, because of the alkali, slightly soapy to the touch. The party followed the creek twelve miles, through copses of aspen and cottonwood along the bottom, to the LU-Bar Ranch. The ranch had a lonesome, slapped-together appearance—it was really just a stone and adobe shack with a few outbuildings—with saddle horses tethered to the porch rail and a spindle of smoke trailing up out of the cookhouse into the big sky.[1]

The place was deserted except for a young cowboy named Irwin Boyd, who'd been left in charge of the ranch while the other cowboys were at a roundup on the west branch of Sunday Creek. Boyd, glad for the company, welcomed the museum party heartily and asked them to spend the night. Hornaday and Hedley rode onto the range on their Indian ponies before nightfall, scouting the territory and looking for game, and when they returned, Boyd had a hot supper ready. That night, Hornaday jotted in his journal, the soldiers and taxidermists crowded inside, sheltered from a light rain, and "there was lots of talk in the shack by candlelight about bad cowpunchers and good ones, deperadoes, fights, outrages, capers, etc."

The next morning, they continued north for eight more miles, where they found a clear spring and stopped to set up the expedition's permanent camp, on Phillips Creek, about eighty miles north of Miles City. They unpacked the wagon, which could go no further in this rugged country, and sent the mule team back to Fort Keogh with a drover. Then Hornaday and George Hedley set about trying to hunt buffalo, if they could find any.

Hornaday and Hedley began scouting the country in a systematic way. They would saddle up the packhorses, load rifles, blankets, and rations for two to four days, and set out in a vast circuit through new territory, covering as much ground as possible each day and making camp under the immense stars wherever night overtook them. Despite the sorrow of their task, Hornaday could not help but feel exultant, spreading out his bedroll in the sagebrush with no sound but the wind around them and the happy crackle of a little campfire. There was no place he felt more at home than out here.

After several unsuccessful forays like this, Hornaday and Hedley went out one day with Boyd and a private from Fort Keogh named Moran, who was riding an Army mule. In the early afternoon, they came trotting over a hill and saw, to their utter astonishment, a bull buffalo calf, cowering in a barren hollow between two high buttes, "as lonesome-looking a waif as ever was left to the mercies of a cold world." He appeared to be only a few weeks old and was wobbly legged as a fawn.[2]

Moments later, they caught a fleeting glimpse of three adults, apparently cows, tearing away over the hilltop. For whatever reason, the little bull had been abandoned by its mother. When the calf saw the two men on horseback approaching, he tried to run, but before he'd gone a hundred yards, they'd caught up to him. Hedley and Hornaday leaped off their horses and tried to grab the calf with their outstretched arms, but he head-butted each of them in turn. Then he kicked the mule that Private Moran was riding. So Boyd threw a lasso around the little rascal and hauled him in. He struggled and kicked, but he was so thin and so weak that his efforts to resist were futile. Hornaday laughed in amazement and delight at the endearing pluckiness of the little calf, who fought at all odds to go his own way. He reminded him of himself.

To all of them, the buffalo calf was "a genuine curiosity." Most buffaloes over a year old are dusty brown, but this one was a "perfect blonde, with coarse, woolly sandy-red hair." Hornaday named him

"Sandy" on the spot. They tied him to a clump of sagebrush and went galloping off after the three adult buffalo that they'd seen running off, but it was too late; the adults, apparently including the calf's mother, seemed to have vanished, as if they'd only been ghosts. Returning to the tethered calf, Hornaday hoisted him onto his horse, with his legs dangling down on either side and a look of wary surprise in his eyes, and carried him back to camp. The next night, Hornaday and Hedley returned to the place where the calf was found and camped there, hoping that the mother would return for her baby. They listened for the sound of buffalo hooves all night, but all they heard was "the occasional chirp of a sparrow breaking the silence" of the moonlit night.

Ten days after they captured Sandy, Hornaday and Hedley finally spooked a couple of adult bulls out of the tree cover along the Little Dry, about fifteen miles from the LU-Bar Ranch.[3] One got away, but Hornaday managed to chase down the other and shoot him from horseback. Once he got his experienced taxidermist's hands on the hide of this animal, which was a large one, standing five feet four inches at the shoulder—the first time he'd ever touched an adult in the wild—he could see right away that the shedding of his winter coat was in progress. A rich mantle of new hair, three to six inches long and of a "peculiar bluish–gray appearance," was coming in over most parts of his body while its old hair, brown, weather-beaten and matted with mud and dung, was being shed. The new hair was coming in unevenly, though: on parts of the bull's hindquarters, there were patches of skin that were perfectly bare, and in other places, only patches of shaggy, old, brown hair, giving the animal a ragged, seedy appearance.

The capture of the little calf and the death of the bull proved beyond a doubt that there were still a few wild buffalo in this region. But Hornaday worried that, given cowboys' penchant for killing game simply for sport, it was "absolutely certain" that within a short time, perhaps even a few months, all the members of this embattled little band of bison would be killed. Nevertheless, he and Hedley decided that the best thing to do was to wait until autumn, when the buffalo's hides would be glossy with new growth and suitable for mounting at the museum, and then return to this same area with enough men and provisions for an extended hunt.

On the way back to Miles City, they stopped to camp at a bleak outpost near a place called Red Buttes, along the Sunday Creek

Trail. That night, by lantern-light, Hornaday was skinning a coyote, a pronghorn antelope, and a couple of sage grouse that the party had shot that day when a lonely looking man driving a horse-drawn buckboard appeared in the circle of lantern-light. The grizzled old man introduced himself as "Doc" Zahl. He seemed to want company, so Hornaday invited him to throw down his bedroll and spend the night with them. The old man happily obliged, and while Hornaday continued his work, Zahl unburdened himself of his story.[4]

He had been a buffalo hunter himself, Zahl said—one of the most celebrated in the territories, in fact. He once killed 120 buffalo in a little over an hour, methodically firing and reloading his Sharps .40–120 buffalo rifle almost continuously, so the barrel got so hot it would sear his skin if he touched it. Zahl had started out on the immense southern herd, down in Texas, but once that was all shot out, he moved north into the Montana Territory and got to work on the northern herd. He was one of the five thousand hunters and skinners who had camped permanently on the Montana plains during the bloody years of 1882 and 1883, finishing off the work in the northern territories. All that killing was hard work, and hard on a man, he said—brutal labor on your back, shoulders, hands, and arms, and months or years sleeping on the cold ground didn't help much, either.

Now that that herd was gone, he and his brother had started a business hauling out buffalo bones by wagon, taking them down to the Missouri and loading them on river steamers. It was lonesome but profitable work, he said; the bones fetched twenty-eight dollars a ton once they were shipped to dealers in St. Louis and elsewhere, where they were crushed up and sold as fertilizer for suburban lawns and gardens—something as unimaginable as heaven out here in this vast, godforsaken emptiness. Zahl said that he and his brother had sold two hundred tons the previous year. He related all this utterly without sorrow or awareness of his own role in the destruction of the buffalo.

When Hornaday told him that he thought that the buffalo was near extinction, Zahl snorted in disbelief. Just a few years earlier, back around 1883, Zahl said, a herd of something like fifty thousand buffalo had crossed the Yellowstone and headed north, up across the Canadian border. They were still up there, hiding out, and they'd come back someday, Zahl said. There were also at least five thousand wild buffalo down in the territories, in little bands here and there. The buffalo weren't gone—there were too many of them to be gone.

Referring to Zahl's numbers, Hornaday commented to his dog-eared journal later that night, "This is a great mistake." From his extensive correspondence, he had learned that in fact, a large herd had crossed the Yellowstone a few years earlier, but they never made it to Canada. Hide-hunters, Indians, and settlers had decimated the herd before they got there. The scattered reports of small droves here and there in the Montana Territory were all that remained. The great ghostly herd, spirited away to Canada, which would return someday to replenish the lost millions, was just a reassuring fantasy, particularly cherished by the hunters who were responsible for the buffalo's destruction.

The spindly legged, sandy-blonde buffalo calf, Sandy, rode in a railroad baggage car when Hornaday, Hedley, and Forney returned to Washington. Hornaday tenderly raised him on cow's milk through that spring and summer of 1886, but one day in July, Sandy ate an enormous amount of damp clover, and before anyone discovered it, he had curled up on the ground and died. Hornaday was anguished by the calf's death. The only hopeful note in this sad end was that at the time of his death, Sandy was three months old, weighed 120 pounds, and stood two feet nine inches high at the shoulder. He'd at least been nurtured, in captivity, past infancy. In letters to friends, Hornaday expressed so much sorrow over the death of Sandy that at least one historian has suggested that the death of the little calf may have inspired one of his greatest creations: the National Zoo at the Smithsonian. If Hornaday could not save the untold millions that were already gone, at least he might be able to preserve the legacy of one small, frightened foundling.[5]

CHAPTER 5

The Last Buffalo Hunt

It was late September of 1886, and along the Yellowstone River outside Miles City, Montana, the shimmering aspen leaves were just beginning to turn, like cascades of tiny golden coins. Four months after his first, exploratory expedition into the territories, Hornaday had once again boarded a westbound train in Washington, but this time he was prepared for an organized, extended hunt. He also was returning with a much better feel for the lay of the land in the rugged coulee country north of the Yellowstone, and of the habits of the few remaining buffalo who remained alive there—if it was not already too late.

This time, he knew almost for certain that there were at least a few animals hiding out in the headwaters of Sand Creek and the Little and Big Dry creeks, probably tucked away up in the heads of the ravines. His great hope was to secure twenty specimens and get back over the Yellowstone within two months, "before the terrors of a Montana winter should catch us afield."[1] Secretary Spencer Baird had asked that Hornaday attempt to secure that many animals because if he was successful, the skins and skeletons could be distributed to other museums, which were as bereft of decent specimens as the National Museum. This expedition was to become the last organized buffalo hunt in Montana, and one of the last in the United States. Hornaday was not unaware of the profound melancholy that hung over the whole affair, like the faint odor of something beginning to go bad.

In his autobiography, written forty-eight years after these events had faded into memory, Hornaday acknowledged his own misgivings over what the museum party was about to do—and begged the forgiveness of future generations for what could arguably be called a crime. But to Hornaday's way of thinking, he was there only to *remedy* the atrocities committed by a criminal enterprise—the million individual crimes of the buffalo-killing industry that grew up in the West in the mid- to late 1800s, and the "criminal indifference" of the government that allowed it to happen.[2]

"If the reader now should feel doubtful about the ethical propriety of our last buffalo hunt, and the killing that we had to do in order that our National Museum might secure a few good wild skins out of the wreck of the millions, let him feel assured that our task was by no means a pleasant one," he wrote, continuing,

> At the same time, remember that the author has made atonement to *Bison americanus* by the efforts that he put forth since 1889 for the saving and the restoration of that species. Never since Juan Cabeza de Vaca killed the first buffalo on the Texas plains did any man ever set forth bison hunting with a heart as heavy, or as much oppressed by doubt, as that carried westward by the writer in 1886.[3]

On this "last buffalo hunt," Hornaday had engaged the services of Irwin Boyd as guide, hunter, and foreman, and Boyd had hired on two veteran Montana cowboys, Jim McNaney and L. S. "Russ" Russell. McNaney was not only a crack shot and champion rider, but he also had a reputation for playing the meanest firelight mouth-organ in all of Montana. He was a former hide-hunter who claimed to have brought down 3,300 buffalo in his day, but he knew the Missouri-Yellowstone Divide as well as anybody, and if anyone could find buffalo in it, it was McNaney. For the buffalo, it was the end of days, and Hornaday could see no way forward but to shake hands with the devil.

Hornaday also brought with him a twenty-four-year-old senior at the University of Kansas named Harvey Brown, whose university had been promised a couple of specimens in exchange for Brown's time, and who proved to be unfailingly cheerful and resourceful on what was probably the most memorable adventure of his life. Hornaday and Brown arrived at the Drover House in Miles City at two in the morning on September 24. The hotel was so crowded that Brown had to finish out the night on the puncheon floor of the barroom, wakened periodically by tipsy cowboys stomping into the bar for a drink, and also by the seemingly indefatigable Hornaday, who stayed up into the wee hours "gassing" with an old fur dealer about buffalo hunting. (Hornaday may have to talked to excess, but he didn't drink that way—he was a teetotaler.)[4]

Again, the quartermaster at Fort Keogh had supplied a six-mule wagon, a Sibley tent and stove, cooking utensils, commissary stores, and even a grizzled old camp cook named McCanna, known as "Mac." The next day, Hornaday bought two months' supplies of commissary stores, a team, and two saddle-horses, and he hired three more horses and a set of double harness. All the cowboys came with their own horses, so that in the whole outfit, there were ten horses, a team, and two good saddle-horses for each hunter, plus a light ranch wagon that could go anywhere, the ATV of its day. The worst of it was that they had to haul 2,000 pounds of oats into buffalo country to feed all those horses, and even that probably wouldn't last the whole trip.

The soldiers of the Fifth Infantry arrived in Miles City to help pack up the wagons on the day of departure, but by mid-afternoon, they were all uproariously drunk, waving whiskey bottles overhead as the team, wagon, and horses made their way out of town. Three miles out of town, on a steep hill, the wagon tipped over and 4,000 pounds of food and supplies went clattering down the hill. McCanna and the driver, who with Hornaday were the only sober passengers, had to supervise reloading the wagon, and they were far from happy about it. By the time they got to Chapman's ranch and set up camp that first night, the soldiers were too "shiftless and drunk" even to put up their tents, so they slept in the open. Hornaday, meanwhile, had the runs. It was an inglorious start for the last buffalo hunt.

By September 29, they had reached the HV Ranch, as desolate and half-finished-looking as the LU-Bar, on Big Dry Creek, about 90 miles from Miles City. Here, they unloaded the provisions from the six-mule wagon, loaded up the wagon with bleached-white skeletons and skulls of buffalo which they'd picked up along the way, and sent the wagon back to Fort Keogh. The cowboys, with their penchant for nicknaming everything for which they felt affection, were by now calling Brown "Browney" or "Flapjack Bill" (after he was discovered secretly making himself a stack of pancakes one morning).[5]

In the following days, Hornaday, Hedley, and the cowboys scoured this difficult country, full of wild and rugged buttes, steep-sided ravines, and badlands, without finding any sign at all of buffalo. But it was the sort of country in which embattled game loved to hide, and on October 13, after almost three weeks in the field, one of the cowboys, Russ Russell, got lucky. In the late afternoon, he came across seven buffalo lying up in the shadows at the head of a deep ravine. As they stumbled to their feet and took off at a dead run, Russell got off a few shots from horseback, but he missed, and they all went thundering away. He chased them for two or three miles, but his horse was tired and the buffalo escaped, heading due south.[6]

Russell brought this great news back to the rest of the hunters at the camp on Big Dry Creek. Hornaday concluded that the cowboy's discovery must mean the buffalo were in the habit of hiding in the shady coolness at the head of these ravines whenever they were disturbed on their favorite feeding grounds further south. The next morning at first light, Hornaday and three cowboys, mounted on fresh horses, returned to Russell's ravine and picked up the trail of the seven buffalo. They followed the trail into the devilishly difficult country that the cowboys called "gumbo ground," where the soil was loose and crumbly, like ashes, and the horses' hooves sank halfway to the fetlocks with each step; where the ground was overrun with deep seams and cracks that could easily turn a horse's ankle or even break a leg; and where the whole confounded mess was interspersed with sagebrush and greasewood. Crossing twelve miles of this in pursuit of the buffalo, Hornaday wrote, was "killing work" and very slow. The ashy soil had one big advantage, though: tracking was easy.[7]

Finally, the animals left the gumbo ground and passed into grassy country near a small stream called Taylor Creek, where tracking was practically impossible. Around noon, the hunters rode up onto high ground and Hornaday surveyed the windswept, treeless countryside with binoculars. About two miles away, resting on the level summit of a small butte, he spotted the buffalo; the original drove of seven had been joined by seven more. Although it was a fragment of the once-mighty multitudes, nevertheless it was the biggest herd Hornaday had ever seen in the wild. The hunters crept up to within 200 yards of the animals and, on a signal, they all began to fire. The buffalo leaped to their feet, unharmed, and bounded away at breathtaking speed, heading for the shelter of the ravines.

Hornaday and the cowboys leaped back in the saddle and took off at a mad gallop, this time directly through a vast prairie dog town, even worse than gumbo ground, which could have snapped a horse's leg should it slip down into a hole at top speed. But none of the horses were injured, and once they'd caught up to the fleeing buffalo, Mc-Naney killed a fine old bull and a beautiful two-year-old or "spike" bull. Hornaday brought down a cow and another large old bull. It was a fine day of hunting, even shot through with the aftertaste of remorse as it was.

For the rest of October, as the aspen leaves turned and then began to fall, the museum party focused their hunt on the heads of the ravines, the buffalo's secret hideouts. By the end of the month, they had taken a total of twelve specimens, with Hornaday, by firelight, spending his evenings painstakingly preparing the skins and skeletons for museum mounting. He cut "SIBO" into the thin, cutaneous muscle that lined the inside of the buffalo hide, a brand which stood for "Smithsonian Institution Buffalo Outfit," the official name of the expedition. It was just the way the old buffalo hunters used to mark their hides in the days of the great slaughter.[8]

Most of the buffalo meat was consumed by Hornaday's hunting party or given to cowboys and soldiers they encountered along the way. Almost all the work of skinning out and skeletonizing the buffalo was done by Hornaday, with help from Harvey Brown, the young student. It was brutal work. "Brown and I worked all day on the buffalo skins, fleshing, washing out blood, etc." Hornaday noted in his journal on October 20. "It is a fearful job to wash the blood out of a skin, a long, cold, tiresome job, freezing to the hands, breaking to the back. Worked all day on 2 skins."[9]

Hunting these last remaining buffalo in this murderous country was doubly difficult because the few that remained alive had probably been shot at before and spooked at the slightest sound. In open country, they also could run like the wind, even though the big bulls could weigh almost a ton. McNaney's technique, once he'd spooked a buffalo into a run, was to fool the buffalo into thinking he'd abandoned the chase, then spur his horse into making a wide circuit of three or four miles, cut in ahead of the buffalo and lie in wait for it behind the crest of a ridge. It took hard riding, but it could be done without killing the horse, and McNaney never seemed to fail. Russ, riding his favorite horse Selim, "an ungainly old beast with a gait like an elephant but staying powers like a steam engine," sometimes used a more straightforward method, actually overtaking a solitary old bull who had a half-mile head start in a straight-ahead race.[10]

This hunt, Hornaday admitted in his journals, was "great sport," partly because it was so difficult and partly because he enjoyed the rugged outdoor life and the friendly rivalry that developed among the hunters. (Jim McNaney won the hunting contest because he was far and away the best shot, coupled with having the canniest intuition about buffalo behavior.) "In our eagerness to succeed in our task, the sad fact that we were hunting the last representatives of a mighty race was for the time being lost sight of," he wrote.

Buffalo were such indomitable animals, particularly the big bulls, that very seldom did they fall with the first shot. Even though they might be gravely wounded, they had to be chased, often for miles, before they were brought down with repeated volleys of gunfire, aiming for heart, lungs, or spine.[11] One day McNaney and Russell shot four buffalo, including a big bull which finally fell eight miles south of where it was first hit. By then it was getting dark, so the cowboys left the bull and returned the next day to skin it out and skeletonize the carcass for later mounting. When they came back the next morning, however, Hornaday and the cowboys came upon a shocking scene: The bull had been stripped of its hide and flesh, its bloody skeleton exposed to the sky, its leg bones broken to get at the marrow, its tongue cut out. The great lionlike head, with its fearsome horns and immense, sorrowful face, was still intact. But one half of the head had been smeared with yellow paint, and the other half with red paint. A tattered bit of red flannel had been tied to one horn and fluttered fitfully in the breeze, apparently as a signal of defiance. Around the denuded carcass, Hornaday found moccasin prints in the sand.

A small band of Indians, thought to be Piegans (members of the Blackfoot nation) were later reported to have been seen in the area a few days earlier. The Piegans, renowned for their skill and savagery as warriors and their prowess at stealing horses, were nomadic peoples who depended on the buffalo for their existence. The decimation of the great herds had brought disaster to these free-ranging people. Ethnographers believe that as many as one-fourth of the Piegans in

Montana died of starvation during the years 1883 and 1884. They had laid claim to the fallen bull—very likely one of the last wild buffalo the tribes of the northern plains would ever see—because they believed that it belonged to them. It was not only the buffalo that was passing away. It was also the end of the ancient ways of the native peoples who revered and depended on them.

But like so many other whites of his time, Hornaday had little understanding or sympathy for the Indians. In fact, he was furious that they'd "stolen" his prize bull, and vowed to get off a shot if he ever came across them. Hornaday had come all the way out to Montana to gather specimens for science, and the specimens turned out to be almost impossible to find. He'd be damned if he'd let the Indians steal them.

Eventually, after weeks of searching, Hornaday's hunting party spotted seven bison resting in the shade of a ravine near Sand Creek, north of the Yellowstone River, at the foot of a rugged, three-square-mile butte Hornaday called the "High Divide." Hornaday and three cowboys, all on horseback, crept to within 200 yards of the herd and then dismounted behind the crest of a hill. They inched up to the rim, drew a bead, and fired, but the bison got to their feet in an instant and went thundering away down the ravine, unharmed. The party pursued them for miles, eventually galloping alongside them and then, one by one, shot all seven animals. Hornaday shot two, a cow and an immense, shaggy-bearded old bull, likely the patriarch of the herd. By then it was getting dark, so the hunters left the buffalo where they lay and returned the next morning. The Indians had not disturbed the prize, but to Hornaday's amazement, the big bull was still breathing. He later recalled:

> [The bull] was still alive, and in a terrible rage. He stood up on his fore legs, pawed the ground, and tore around as far as he could. Tried hard to get up, but could not. His eyes fairly flashed fire. We stood at a safe distance awhile and studied him, then, as it was getting late, I drew up, aimed for his heart, and fired. The blood gushed out of the hole, and the old fellow gave a great shudder. He struggled mightily for a moment, then his head slowly sank until it touched the ground. Rising on his fore legs, he threw his head high into the air until his nose pointed at the sun, and his eyes rolled in agony toward the sky. He opened his mouth

and the blood ran out. An instant later, he fell suddenly prone upon his side, and his left fore leg, by a strange coincidence, pointed straight at me and shook like a mighty arm in reproach and condemnation.[12]

Finally, after two months in the field, the Smithsonian party had reached a total of nineteen buffalo skins, one shy of their target of twenty. They decided to pack up and head back towards Miles City, hunting and camping along the way.

By now it was late November; they'd already had one forty-eight-hour Montana blizzard, which kept them huddled in their camp for two days, feeding firewood into the little Sibley camp stove, supplying oats to the storm-beaten horses and playing draw poker for gunwads. Finally, the weather cleared, but the hunters decided it was about time to call it quits. They packed up the wagon and prepared to head south. But before they did, Hornaday told the cowpokes, he was going to let them pilot the wagon because he wanted to kill another big bull "before this thing is over." On November 22, Harvey Brown noted uneasily in his diary that it had snowed all night and was five below zero at dawn; two degrees at one p.m.; and already four below at nine p.m. "The terrors of a Montana winter" were fast approaching.

But the light snow made conditions perfect for tracking, so Hornaday and McNaney rode out away from the wagon train in search of game. They had crossed two or three snowy ridges, then began descending through steep country toward a dry river bottom, when Hornaday spotted the light-brown humps of three buffalo, about 200 yards away.

The buffaloes appeared to be a youngster, perhaps two years old; an old cow; and an immense bull, the largest Hornaday had ever seen. He and McNaney jumped off their horses and ducked behind a clump of sagebrush, but the animals spotted them and took off through the snowy ravine at a slow trot, kicking up a spray of snow as they ran. Hornaday stood up, squared himself into a wide stance, and got off a couple of shots with his .44–40 Winchester buffalo rifle, but both bullets missed.[13]

McNaney had better luck, or better aim. Hornaday saw a cow go down, and watched as the other cow and the great bull hightailed it over the hill. He slammed a few more cartridges into his Winchester, leaped onto his Indian pony, Brownie, and took off at a gallop through the snowcovered sagebrush. Brownie was a splendid, high-spirited animal, and he mounted the hill and flew down the other side like the wind until he drew even with the fleeing pair of buffalo, who were tearing away down the ravine with wads of snow flying up from their hooves. The bull, seeming to sense that he'd been caught, stopped suddenly and whirled around to fight, his head lowered, shovel-shaped horns thrust outward like an invitation to death. Hornaday fired once for his lungs, but the shot was low. He fired a second time at his shoulder, and the beast went down, head foremost, in the snow. Without waiting to watch what happened next, Hornaday took off in pursuit of the cow, but she escaped. He reined Brownie back around sharply, and trotted back to the fallen bull. The bull was still alive and sitting up where he'd fallen.

As the bull saw Hornaday coming back, he staggered to his feet—despite what appeared to be a broken leg—and began trundling off over the snowy hill. Just over the crest, the bull halted again, panting, blood pouring down his shoulder, head lowered for a fight. When he panted, a spray of bright blood appeared on the white snow. Hornaday pulled Brownie up to within thirty yards of him and "gazed upon him with genuine astonishment. Not until that moment had I realized what a grand prize had fallen to me." He continued:

He seemed to me then, ay, and he did later on, the grandest quadruped I ever beheld, lions, tigers, and elephants not excepted. His huge bulk loomed up like a colossus, and the height of his great shaggy hump, and the steepness of its slope down to his loins, seemed positively incredible. . . . His massive head was crowned by a thick mass of blackish-brown hair lying in a tumble of great curly tufts, sixteen inches long, piled upon on each other, crowding back upon his horns, almost hiding them, and quite onto his shoulders. . . . The upper half of each foreleg was lost in a huge bunch of long, coarse black hair, in which scores of cockleburs had caught and hopelessly tangled. The body itself and the loin quarters were covered with a surprisingly thick coat of long, fine, mouse-colored hair, without the slightest flaw or blemish. From head to heel, the animal seemed to possess everything the finest buffalo in the world should have, and although by that time no stranger to his kind, I sat gazing upon him so completely absorbed by wonder and admiration that had he made a sudden charge he might easily have bowled me over.[14]

The immense bull stood there in the snow with his feet braced apart, head lowered, eyeing the hunter fiercely, with the whites of his eyeballs showing. His head sank very low a couple of times, then he abruptly lifted it and glared at Hornaday, panting. He pawed the wet snow with his wounded foreleg. He was a formidable adversary, a truly noble combatant, and he was not prepared to surrender.

"With the greatest reluctance I ever felt about taking the life of an animal," Hornaday wrote later, "I shot the great beast through the lungs, and he fell down and died."[15]

When he and McNaney laid the big bull out in the snow and took measurements, he turned out to be five feet eight inches in vertical height at the shoulder; nine feet two inches end to end, from the tip of his nose to the back of the thigh; eight feet four inches in girth around the chest; and according to Hornaday's reckoning, must have weighed about 1,600 pounds. When he dressed the animal out, he turned out to have four old bullets buried in his body; more than one hunter had aimed to have him as a trophy but failed. The horns of bulls taken in their prime were smooth and glossy-black, almost as if they'd been rubbed with oil, but this was what the old buffalo hunters called a "stub-horn." That meant that this was an old bull whose horns had begun to peel off in layers at the base, leaving a thick, blunt stub, with only the tip of what was once a glossy horn showing through at the end. Because bison add a ring each year around the base of the horn, just as domestic cattle do, Hornaday judged that the bull was about eleven or twelve years old (in an animal whose natural life-span was roughly twenty-five years). His tongue and lips were bluish-purple; his hooves were jet black; and his eyes, with a pear-shaped iris, were reddish brown.

Hornaday lovingly noted all these details as he prepared the skin for mounting. Later, this superb animal would become the principal figure in Hornaday's famous bison group that was displayed for sixty years at the Smithsonian. Later still, the bull became even more famous when he was used by the Treasury Department as the model for the bison depicted on the ten-dollar bill that went into production in 1901. Greengrocers, housewives, gamblers, shopkeepers, and petty criminals all made contact, however fleetingly, with the great bull who went down in the Montana snow that long-ago afternoon. The mighty bull, though fallen, served Hornaday's larger purpose of bringing "wildlife to the millions" and so played his role in halting the extermination of his species.

On the night of November 25, a ferocious blizzard came shrieking down from the north country, temporarily trapping the museum party in their camp on Porcupine Creek. The temperature dropped to sixteen below zero that night; Hornaday watched a pail of water standing within four feet of a blazing campfire freeze over solid in ten minutes. That dreadful winter, which came to be known as the Winter of the Blue Snow, would later be remembered in plaintive lines from a cowboy song:

> I may not see a hundred
> Before I see the Styx,
> But, coal or ember, I'll remember
> Eighteen eighty-six
> The stiff heaps in the coulees
> The dead eyes in the camp
> And the wind about, blowing fortunes out,
> Like a woman blows out a lamp.[16]

The Smithsonian Expedition broke camp on December 15, during a brief thaw in the weather, packing the wagons with boxes of specimens, food, and camp supplies, saddling up the horses and ponies and heading back home. Hornaday knew that if the museum party did not get out of camp very soon, they could be in serious trouble. It was bitterly cold; they were running out of food for both men and horses; the snow made the Sunday Creek Trail almost impassable; and the Yellowstone River would soon be so choked with treacherous running ice that the ferry to Miles City would be closed for the season.

Despite the hunt's lingering sorrow, it had been hugely successful, producing twenty-two fresh buffalo skins, forty-four skulls, eleven skeletons, and various other skins and bones collected along the way. Hornaday reported to Secretary Baird that it was "the finest and most complete series of buffalo skins ever collected by a museum." The buffalo, of all ages and sexes, would be an extremely valuable addition to the Smithsonian collection, with enough left over to distribute to other museums.

Even so, Hornaday's grim prediction, in 1889, that all the wild buffalo would be gone within ten years proved prophetic. In the winter of 1893–94, poachers killed 114 of the last band of wild buffalo cowering in the newly created Yellowstone National Park. And in 1897, the last four free-roaming buffalo were found in a high mountain valley in Colorado and shot. The hunters must have been exultant. They had succeeded in killing off the very last wild buffalo on the planet. It was only because there were a few animals still sheltered in private reserves or zoos, which would later be used to seed new herds, that the buffalo survived at all.[17]

CHAPTER 6

A Mysterious Stranger

One winter afternoon in 1888, about two years after his return from the Montana Territory, William Temple Hornaday was kneeling in the ersatz buffalo grass and sage of an immense museum display in the Hall of Mammals, at the National Museum in Washington. The diorama, the most ambitious undertaking of his celebrated career as a taxidermist, was housed in the largest display case ever made for the museum: sixteen feet wide, twelve feet deep, and ten feet high, surrounded by a burnished mahogany frame. In addition to its size, what was genuinely new about the exhibit was that it was an immense glass cube, its contents visible from all sides. Virtually all other museum displays of the eighteenth and nineteenth centuries were visible from only one side, or at most two sides. This was to be, Hornaday hoped, his masterpiece, his Sistine Chapel of celebration for a vanishing—and perhaps vanished—species.[1]

The museum's chief taxidermist had his sleeves rolled up above the elbows and was wearing a full-length oilcloth apron. As was the Victorian custom, he also was absurdly overdressed for the occasion, wearing a white turnover collar and tie. On his face, along with brush-strokes of plaster of paris, gray sculptor's clay, and genuine Montana dirt (brought back for this exhibit on the 1886 expedition) was a look of ferocious focus, like a surgeon preparing to make an exact-ing incision. Scattered around him in the grass were a carpenter's bag of taxidermy tools—flat pliers, cutting-pliers, two kinds of forceps, three-cornered files of various sizes, a huge glover's needle stuck in a bar of soap, a glue-pot.[2] They were the tools with which he was con-juring the dark arts of resurrection. Towering above him, stuffed and mounted but so real it seemed ready to snort, was the lordly bison bull he had brought down in the Montana snow two winters before. Nearby stood the half-completed figures of a two-year-old "spike" bull, a yearling, two cows, and Sandy, the little blond calf who had perished, making this whole display a kind of sepulchre of innocence.

A heavy canvas privacy screen had been drawn around the four-sided exhibit to shield Hornaday and his assistants from rubberneck-ers trying to get a premature peek; but even so, Hornaday could still hear the laughter and footfalls of museumgoers echoing through the high-ceilinged hall. Unperturbed by these distractions, he devoted his tenderest attentions to re-creating the scene, an imagined moment on the northern Great Plains in which an alpha bull, several cows, and a calf stopped to drink at a little alkaline watering hole (re-created out of layered wax and glass to give the illusion of depth). Nearby lay a couple of bleached buffalo skulls, discarded by hunters who had lain in wait at the spring.

Hornaday was not a man above wondering about his place in his-tory. As he worked, in fact, he was nearly as enthralled by the idea that this six-figure habitat group would become the masterpiece for which he was remembered, as he was about celebrating a vanishing species. Before he was through with this exhibit, he would feel compelled to speak directly, though secretly, to future generations whom he feared might not remember him. One day almost seventy years later, in 1957, the curatorial staff at the Smithsonian was finally taking down Hor-naday's buffalo group—which had been on prominent display at the museum's ground-floor entrance, greeting millions of visitors with forbidding glass eyes for more than six decades—when one of the cu-rators discovered a small metal box embedded inside the floorboards at the foot of the great bull. Inside were a few yellowing newspaper clippings, a couple of sketches of buffalo, and a handwritten note, in Hornaday's flamboyant script:

> To my illustrious successor: The old bull, the young cow, and the year-ling calf you find here were killed by yours truly. When I am dust and ashes, I beg you to protect these specimens from deterioration and destruction as they are among the last of their kind. Of course they are crude productions in comparison with what you may now produce, but you must remember that at this time, the American School of

Taxidermy had only just been recognized. Therefore give the devil his due and revile not Wm T. Hornaday[3]

It was a jocular greeting to a new generation of taxidermists (if in fact there was one), an anguished warning of impending doom, and a look beyond the petty politics and recriminations of his own day. He was not unaware that his rapid rise to the top of such an august institution, at such a young age, coupled with his brash and sometimes strident manner, had created a dark undertow of criticism. By 1888, his detractors had begun grumbling (mostly in private) that Hornaday was simply a fame hog, constantly making bombastic public pronouncements to attract attention, constantly in the papers, railing about the coming calamity facing wildlife to get himself a few more column inches of glory. And it's true that his name, face, and opinions were in the newspapers so frequently that he'd hired a clipping service and begun filling fat scrapbooks with all his public notices. "Vindication of America's Greatest Wildlife Champion" read one; "Zoo Man Convinced of Evolution Theory" read another.[4]

Well, so be it, he thought. What did he care what lesser men thought? What he was doing with his life got attention because it was urgently important. To his mind, nothing was *more* important than saving the natural world from the grim annihilation he'd seen in Montana and all across the west—the violated corpses, the acres of bones.

The planet was burning! If he yelled "Fire!" did that make him an egotist?

During the previous winter and spring, as he worked feverishly on the great bison display, he'd written an eight-part series called "The Last Buffalo Hunt," about his adventures and discoveries in Montana, which had recently run in twelve major newspapers from New York to San Francisco. It had brought him a new round of acclaim, but it also drew attention to the awful crime in progress in the West. Since the articles appeared, a steady stream of curiosity-seekers, as well as the occasional important visitor, had begun showing up at the half-completed exhibit in the Hall of Mammals. Although the average gadabout was not allowed behind the privacy screen, official visitors would be ushered into the display case from time to time to be introduced to the museum's chief taxidermist.

Now, as Hornaday hastened to prepare the remaining buffalo for the exhibit's opening in March 1888, the privacy screen was flung open and a stranger stepped boldly into the display space, unaccompanied by any official envoy.[5] Hornaday flicked him a glance, with momentary irritation, and then returned to his work on a troublesome seam in the yearling's hide.

Professor Goode said you wouldn't mind if I came down here and had a look, friend, the stranger said in a congenial sort of way.

Hornaday bridled at this uninvited familiarity. The stranger wasn't his "friend." He had no idea who this fellow was: a hale-looking young man in his late twenties, with a bull-like head and a square jaw.

My God, look at that thing, the young man said, gesturing at the bull. *You bagged this animal?*

Hornaday grunted his assent.

Stub-horn—an old one. Fourteen, fifteen hundred pounds, I'll bet. That's probably one of the biggest bulls ever taken. What did you use?

.44–40 Winchester.

Nice piece. Not much recoil. Anything over a hundred yards, you can practically see that bullet drop down like an artillery shell. Where'd you shoot 'im?

Montana Territory. Missouri-Yellowstone Divide, north of Miles City. If you know that country.

Sunday Creek Trail?

Yep.

Hornaday shot another glance at the man. Not many people in Washington, D.C., would have appreciated the sterling virtues of the new .44–40 center-fire Winchester rifle, or recognized that the bull was what the old hide-hunters called a "stub-horn," much less known about the Sunday Creek Trail.

How do you happen to know that country up the Sunday Creek Trail? Hornaday asked finally.

Used to have a ranch on the Little Missouri, near Cannonball Creek. But I'm out of the business now, after the winter of '86. No money in ranching, just a world of grief.

Hornaday could contain himself no longer.

I don't believe we've been properly introduced.

Oh, beg pardon, the young man said, shoving out a big, square hand. *The name's Theodore—Theodore Roosevelt.*

Although he was only twenty-eight years old at the time of their first meeting, Theodore Roosevelt was already marked for fame. Hornaday recognized his name because it had been all over the papers: he'd just been defeated in a highly publicized run for the mayoralty of New York City, having campaigned—honestly, but perhaps foolishly—as "The Cowboy from the Dakotas." Hornaday also already knew that Roosevelt once owned a ranch near Medora, in the northern Dakota Territory on the Little Missouri, not far from the place where these animals had been taken.

On that wan winter day when their paths first crossed, these two fierce and ambitious young men forged a bond that was to last for the rest of their lives. "In our first hour," Hornaday later wrote of this first meeting, Roosevelt "told me a serious secret, and we dealt in secrets forever after. I think I proved that I knew how to keep things that should not be told—and he told me many mighty interesting things that, while new, never appeared in print."[6]

The two men were natural companions. They loved the West, wildlife, guns, horses, and the open air. They were both hunters and adventurers, men whose souls came alive under the blue sky. They knew what it was like to live rough and take risks, to work for days in the saddle, to confront a tiger or an elephant at close quarters, or to wade chest-deep through the snake-infested swamps of the Orinoco. They shared a cowboy's scorn of effete Easterners (even though they'd both grown up east of the Mississippi, and Roosevelt was born in Gotham itself). They both sensed, at a gut level, that all across the continent, birds and game were being hunted down at a much faster rate than they could possibly reproduce, that the whole natural world was careening toward disaster. This was so seldom acknowledged in public that it was almost as if *this* was the great secret that they shared.

There were many other things of a more personal nature that the two had in common. They were about the same age (Hornaday, at thirty-four, was six years older than Roosevelt). Both men had lost their parents when they were still very young and had had to pull on a grown man's boots prematurely. (Hornaday lost both his parents when he was only thirteen; Roosevelt was nineteen when his father—"the greatest man I ever knew"—died, and twenty-six when his mother died of typhoid fever). They were both writers. Hornaday's book *Two Years in the Jungle* had created a huge following and a hunger for his further exploits, and Roosevelt—a man who seemed to pack ten times as much life into every hour as a normal man—had once written, in a period of less than three months, a biography of

Missouri senator Thomas Hart Benton *and* a celebrated four-volume series called *The Winning of the West.*

One other thing the two young men had in common was that they'd had to overcome physical frailty and vulnerability. Hornaday had always been smaller than his peers, and he was forever over-compensating with sheer pugnacity, as if he could *will* himself to be taller. Roosevelt, on the other hand, had been so sickly as a child—he suffered extremely from asthma—that his father built a gym at the family home in a brownstone on East Twentieth Street in New York City. "You have to *make* your body," his father had demanded, and "Teedie," as he was known as a child, struggled to pack muscle onto his quivering, twiglike frame. Teedie remained so frail, though, that he could not attend school and was taught instead by tutors at home until he enrolled at Harvard at age eighteen. A couple of years later, after attending law school, he served for three terms in the New York State Assembly. But he still appeared weak and effeminate and wore foppish side-whiskers, a gangly Harvard man trying to be a grownup. His fellow assemblymen ridiculed his "squeaky" voice and dandified dress, calling him "Punkin-Lilly," "Jane-Dandy," and "our new Oscar Wilde."[7]

Both of these men had found true love in their lives; but for only one of them would it last. Hornaday's love affair with his wife, Josephine, would endure for almost six decades, until his last breath. "This morning—'it bein' Sunday'—I had a long think, all about you," he wrote to her in 1899, "about our first acquaintance, the middle and the end of our courtship, and the 19 1/2 very happy years following. . . . Dear old Heart, dearest Love, the years have made me so fond of you, and so dependent on your love and your daily smiles that when you are gone I am lost!"[8]

Roosevelt, too, experienced early love of a shattering intensity. He was twenty years old when he met Alice Hathaway Lee at her parent's house in Chestnut Hill, Massachusetts.[9] It was October 1878; she was seventeen. He was smitten as soon as he saw her, and he wooed her for over a year, during his senior year at Harvard, before he won her. They were engaged on January 25, 1880. A few days later, Roosevelt rode his sleigh through a snowstorm over to Chestnut Hill, "the horse plunging to his belly in the great drifts, and the wind cutting my face like a knife," he later confided to his diary. "My sweet life was just as lovable and pretty as ever; it seems hardly possible that

I can kiss her and hold her in my arms; she is so pure and innocent and so very, very pretty. I have never done anything to deserve such good fortune." Perhaps because he was so beside himself with joy, on his way home the sleigh tipped over in a snowdrift and he was "dragged about 300 yards, holding onto the reins, before I could stop the horse."[10]

By summer, his feelings for Alice Hathaway Lee seemed only to have intensified. He wrote in his diary on July 4, 1880, a Sunday: "In the afternoon I took my darling on a long and beautiful walk through Fleet's woods. How I love her! And I would trust her to the end of the world. Whatever troubles come upon me—losses or griefs or sickness—I know she will only be more true and tender and loving than ever; she is so radiantly pure and good and beautiful that I almost feel like worshipping her. Not one thing is ever hidden between us. No matter how long I live, I know my love for her will only grow deeper and tenderer by the day; and she shall always be mistress over all that I have."[11]

Theodore Roosevelt and Alice Hathaway Lee were married four months later, on October 27, 1880, on his twenty-second birthday. But her radiance and goodness and beauty would illuminate his life for only a little more than three years. On the morning of February 12, 1884, Alice gave birth to their first child, a girl they named Alice Lee Roosevelt. But the child's mother became gravely ill, and on the terrible morning of February 14, 1884, she died. By an awful irony, Roosevelt's mother had died a few hours earlier, in the same house, on the same day.

Beside an enormous scrawled "X," Roosevelt wrote in his diary on the day of Alice's death, "the light has gone out of my life."[12] He remained inconsolable and refused to talk about Alice, publicly or privately, for the rest of his life. His father had died at forty-six; his mother at forty-eight; and now his beloved Alice at twenty-two. The historian David McCullough wrote that for Roosevelt, "the sole, overwhelming lesson was the awful brevity of life."[13]

A year before Alice's death, in 1883, Roosevelt had gone West to the territories with the intention of bagging a buffalo before they were all gone. It was a kind of boyish lark. He succeeded in shooting his first buffalo, and it made him so happy he did a crazy little war dance.

"I've never seen anybody so happy about anything," a friend of his said. He had his picture taken in a foppish Western outfit, holding a muzzle-loading rifle—Oscar Wilde in buckskins. He even took off his rimless spectacles for the picture, even though he was nearsighted and could barely see without them (he often had several extra pairs sewn into his clothes). But something else happened on that trip to the Dakota Territory. Once Roosevelt got a look at that wide-open country, with its molten sundowns, its totemic buttes, and the seeming limitessness of the sky, he liked it so well that he threw in with a couple of other men and bought a small operation on the Little Missouri called Chimney Butte Ranch. He bought a few cattle and horses and called himself a cowboy.

He was enormously pleased with himself when he returned to New York to his pregnant wife, Alice, and the house he'd built in Oyster Bay called Sagamore Hill. But just a few short months later, his wife and mother were both dead, and he was inconsolable with grief. He was only twenty-six years old, but "for joy or for sorrow, my life has now been lived out," he confided to his diary.[14]

Roosevelt began returning to the ranch in the Dakotas, sometimes four or five times a year, but now these visits no longer were merely youthful escapades. Those who knew him said that Roosevelt struggled to keep from sinking into a melancholy listlessness during this period. He withdrew from friends. He seemed distant and distracted. A man of action, he hardly seemed to know what to do. He threw himself into the bruising physical work of the ranch, into the West, into the possibility of oblivion in that enormous country. Now he seemed to be restlessly seeking a new life, some new purpose in his life, and even a new self.

Roosevelt's younger cousin, Nicholas, later observed that he "took obvious delight in the apparently pathological extremes" of his adventures in the Dakotas, "rides of seventy miles or more in a day, hunting hikes of fourteen to sixteen hours, stretches in the saddle in roundup as long as forty hours."[15] He was embracing what he called "the strenuous life," a manly life of physical extremes and great personal risk, which was perhaps also a way of avoiding too much introspection.[16]

In a sprawling country famous for transformations, and out of the bottomless grief of all his losses, Theodore Roosevelt began undergoing one of the most remarkable transfigurations in American history. Over two or three years, the effete, side-whiskered "Punkin-Lilly" of the Harvard Club and the Upper East Side morphed into a genuine Dakota cowboy—not the dandy *faux* cowpoke in the early posed photographs, but a lean and rangy cattleman, with a craggy, wind-burned face and a fighting physique. He had steeled his body and his soul to survive. He had been transformed by his grief. Alice Hathaway Lee was still there inside him, as she would always be, guttering like a radiant candle flame, but he chose never to mention her again, as if to do so might cause his rough-hewn cowboy avatar to crumble like a tower of sand.

One of his neighbors on the Little Missouri, a rancher named Frank Roberts, later said that Roosevelt "was rather a slim-lookin' feller when he came out here, but after he lived out here his build got wider and heavier ... he got to be lookin' more like a rugged man." He earned the cowboys' respect by working long hours in the saddle, by lassooing and branding and sleeping on the ground like everybody else. He went up against cattle thieves and lawless gangs and learned to break and ride wild cow ponies. He became as robust and fearless as any frontiersman. His experiences in the Dakotas "took the snob out of me," Roosevelt later said. It did something else, too: "I have always said I would not have been President, had it not been for my experience in North Dakota."[17]

Like Roosevelt, William Temple Hornaday was a man of almost inhuman ambition. Back in the winter of 1886, before his train had even returned to Union Station in Washington after the "last buffalo hunt," Hornaday had laid out four strategic tasks for himself. Together, they would involve enough effort to consume several lifetimes, but he immediately began pushing ahead on all four tasks simultaneously. Newly energized by abject fear, he became a blur of action.

His first strategic task would be to organize, create, and complete the magnificent six-figure habitat group of bison for display at the National Museum. Nothing could communicate the almost transcendant nobility of these animals but the animals themselves, displayed in their natural habitat.

The ideal thing, of course, would be to show the American public the living, breathing animal, just as Hornaday had seen them on the great plains—the big bulls breaking into a gallop, throwing up clots of snow; the frightened cows, crowding together to protect their young;

the sound and the smell and the thrill of them. But that was impossible—and even seeing them in a zoo was improbable because there was only one real zoo in America at that time, and that one was only twelve years old—so Hornaday would have to show the American public six mounted animals, re-created with as much realism as his talents could conjure.

To reconstruct these animals out of the formless skins and bones the party had brought back from Montana, Hornaday would use the multistage "clay manikin process" that he had developed at the taxidermy table, which was a dramatic improvement over the primitive "rag-and-stuff method" of the eighteenth and early nineteenth centuries. First, he completely discarded all the bones and innards of the animal (in the process, eliminating the skeleton as a source of support). Then he carefully cleaned, dried, and preserved the skin, cutting around bloodstains, bullet holes, and other evidence of a violent death. Then he sculpted a plaster cast of the buffalo's body, supported by a wooden frame or armature wrapped in rope. This artful creation, called a *manikin*, then was coated with textured clay to give the animals' forms their final contours. Essentially, he had created a life-size statue of a buffalo, over which the preserved skin, head, hooves, and other parts were stretched. In his famous 1891 textbook *Taxidermy and Zoological Collecting*, Hornaday maintained—with his usual bravado—that the clay manikin method was the only proper way to "produce a specimen which fitly represents the species." But not everybody could do it. The task required the field observations of a wildlife biologist, the deft artistic hand of a sculptor, and the practical ingenuity of an engineer, especially when it came to re-creating the 1,600-pound bull.

What Hornaday wanted to do was, as far as possible, simply "bring 'em back alive"—to display birds, mammals, and now buffalo as he had actually seen them in their natural habitat, in a scientifically responsible way, so that the public could actually *see* things that they had never seen before. Even seeing live animals in a zoo did not really convey what the animals looked like in their natural habitat. Animals were so embedded in their habitats, having actually been *created* by their surroundings, that the two could not really be separated, Hornaday believed.

This was especially true of the American bison, which was a creature of the immense vastnesses of the great plains. To a large extent, the buffalo was a physical embodiment of those huge spaces, that vaulting sky, those unimaginable distances. It was a touching irony that, in actuality, Hornaday was re-creating this sense of imagined immensity inside a sixteen-foot-by-twelve-foot-by-ten-foot glass box, in a museum, in a city more than two thousand miles away from the place these animals had lived once. Even so, what Hornaday was trying to do in this exhibit was communicate what he had seen out on the Missouri-Yellowstone Divide, glimpsing the last remnants of the buffalo herds in mixed groups of bulls, cows, and calves. He wanted to bring museum visitors from all over the country closer than they had ever come—perhaps, regrettably, closer than anyone *would* ever come—to *Bison americanus* in the wild. His great aspirations seemed fulfilled when, in 1888, a scholarly survey of American museum taxidermy called Hornaday's buffalo group "a triumph of the taxidermist's art, and, so far as known, it surpasses in scientific accuracy, and artistic design and treatment, anything of the kind yet produced."[18]

Hornaday's second strategic task was to write an angry book about the history of the buffalo slaughter and distribute it as widely as possible. He'd call it *The Extermination of the American Bison*, as if the end of the species were a fait accompli. On the train back home, and later in his small upstairs study in Washington, late at night, he began pounding out this furious testament and call to arms.

The third, and perhaps most ambitious, task was to take the first steps toward creating a national zoo in Washington, D.C. All the great cities of Europe had public zoological gardens, but there was nothing of the kind in the young nation's capital. He began imagining that a small herd of live bison might be kept in a spacious enclosure and perhaps, if captive breeding proved possible, the herd might grow to the point where some animals could be released into the wild. It would be the first reintroduction of captive-bred animals into a wild population ever attempted.

Last, Hornaday felt that he neeeded to create some kind of a political organization that would draw attention to the deadly peril facing the buffalo and harness the public's outrage in order to *do something*. He'd lobby Congress to draft legislation that would stop the buffalo slaughter and create reserves and ranges in the West to the bring the bison back from the precipice of extinction, if possible.

But the task of setting up a political organization, Hornaday recognized, was not one that he was terribly well suited for. He felt far more at home at a taxidermy worktable or in a rude hunting camp than hobnobbing with the muckety-mucks on Capital Hill or the power brokers of Wall Street.

Enter his new friend, Theodore Roosevelt (who hated the name "Teddy," because that's what Alice had called him). With more of a natural instinct for politics and better connections in high places, Roosevelt also was envisioning one of the first conservation organizations in America. The year before he and Hornaday met, Roosevelt had formed an organization he called the Boone and Crockett Club, a conservation group named after two of Roosevelt's heroes, Daniel Boone and Davey Crockett. These men, who were exemplars of "ethical hunting," the notion of the "fair chase," and lovers of wilderness, would stand as the guiding lights for a group of a hundred affluent New York big-game hunters, which would later became one of the most influential conservation groups in the United States.

But Hornaday wanted to create an organization that would address the terrible plight of the buffalo specifically. So in the months following their initial meeting at the National Museum, Hornaday and Roosevelt began laying the groundwork for creating an organization to be called the American Bison Society. Hornaday would serve as the organization's first president, running its day-to-day affairs and being its public face and spokesperson. The "honorary president" would be the up-and-coming political powerhouse Theodore Roosevelt, a man who seemed destined for great things indeed, but whose dance card was already almost completely full. Roosevelt began lunging up the ladder of power, often taking two steps at a time. He was appointed New York City police commissioner, then assistant secretary of the Navy, then elected governor of New York, then vice president, and then (after the assassination of President William McKinley in 1901), president of the United States. The inauguration took place six weeks before his forty-third birthday.

Even in his ascent to the pinnacle of power, Roosevelt never forgot William Temple Hornaday or left him behind. "Whenever you really, *really* need me, when you can't get any further, call me," Roosevelt had told Hornaday.[19] Throughout his two terms in the Oval Office, Roosevelt regularly sent Hornaday invitations to lunch so that the old hunter-naturalists could dine in luxurious privacy and talk shop. But such access to power had come only in the nick of time. In the summer of 1887, inspired by Hornaday's successful bison hunt for the Smithsonian, a collecting party from the American Museum of Natural History had gone West to procure a few specimens of *Bison americanus* of its own. Using local guides, these seasoned hunters scoured the Missouri-Yellowstone Divide for three solid months.

But they did not find a single living animal.

CHAPTER 7

"A Nobility Beyond All Compare"

In the months after Hornaday returned from the Montana Territory, "dazed and stunned," he was like a man possessed. What he had witnessed on the frontier frightened him to the marrow. No one back East seemed to grasp the magnitude of the slaughter; no one could hear the implacable silence or see that windswept ocean of bones where once had roamed numberless herds of a species that had once been the undisputed lord of the great plains. What was worse, almost no one besides himself seemed to care that the slaughter was happening.

Now, in addition to his work on the monumental six-figure bison group, the formation of the American Bison Society, and his first attempts to create a national zoo in Washington, he sat down to write a book that one historian later called "the most forceful protest ever written against the criminal matter in which the buffalo were nearly exterminated."[1]

Professor G. Brown Goode, Hornaday's boss at the National Museum, had given him permission to write his book, but only after working hours. Night after night, month after month, Hornaday labored away on his manuscript, no longer crouched in the lantern-light of a remote Western hunting camp or jungle outpost, but in an upstairs study in the small rented house he shared with Josephine. He wrote like a man on fire, convinced that this could be the last written record of a species that soon would vanish from the earth. He had decided to call his book *The Extermination of the American Bison*, as if the saddest possible outcome had already occurred.

Because he intended for this book to be not just a raging polemic but also a serious scientific monograph, Hornaday began by describing the nature and range of the species, making the point that the bison had been very likely the most abundant quadruped that ever lived on the planet. He moved on to the more subjective judgment that, in his view, *Bison americanus* was also arguably the most magnificent ruminant in the world. The only other animals that came close were the Indian bison, or gaur (*Bos gaurus*); the European bison (also known as the *wisent*); and the aurochs, an extinct ancestor of domestic cattle. But the gaur seemed "more like a huge ox running wild," and the auroch, though taller than an American bison, was also leaner and leggier, and it lacked the bison's lionlike pelage, or mane. Its hair was sparse and thin, completely unlike "the magnificent dark brown frontlet and beard of the buffalo, the shaggy coat of hair upon the neck, hump, and shoulders, terminating at the knees in a thick mass of luxuriant black locks." All things considered, the American bison had a "grandeur and nobility of presence which are beyond all comparison amongst ruminants."[2]

In the following pages of his book, Hornaday laid out the biology and habits of the species. In addition, in melancholy detail, he described the story of the slaughter, the numbers killed, the methods used, the steady disappearance of the great herds, and the approaching end.

"There is no reason to hope that a single wild and unprotected individual [buffalo] will remain alive in ten years hence," Hornaday wrote at the conclusion of his book, dated May 1, 1889. A buffalo, he said, "is now so rare a prize, and by the ignorant is considered so great an honor (!) to kill one, that extraordinary exertions will be made to find and shoot down without mercy the 'last buffalo.'"[3]

In fact, he was off by only a couple of years.

One deadly problem for the species, he explained, was that a buffalo "would very often stand quietly and see two or three score, or even a hundred, of his relatives and companions shot down before his eyes, with no other feeling than of stupid wonder and curiosity."[4] The bison's apparently dim intelligence made possible one of the easiest and deadliest forms of hunting, that of the still-hunt, and "of all the methods that were unsportsmanlike, unfair, ignoble, and utterly reprehensible, this was in every respect the lowest and the worst." Hunting buffalo from horseback was difficult and dangerous; it required too much skill and too much time. (William F. Cody, or "Buffalo Bill," was one of the few white hunters who had the skill to hunt from horseback, claiming to have brought down 4,280 buffaloes in eighteen months during 1867–68.)[5] Most of the buffalo hunters in the West were not only without skill, they were also both greedy and lazy, Hornaday wrote, and "if they could have obtained Gatling guns with which to mow down a whole herd at a time, beyond a doubt they would have gladly used them."[6]

During the years 1871 to 1873, when still-hunting (or "sneak-hunting") was at its worst, all a hunter had to do was get up at daylight in his camp on the range and walk to the nearest buffalo herd, usually less than three miles. He'd be well-armed, usually with a huge breech-loading Sharps rifle weighing almost twenty pounds, and with 75 to 100 loaded cartridges in his ammunition belt or his pockets. Then he'd creep up on the herd, keeping low and out of sight—some still-hunters wore gunny sacks with holes cut out for eyes and arms—and once he'd gotten to within 100 to 250 yards, he'd settle into a comfortable position. If the herd was moving, the animal in the lead would be the first one shot; if the herd was at rest, the oldest cow was generally the leader, and she'd go down first. She would stagger, blood pouring from her nose, fall to her knees, and then drop. The others would gather around her, bawling plaintively, confused and frightened. But they wouldn't run. The hunter would wait, perhaps a full minute—the trick was not to fire too rapidly—and then blast another animal, and another. Sometimes the rifle would get too hot to use, and the hunter would have to wait for it to cool off.[7]

In this way, even the laziest, stupidest hunter—even a drunk one—would find himself surrounded by mounds of corpses within a half-hour's time. Then all he had to do was start skinning or, better yet, hire somebody else to do the skinning. Such was the slaughter that was taking place in the West. In eight years, between 1876 and 1884, a dealer in New York City called Mssrs. J. & A. Boskowitz reported handling 246,175 buffalo skins, Hornaday reported. And that was just one middling dealer. By Hornaday's count, if you totaled up all the buffalo hides shipped by all the railroads between 1872 and 1874, the total number of buffaloes slaughtered by whites added up to 3,158,730. Perhaps most appalling of all, more than half of these animals—1,780,481—were simply killed and left to rot; the blood-tide ran so high and so fast that hunters and skinners were unable to keep up with the overwhelming task of harvesting all those hides, tongues, and meat. The absolute extermination of the buffalo was in-evitable, and in an astonishingly brief period of time. In some ways, the near-extermination of the buffalo can be thought of as a failure of the national imagination: they were at one time so unimaginably abundant that almost no one could conceive of a day when they had vanished entirely. Yet that day very nearly arrived.[8]

In Hornaday's telling of this tragic, epic story, whites were al-most completely to blame. The Plains Indians had a much thriftier and more sustainable relationship with the buffalo, using the meat for food; hides for warmth and trade; skins for teepees; stomach and intestines for containers for cooking, storage, and transport; and dung for fuel.[8] Even the way they hunted the buffalo—generally on horse-back, wading into the undulating herds with nothing but bow and arrow—seemed to demonstrate honor and respect for the animal, in contrast to the grim, meaningless carnage of blasting away from a hid-den location with a large-bore rifle. "It was the buffalo that undergirt the economy [of Indian life] and mightily influenced society, religion, and warfare," one historian wrote.[9]

Even so, the native peoples got their share of blame. They, too, sometimes got so carried away by the buffalo's multitudes that they became participants in the slaughter. In his book, Hornaday retold a story from George Catlin, who told of arriving at the mouth of the Teton River, in the Dakotas, in 1832. He saw that "an immense herd of buffaloes had showed themselves on the opposite side of the river." Shortly afterwards, a party of 500 or 600 Sioux warriors forded the river on horseback and set about decimating the herd. They came back about sunset with 1,400 fresh buffalo tongues, which they sold to white soldiers for a couple of gallons of whis-key. (Arguably, these Sioux were red men who had been corrupted by the white man's liquor.) "Not a skin or a pound of meat, other than the tongues, was saved after this awful slaughter," Catlin wrote. The destruction of the buffalo was not so much a white man's crime as a human crime.[10]

During the terrible winter of 1886–87, some Indian tribes in the Northwest Territory that had once lived on the buffalo were so des-titute, and so close to starvation, that some Cree resorted to canni-balism. But Hornaday pointed out that, like the white man, many tribes had been reckless and foolish with the buffalo, and now they were paying the price for the wanton slaughter. "The buffalo is his own avenger, to an extent his remorseless slayers little dreamed he ever could be."[11]

Among the people who actually cared, blame was almost universally heaped upon the government for allowing the slaughter to happen on public lands. In fact, between 1871 and 1876, various laws were introduced in Congress to protect the buffalo, but all of them, to one degree or another, failed.

In his book, Hornaday briefly summarized the tragicomic fate of one bill, H.R. 921, which was introduced in the House by Mr. Fort of Illinois on January 5, 1874. The bill was simple, making it unlawful for any person who was not an Indian to kill or wound any female buffalo within the boundaries of any of the territories of the United States. Violations would result in a fine of $100; and second violations, a jail sentence of not more than 30 days.

S. S. Cox, the gentleman from New York, stood to object that old hunters said it was impossible to tell the sex of a buffalo while it was running, and also that the bill gave preference to the Indians. (Years afterward, Hornaday commented that "I know of no greater affront . . . to the intelligence of a genuine buffalo hunter than to accuse him of not knowing enough to tell the sex of a buffalo 'on the run' by its form alone.")[12]

Fort replied that he had been told that it was possible to distinguish the sexes, and the point of the bill was to the stop the wanton slaughter, in which thousands of buffalo were being taken simply to cut out their tongues.

Cox persisted, stating that he wanted the clause excepting the Indians removed. He pointed out that the secretary of the Interior, Columbus Delano, had already told the House that "the civilization of the Indian was impossible while the buffalo remained on the plains."

Mr. B. C. McCormick, of Arizona, read into the record an article from the *Santa Fe New Mexican*, which called the buffalo slaughter "wantonly wicked, and should be stopped by the most stringent enactments and vigilant enforcements of the law. . . . One party of sixteen hunters report having killed twenty-eight thousand buffaloes during the past summer. It seems to us there is quite as much reason why the Government should protect the buffaloes as the Indians."

McCormick went on to say, "It would have been well both for the

Indians and the white man if an enactment of this kind had been placed on our statute-books years ago. . . . I know of no one act that would gratify the red man more."

Charles Eldredge, of Wisconsin, offered that "there would be just as much propriety in killing the fish in our rivers as in destroying the buffalo in order to compel the Indians to become civilized."

Mr. Conger said, "As a matter of fact, every man knows the range of the buffalo had grown more and more confined year after year; that they have been driven westward before advancing civilization. . . . There is no law that Congress can pass that will prevent the buffalo from disappearing before the march of civilization . . . They eat the grass. They trample upon the plains upon which our settlers desire to herd their cattle and their sheep. They are as uncivilized as the Indian."

Despite all the debate and recriminations, in the end, H.R. 921 passed the House.

In the Senate, there was some haggling about the clause "who is not an Indian," with some senators arguing that it showed favoritism to the red man, but ultimately, it passed the Senate after a third reading. Then it went to the desk of President Ulysses S. Grant, that dear old friend of William Tecumseh Sherman. And there the bill was "pocket-vetoed"—it died simply by being ignored. Inaction became action. In despair, Hornaday realized that the enemy's power extended all the way to the very pinnacle of the U.S. government, 1600 Pennsylvania Avenue itself.

It revealed worlds about Hornaday that, observing the ineffectualness of Congress and the indifference of the president, he concluded that the problem was democracy itself. "The necessary act of Congress was so hedged in and beset by obstacles that it never became an accomplished fact," he wrote. If this had been a monarchy—if, for instance, William Temple Hornaday had been king—a reasonable law to protect the buffalo would have been created within the hour. The fear and sorrow of the approaching extermination made him long for unlimited power to change the world. But he didn't have that power. And the slaughter went on.

A few of the Western states and territories passed vague, feeble laws attempting to protect the buffalo, but like most other game laws in the West, they amounted to nothing at all. "I have never been able to learn of a single case, save in the Yellowstone Park, wherein a western hunter was prevented by so simple and innocuous a thing as a game law from killing game,"[13] Hornaday wrote. The Western "ethic" of hunting was, essentially, to kill as much as you could before the other man did, and do so quickly before your game was all killed off.

By the early 1880s, it was even increasingly argued that stopping the slaughter was impossible—that extermination was inevitable. Even George Bird Grinnell, one of the most prominent conservationists, had begun to say so. And, of course, there was General Philip Sheridan, Sherman, and Delano arguing that extermination would actually be a good thing, by decimating the heathen Indian and opening up the West to the golden possibilities of white civilization. Hornaday railed against all of this as "weakness and imbecility." It all came down to national will, he said, and to money. If a code of game laws were put in place, and game wardens were paid a salary (a fifty-cent tax on every buffalo robe would pay for all the wardens needed), the slaughter could be brought under control in short order.

But it wasn't. So the slaughter went on, year in and year out, even though the ultimate outcome became more and more inevitable as time went by. Far from the marble palaces of power in Washington, meanwhile, the people whose lives would be most affected by the fate of the buffalo—the Indians—were almost entirely drowned out. Few spoke English. They were embattled; they were starving; they were desperate. Knowing full well the peril of their situation, the native peoples had turned their eyes to the ancient gods and the ancient myths. In the fall of 1885, a young surgeon named O. C. McNary, stationed with A Troop, Fifth Cavalry, in the Indian territory, was present when several ragged bands of Cheyenne came into the stockade. Through sign language, McNary was able to communicate with the Cheyenne's chiefs, Stone Calf and Little Robe.

"The chiefs were greatly troubled over the disappearance of the buffalo," McNary wrote later. "They told me that the great spirit created the buffalo in a large cave in the panhandle of Texas; that the evil spirits had closed up the mouth of the cave and the buffalo could not get out. They begged me to get permission from the great father in Washington for them to go and open the cave, and let the buffalo out. They claimed to know the exact location of the cave. They even wanted me to accompany them."[14]

—ⅢⅢ—

By 1887, when Hornaday was engrossed in writing his book, he and a few other naturalists had begun to ask a basic question, by which to measure the extent and speed of the slaughter: "What was the original number of bison who once roamed the great plains?" The answer that would eventually work its way into the popular imagination was "Sixty million." And the origin of this almost unimaginable number—later disputed—was Mr. Hornaday's book.

One of the first people to actually begin doing the math on the original numbers of buffalo in the West, as well as the numbers of the great slaughter, was Colonel Richard Irving Dodge, former aide-de-camp to General Sherman and commanding officer of a remote outpost called Fort Dodge, in southwest Kansas near the Cimarron River. In 1871, Dodge took a trip in a light wagon along the Arkansas River, Hornaday wrote. During twenty-five miles of this thirty-four-mile trip, Dodge said he passed through an immense herd of buffalo travelling perpendicular to his route.[15]

In 1927, the details of Dodge's trip, mentioned in Hornaday's book, caught the attention of Ernest Thompson Seton, the popular nature writer and illustrator, who was struggling to come up with an estimate of the original size of the buffalo population in the Americas. He studied historical accounts of early explorers and the accounts of hide-hunters, tried to calculate the number of hides shipped East in old rail records, and attempted to calculate the number of animals the Western grasslands could support. Ultimately, he fell back on Dodge's story. Like a mathematical sleuth, he calculated that a herd could travel twenty miles in a day, and since Dodge was in the herd most of the day, he deduced that the herd must have covered an area of about twenty-five miles by at least twenty miles. Making the very conservative estimate that there were about twelve buffalo per acre, Seton concluded that the herd comprised "at least" 4 million animals. By drawing a line around every reported location of bison herds in North America, he came up with a total potential range of 3 million square miles. If the herd that Dodge saw represented all the animals in 200,000 square miles, and 200,000 square miles goes into 3 million square miles fifteen times, the resulting number, he concluded, would be 60 million.[16]

(More recently, zoologist and author Tom McHugh, in his 1972 book *The Time of the Buffalo*, suggests that estimate may be too high by half. By computing the entire range of the great Western grassland—about 1.25 million square miles—by the "grazing capacity" of the land—a term that ranchers use to measure how many animals can graze in a given area without overgrazing it, which averages out to about 25 acres per buffalo, or 26 buffalo per square mile—McHugh came up with a total of about 34 million. Subtracting 4 million to account for other browsers like pronghorn antelope, elk, and deer, he came up with 30 million buffalo.)

Whatever the actual number, however, it was stupendous. The awe of the earliest white observers, who described the herds with phrases like "numberless numbers," "teeming multitudes" and "like the fishes in the sea" seemed apt, though feeble and inadequate to the task of naming such a glory.[17]

It may well have been that the whole compulsion to attempt a census of something as seemingly incalculable as the bison herds was brought to the great plains by white settlers. The native peoples existed in a state of ritual or cyclic time, time without beginning or end, and the great herds were the living embodiment of this sense of limitlessness, of infinity, of superabundance. They did not need to count. But white settlers, with their belief in linear time, of beginning and end, were compelled to count the buffalo in an effort to quantify, describe, and somehow control them. Ironically, once the counting began, so did the countdown toward extinction.

Richard Dodge was also a math sleuth, and he began attempting to calculate, in raw numbers, the magnitude of the bison slaughter in the west. He began his investigation by focusing on the three years of 1872, 1873, and 1874, during the heyday of the massacre. He contacted the Atchison, Topeka, and Santa Fe railroad and was informed that, during that three-year period, the railroad had shipped 469,453 buffalo skins to market back East. But that was only a part of the total. When he tried to discover what the other railroads had shipped during those same three years, he was met with caginess and obfuscation. The railroads did not want to tell him, he concluded, for fear that this lucrative trade might be curtailed by legislation. Nevertheless, Dodge ultimately came up with numbers similar to those earlier calculated by Hornaday—more than 3 million killed in one three-year period alone.[18]

Colonel Dodge seemed to grasp the consequences of this saturnalia of blood, and he wrote feelingly about the effects it had had on the native peoples. "Ten years ago, the Plains Indians had an ample supply of food," he wrote in 1882. "Now everything is gone, and they are reduced to the condition of paupers, without food, clothing, shelter, or any of those necessaries of life which came from the buffalo." Professional white hunters, he observed, often "too lazy or shiftless to make a living in civilization," were encamped in rough huts on the plains, and "in season or out of season, they kill everything that comes in their way. . . . It is sad to reflect that there is [an] enemy against which nature has made no provision, and from whose ravages there is no escape, and that in a very few years all the larger animals of the plains must inevitably be extinct. This enemy is man."[19]

In Hornaday's bitter "war for wildlife," Colonel Dodge was clearly on the side of the friends. Not only had he grasped the majesty and magnitude of their original population, he had seen and described what was happening to the buffalo more precisely than any other man, white or red. He had not only seen but felt the impact of this terrible profligacy on the Sioux, the Cheyenne, the Arikara, the Pawnee, and the Crow. He had peered into the book of the future and seen the awful calamities that were waiting there.

But wait. For in one of several books that Dodge wrote, called *The Hunting Grounds of the Great West: A Description of the Plains, Game and Indians of the Great North American Desert*, he also described a jolly twenty-day hunt in October 1872. Besides himself, there were four other members of the hunting party—three British visitors and another office of the post. Hunting was the primary amusement for soldiers garrisoned at bleak outposts in the West, and when there were visitors, especially those from overseas, the hunting parties lasted for weeks. Colonel Dodge dearly loved to hunt; General Sherman, in an introduction to another of Dodge's books, later called him "a capital sportsman."

In this case, Dodge's five-man party ranged down along the Cimarron River watershed to the southwest of the post, and when they returned, they had joyful news. They had shot not 1, not 10, not 100, but 127 buffalo, or more than 6 each day. As if that were not enough, they had also shot 2 deer. And 11 pronghorn antelope. Also 154 wild turkeys, 223 teal, and 84 field-plover. They encountered 7 raccoons and shot them all. Also 2 badgers. And 9 hawks. And 3 owls. Also 5 geese, 45 mallards, 49 shovelbills, 57 wigeons, 38 butter-ducks, 3 shell-ducks, and 17 herons. They also shot 187 quail; 32 grouse; 6 cranes; 12 jack-snipes; 33 yellowleg snipes; a pigeon; a few doves and robins; a bluebird, "for his sweetheart's hat"; and 11 rattlesnakes. Oh, and 143 meadowlarks—meadowlarks!—whose only crime was to warble like glory and be a target. In all, the total number of carcasses produced by Colonel Dodge's merry hunting party was 1,262. It was such a success-ful hunt that the next year, the Brits came back and the same group (minus one) hunted the Cimarron River drainage and killed almost the same number of birds, mammals, and reptiles. They were a little puzzled that there wasn't quite as much game the second year, but they must have been pleased nevertheless.

If this wanton hunter was on Hornaday's side, who was against him? Those enemies became ever more strident as time went by, as re-ports from the Indian wars became ever more disturbing. The voices of General Sherman, Interior Secretary Delano, and President Grant (by his silence) had now been joined by other influential voices, such as Senator James Throckmorton of Texas, who, in a calm, seemingly reasonable voice, observed to his fellow congressmen that "it would be a great step forward in the civilization of the Indians and the pres-ervation of the peace on the [frontier] if there was not a buffalo in existence."[20]

It was as if the enemy were providing every farmer, every settler, every hide-hunter, and every sportsman, with a sanctimonious ratio-nale for locking, loading, and blasting away at anything that moved without remorse or restraint. "Shoot a buffalo, starve an Indian," Gen-eral Sheridan had said, which was like a simple how-to manual for the Indian wars in the West. But now it was even the reasonable people, the "friends," the "conservationists," who seemed to lack any sense of restraint or respect for wildlife. There seemed to be absolutely no sense of natural limits, much less remorse at what they'd done.

And, if the truth be told, in his younger days, William Temple Hornaday had been entirely too quick on the trigger himself. He was not beyond blame. His rationale was that game was plentiful when he was a young man, and all the animals he shot (or almost all of them) were procured in the service of science. Still, he confessed in 1913, "When game was plentiful, I believed that it was right for men and boys to kill a limited amount of it for sport and for the table. I have been a sportsman myself; but times have changed, and we must change also."[21]

These lines were the closest William Temple Hornaday would ever come (at least in print) to repentance. They were a veiled admission of his own guilt, although he never did admit guilt directly, and a frank acknowledgment of the transformation that was underway in his own life. Even though the hour was late, William Temple Hornaday was waking up. He had begun to see, perhaps more clearly than anyone in the country, what was happening to the wildlife of the United States. A single hunting party could blithely kill more than 1,200 living things, with no thought at all that they might be committing a crime. Such a bloody spree was not considered a massacre—it was considered a successful hunt. It wasn't a crime against any particular manmade hunting law—because in most places there weren't any laws to speak of at all (or if there were laws, only laughable "enforcement"). Whatever laws there were had been written by hunters, or their lackeys in Congress. A British sportsman could come to the New World, go out each morning, lay waste to every living thing in sight, and then go back to camp and hoist a brandy to a day's work jolly well done. It was as if the New World seemed to be so overflowing with game that it was necessary to invite a few friends in from the Old World to assist in the slaughter.

The crime was against something much more ephemeral and far away. It was a crime against the whole natural world, the entire web of life. It was a crime against the people of the United States, and against the native peoples of North America. If ownership is nine-tenths of the law, one also could say it was a crime of ownership, because the tiny fraction of people who were hunters were treating the game of the United States as if it belonged to them alone, and not to the Sioux, the Pawnee, and the Crow; to the people of Cleveland and Portland and Boston and Peoria and Miami; and even, in some sense, to the people of London, Madrid, and Singapore. It was a vague, strange, overarching concept that was new in the New World—an ethic of morality toward the natural world.

The ethic of moral outrage would be one of William Temple Hornaday's finest contributions to the growing war for wildlife. And, like Colonel Dodge, so would doing the math. In his book *Thirty Years War for Wild Life*, Hornaday calculated that by 1931, 6,493,454 licensed hunters, plus more than a million unlicensed ones, took to the woods during every hunting season in the United States in search of game. This, he pointed out, was more armed men and women than

all the active standing armies in the world. Even so, all these hunters represented only about 3 percent of the total population, and "the
game of North America does not belong wholly and exclusively to
the men who kill! The other ninety-seven percent of the People have
vested rights in it, far exceeding those of the three percent. Posterity
has claims on it that no honest man can ignore."[22]

Combine the fearsome firepower of this army of hunters with
their misplaced sense of entitlement, and the result was inevitable.
The story of the bison in the West was simply the most conspicu-
ous tragedy that was unfolding; all across the country, other, smaller
tragedies were unfolding at the same time—sometimes as small as
a single meadowlark. But taken together, all the individual crimes
amounted to a great dark shadow, still as death and unfathomably
huge, slipping down over the world.

PART TWO

The Heedless Hunter

CHAPTER 8

Explorations and Adventures
in Equatorial Africa

Will Hornaday was all of nineteen years old when he marched into his employer's office in Rochester, New York, one morning in May 1874. His new boss, Professor Henry Augustus Ward of the famous Ward's Natural Science Establishment, was the most renowned merchant naturalist in the United States, whose firm supplied gemstones, fossils, bones, and skins to museums, schools, and private collectors across the country and overseas. His office was a huge, tin-ceilinged room with books lining the walls and a cozy litter of maps, scientific papers, photographs, drawings, and all the detritus of a life spent gathering scientific specimens of all kinds. A small curiosity cabinet held geodes and fossils; iridescent African butterflies, identified by their scientific names, in a glass case; a jaguar skull from the Matto Grosso; and a plaster cast of a fragment of mammoth tusk, shattered in some ancient duel.[1]

Ward, seated in a comfortable swivel chair, glanced up from the papers on his desk and leveled his frosty gray eyes at the young man standing in front of him. Ward wore a distinguished-looking graying beard that framed a handsome, refined face, and his suit, bought in London, was far more sumptuous than that of nearly any other man in Rochester. He was quite small, with tidy, acquisitive little hands, but he had the commanding presence of a diminutive man overcompensating for his size. It was said that Ward's voice could split the air like a foghorn and was capable of being heard a quarter-mile away.[2]

"Professor Ward," Hornaday announced, with elaborate casualness, "I'm going to du Chaillu's country in West Africa on a collecting expedition for gorillas. Is there anything in particular that I can do for you over there?"[3]

Ward could hardly believe his ears. He'd hired this young stripling as an underpaid "assistant workman"—basically a tub-scrubber—all of six months ago, and now Hornaday was proposing to mount an expedition to one of the most remote and dangerous places in the world. It was like an eighth-grader proposing to row across the ocean.

"I've got $800 in cash saved up, and I could get $1,000 more to finance the trip," the boy went on, with an air of supreme confidence. "I'm competent to be a collecting naturalist. I'm a crack shot, I'm good in the woods, I don't mind roughing it, and now I know how to prepare skins and skeletonize specimens. I want to go to Africa because I want to go someplace where I could be sure to make the investment count."

When Ward had hired Hornaday, fresh out of Iowa State University with limited experience as a taxidermist in the college museum, he did not quite recognize what he was getting. Determined to excel at his new job, Hornaday had thrown himself into his labors (however menial) with a vengeance, working from seven in the morning to six at night, or even later, and in his spare time, he read zoology textbooks or pored over Professor Ward's catalogs, which, being Ward's life work, were marvels of scientific precision even as they radiated the deep luminosity of true passion, like radioactive minerals. The catalogs were a sort of Sears, Roebuck of natural history specimens and were in fact so comprehensive and entertaining that they were used as textbooks in some college classrooms. One cast of a fossil skeleton of a prehistoric *Plesiosaurus*, for instance, was described this way:

> SKELETON *on slab. The Plesiosaurus was first discovered in 1822, by Conybeare and De la Bleche. Cuvier thought "its structure the most singular and its characters the most anomalous that had been found amid the ruins of a former world." "To the head of a Lizard (wrote Buckland) it united the teeth of a Crocodile, a neck of enormous length, resembling the body of a Serpent, a trunk and tail having the proportions of an ordinary quadruped, the ribs of a Chameleon, and the paddles of a Whale."*[4]

When Professor Ward had agreed to give Hornaday a job, the aspiring young naturalist could hardly believe his good fortune. He didn't mind if his salary was barely a pittance, or that he had to live in a drafty rooming house in Rochester. He would be getting invaluable training for his life's calling. A few years earlier, as a still-aimless sophomore at Iowa State, he'd been walking across the campus one day when he'd suddenly struck on a direction for his life: "I will be a zoologist, I will be a museum builder!" Later in life, he recalled this realization bursting upon him. "I will fit myself to be curator. I will learn taxidermy under the best living teachers—I will become one of the best in that line. That settles it! I will bring wild animals to the millions of people who cannot go to them!"[5]

Will Hornaday's grandfather, Ezekiel, settled the family farm in Indiana back in 1823. At that time, Indiana was the edge of the Western frontier. Ezekiel built a small, tidy farmhouse near the little town of Plainfield, just outside Indianapolis, underneath a grove of immense shade trees that were the remnants of the primeval forest that covered Indiana in ancient days. Will's father, William, was born in that farmhouse and grew up working the farm. But gradually the poor, claylike soil grew increasingly infertile and William began casting a restless eye westward. Eighty acres of tired dirt was simply not enough land to support the family, William realized, but land in Indiana was too expensive to increase the farm's productivity by simply buying more acreage. He also wanted to help his boys buy farms of their own when they were grown, and land prices made that impossible as well. Then, in quick succession, a severe drought and a cholera epidemic swept through the Ohio River Valley. Farmers began putting their old played-out farms up for sale, cheap, and going west.

In the spring of 1857, William Hornaday, his wife Martha, and their seven children—including two-year-old Will—climbed onto a creaking buckboard wagon and headed west to Iowa, with their horses, cows, goats, and chickens trailing out behind like a small-town circus. Iowa, with its inexpensive farmland and its legendary topsoil—three feet deep, black as tar, and with the consistency of chocolate cake—was what California would become to a later generation of restless Americans: the Western frontier, the promised land. Farmers flooded out of Ohio, Indiana, and Illinois in astounding numbers, heading west. Huge traffic jams of wagons, horses, and cattle clogged roads passing through southern Illinois, women in their scoop-shaped sunbonnets, pots and pans clattering from the wagon-bows. At one point near Peoria, Illinois, in the late 1850s, an observer counted more than 1,700 wagons passing in one month.[6]

William and Martha were a bit of an oddity in the 1850s: a blended family. Both of them had lost previous spouses to illness, and both brought children from the previous marriage to the new one. William had had five children by his previous wife, four boys and a girl; and Martha brought with her two boys, including Will.

When the family got to Iowa, William succeeded in buying a 270-acre farm near the town of Eddyville, on the Des Moines River. People had warned that hucksters were overselling Iowa, but for William Hornaday, the place stood up to the promise. The farm in Eddyville was where William Temple Hornaday came of age (although he made frequent trips back East to visit relations in Indiana), and where he came to love the natural world, the deep timber and river thickets filled with birds and animals and the thrill of discovery. "It was game country in those days and I loved the woods," he recalled later in life. "Love of all wild things came naturally."

Older people, especially hunters, said the wildlife in Iowa just wasn't what it once was. But to Will Hornaday, the farm and surrounding woods and fields seemed to be teeming with life. It was easy to miss the fact that the last remnants of a forgotten world were passing away in plain sight. Droves of American elk were not uncommon on the prairie in those days.[7] Bobcats and "prairie wolves," or coyotes, were so widespread that it wasn't until the 1880s that farmers in Iowa could succeed in raising sheep profitably, according to a history of Dickinson County in the nineteenth century. There were even a few buffalo left in Iowa when Will was a boy—the last pair of wild bison were thought to have been shot while resting on a bluff overlooking the Little Sioux River, in northwest Iowa, in 1863. Once Will even saw a wolf—not a skulking coyote, but a shaggy gray timber wolf—loping across a distant field in broad daylight. He did not quite grasp that this lurking marauder, denizen of the darkest woods of the human imagination, was an artifact of the fast-fading wilderness.

The Civil War years marked the beginning of a long, sad downward spiral for the Hornaday family.[8] Will's two big brothers, Clark and Calvin, both enlisted in the Union Army with great enthusiasm when President Abraham Lincoln put out the first call for troops. Clark joined the Seventh Regiment in Indiana, but a few years later, while fighting with the army of the Potomac, he was grievously wounded and later died in a hospital in Philadelphia. Calvin came home from the war unhurt, but by then he and Will were the only ones left to help their father run the farm, all the other siblings having grown up and moved away. Then Calvin became crippled with rheumatism and became bedridden. The burden of running the sprawling farm fell on Will's parents, who were getting on in years, and on Will, who was still just an adolescent mostly interested in roaming the woods and fields. His father's grand American dream of buying a big spread that he could one day share with his sons now seemed like nothing but a boulder on his back. The health and spirit of both his parents seemed very nearly broken by the struggle of keeping up the farm, as well as by the sorrow of Clark's death in the war. His father was forced to sell the farm in Eddyville and moved what was left of the family to a much smaller place, on a twenty-acre parcel of land near Knoxville, Iowa.

In 1866, when Will was eleven, his mother died. Three years later, his father also died, and the Knoxville farm was sold and all the family's possessions were auctioned off. The dream had come to an end. Will was fourteen years old and quite alone; by then, all his brothers and sisters had moved away or were dead. He went to live with relatives in Indiana temporarily, but eventually he wound up living on an enormous stock and hay farm near Paris, Illinois, owned by his uncle, Allen Varner, a Civil War veteran known as "the hero of Chickamauga." Will Hornaday proved a willing hand, but after a year, he was clear about one thing: he never wanted to be a farmer.[9]

It was when he was living with his Uncle Allen in Indiana that Will Hornaday first made the discovery that something called "taxidermy" existed. His older half-brother, David Miller, had taken him into Indianapolis on a shopping trip, and they walked into a bustling gun and tackle store operated by a man named Ambrose Ballweg. The store was filled with wonders, from Kentucky squirrel rifles to fly-casting rods to shelves of sparkling fishing lures, line, and sinkers. To his astonishment, Will saw, in a glass case on a high shelf, a half-dozen ducks, all mounted and "stuffed" so realistically they looked as if they were about to quack. Riveted by this discovery and compelled to understand the spell that made it possible, he convinced David to ask Mr. Ballweg how it had been done. But Mr. Ballweg was no help. He told the boys that he'd just bought the ducks somewhere back East, and had no idea how taxidermy worked at all. But that moment remained seared in Will's memory, like a brand.

Like most nineteenth-century boys raised on a farm, especially one near what was then the Western frontier, Hornaday grew up shooting a rifle. Learning how to shoot and hunt was considered part of a boy's natural education, so it was practically an automatic reflex to lock and load at the sight of any creature other than domestic livestock spotted on the farm. Woodchucks, crows, hawks, foxes, rabbits, deer—they all became a target of flying lead if they got close enough. But Hornaday's father and two older brothers, Clark and Calvin, who taught Will to hunt, were more compassionate than their Iowa neighbors. They were, Hornaday remembered, "kind-spirited and humane," and they never hunted animals they did not intend to eat, nor did they harm the birds around the house that became almost tame during the winter months while feeding on kitchen scraps.

Still, Will became a lethal shot almost as soon as he'd grown out of short pants, and once or twice, he couldn't resist pulling the trigger when he knew he shouldn't. Over the years, he confessed later, he shot a prairie chicken (also known as the pinnated grouse), a woodpecker, and a little green heron. The heron especially fascinated him, and he studied its wings, beak, legs, and underplumage in awe "to see how they were made and put together and what they were fitted to do."[10] But each time he killed one of these living things without good reason, he was tortured by pangs of doubt and guilt. A child's emotional response to the killing of a bird or animal is a kind of Rorschach test of character: some children feel remorse; some don't. Will Hornaday was one of those who did.

Seeing the mounted duck at the sporting goods store in Indianapolis was deeply significant for Hornaday because it seemed to provide a solution to the "problem" of guilt and death, historian Gregory Dehler argues in a dissertation about Hornaday's later years as a wildlife crusader. Dehler points out that Hornaday had grown up in a household permeated with the tenets of the Seventh-day Adventist Church, a faith that preached the imminent Second Coming of Christ and the absolute truth of the Ten Commandments. In fact, the Ten Commandments were prominently displayed in the family home, and a white-bearded Seventh-day Adventist preacher was a frequent visitor at the Hornaday house while conducting revivals in the area. Still, Hornaday remembered his upbringing as "profoundly moral; and significantly but not painfully religious." As a boy, he learned not to be drunk, dishonest, lazy, or quarrelsome, and not to lie, cheat, or steal (though he also loved a good brawl, sometimes played cards in the living room, and once, in an act of flagrant rebellion, even flew a kite on Sunday).[11]

Nevertheless, his shame at the deaths of birds and animals that died in his hands was tinged with the soul-sickness of sin. When he discovered that taxidermy existed, it was as if a light went on: here was a way of "resurrecting" dead birds and animals, bringing them back to life as Christ had been brought back to life. At the same time, the bird could serve to educate the masses—millions, perhaps—about the beauty and importance of wild things. The inner shame and torment he felt about hunting could be channeled into a noble purpose.

At this and other moments in American history, Dehler points out, it was not uncommon for crusaders of various kinds to transfer evangelism to "pseudo-religious social causes." Will's Seventh-day Adventist upbringing taught him that ethics and values were absolute, and that evangelism was the highest and most important calling of humankind. It was not too much of a stretch to substitute the well-being of nature for the spiritual suffering of humanity. "Although he never assumed the pulpit," Dehler writes, "William Temple Hornaday spent his life preaching his causes in the most absolute terms, requiring the most immediate response from his 'congregation.'"[12]

By the time he was sixteen, Hornaday was casting about, trying to decide what to do with the rest of his life. His legal guardian, Benjamin Auten—a confirmed bachelor who was one of the wisest, kindest, and most loveable of men—suggested dentistry,[13] but Will hated the idea and succeeded in avoiding it. He considered becoming a newspaper editor because he liked "reading, writing and declaiming." He applied for a job at a local newspaper by boasting in a letter to his prospective boss that he was "a corking good speller and could write some," and concluding, "What can you do for me?" "Not a thing," the editor replied.[14]

He went to another editor, who seemed amazed and delighted by the boy's gumption but who made him realize he really wasn't sufficiently well educated to be a newspaperman. After all, Will Hornaday—like so many other young men of his day—had never even been to high school.

Finally, Will decided to see if he could get into college. He enrolled at nearby Oskaloosa College, even though he did not qualify for a scholarship. For a year, he struggled with his studies and with his bills, knowing full well that he had no family to fall back on if he failed. The next year, he qualified for a county scholarship and transferred to Iowa State Agricultural College (later Iowa State).

One day in his first year at Iowa State, he heard that the college president, A. S. Welch, had offered a ten-dollar award and a job as a taxidermist to any student who could mount a specimen suitable for the college museum. Hornaday borrowed a small-bore rifle, went out and shot a squirrel, then stuffed it full of tow. He mounted it in a sitting position with small black buttons for eyes and a hickory nut in its paws. When he proudly presented his trophy to the president, Welch just chuckled and told him it was "not good enough for the museum." It was then that the veil fell from Hornaday's eyes, and he realized what he'd created was a "monstrosity."[15]

Later, Hornaday became a pupil of Professor Charles Bessey, the distinguished botanist and zoologist. Bessey liked Hornaday's fire and his great enthusiasm for anything having to do with natural history. It was Bessey who gave the boy his second chance at taxidermy. A farmer had shot an American White Pelican on its migratory passage over Iowa, and he'd brought the immense white carcass to Bessey because he thought it might be stuffed for the campus museum. Laying out the fallen bird on a dissecting table in front of Hornaday, Professor Bessey had taken down an enormous volume from his bookshelf—the majesterial *Birds of America*, by John James Audubon. Using Audubon's color plate of the white pelican as a template, he showed Hornaday how to bring the bird back to life with wire, stuffing, glue, glass eyes, and a sense of reverence for the splendor and complexity of birds.[16]

Though the plates in Audubon's famous book seemed to vibrate with life, in order to paint his subjects in such detail, Aubudon had been forced to shoot the birds with small shot (or pay someone else to shoot them) and then prop their lifeless bodies up in realistic positions. His devotion to nature and his desire to share it with the world required that Audubon—like Hornaday—first strike a dark bargain with death.

It was Professor Bessey who first told Hornaday about Ward's Natural Science Establishment, in Rochester, and the very same day he heard about it, Will Hornaday wrote Professor Ward a letter:

Ames, Iowa
11 April, 1873
Prof Henry A. Ward
Rochester, N.Y.

Dear Sir,

I want to learn taxidermy in all its branches. I understand that
you are doing a large business in that line, and so think it likely
that I can gain useful information as to the best place or chance of
studying the art. Wish to ask in the first place is there is *any chance*
of learning in your establishment. I have considerable knowledge of mounting birds, and stuffed many specimens for the
College museum last year. But my knowledge of the art is limited
and it is my wish and determination to make a first class taxidermist. What can you do for me?

Respectfully yours,
W. T. Hornaday[17]

Ward, as amused as he was intrigued by Hornaday's forwardness,
wrote back immediately, and after some correspondence—during
which he urged Hornaday to finish school before coming to work for
him—he invited the young man to come to Ward's as a kind of low-
ranking apprentice. Hornaday took a train to Rochester the instant
he graduated.

Working at Ward's, Hornaday would later write, was like spending every day in a "signal station," in which invitations to romance from
exotic locales all over the world came pouring in. Isadore Prevotel,
Frederic Lucas, and the other older taxidermists not only seemed to
have visited every remote place on the planet, they also had narrowly
escaped death somewhere. Almost every day, a crate of skins or skeletons would arrive at the taxidermy shop from some steamy jungle or
mountain fastness, like a summons from a lost world.

In the Cast Building, Hornaday watched workmen making plaster
replicas of prehistoric creatures, from the shambling, shaggy mast-
odon to the triceratops. There was even a fantastic casting of a *Mega-
therium*, or giant ground sloth, fourteen feet high and twenty feet
long, as big as an elephant—proof that Professor Ward's collection
was on a par with the greatest museums in America. In the Osteology

Building, a different kind of specialist pieced together the skeletons of animals living and long gone, from wolverines and tigers to immense prehistoric crocodiles. Another building served as a carpenter shop; the Long Museum—despite a disapproving placard at the compound's entrance warning curiosity-seekers that "THIS IS NOT A MUSEUM"—was essentially a musuem or storehouse where finished specimens were kept; and Cosmos Hall was where Professor Ward kept his mineral and fossil collection, which was so extensive it was obvious to Hornaday that he must be one of the world's greatest collectors.[18]

But it was the Taxidermy Building that captured Hornaday's interest with the swoon of young love. Reeking with the smell of camphor and creosote, chemicals used to store skins before they were mounted for exhibition, it was a regular Noah's Ark of species from around the world. Hornaday later wrote that he couldn't walk into that room without feeling he was being watched, by a black jaguar, a bull elephant, a wildebeest, or some other creature in the process of being resurrected on the mounting-tables. Years later, he described the thrill of it all:

> To me, the romance and glamour of Ward's museum was as fascinating and compelling as the stage and footlights are to the confirmed actor. Up to that time, nothing else of the kind had entered into my life. At that one spot, the jungles of the tropics, the game-haunted mountains and plains, and the mysterious depths of the seas seemed to contest for the privilege of pouring in day by day their richest zoological treasures.[19]

Hornaday had been working at Ward's for six months, spending most of his waking hours in the company of older men who had exotic field experiences in far-off places. But Rochester was about as far-off a place as he'd ever been in his life. Now, he felt, he was ready to test his mettle against the world. After all, he was nineteen years old, a grown man. It was time to mount an expedition of his own, just like Paul Du Chaillu had in Africa. When Du Chaillu left on his first expedition, the one that made his name famous around the world, he had been only twenty.

When Hornaday marched into Professor Ward's office that May

morning and dropped the name of Paul Du Chaillu, it was a name that was no doubt familiar to a majority of households in America. Fifteen years earlier, in 1859—the same year Charles Darwin published his famous book on the origin of species—the French-American explorer had emerged from the trackless jungles of Gabon after a four-year expedition with conclusive proof of the existence of the hairy, upright-walking "ape-man" of the jungle, which had long been rumored but never confirmed. Although the myth of such a creature had persisted since Roman times, it was not until 1847 that Dr. Thomas Savage, an American missionary in Africa, had produced an actual skull of the beast. The skull was shocking: heavy and low-slung, it looked vaguely human, but with thick ridges over the brows and a long sagittal crest across the top of the head. Then, two years later, another explorer produced an entire skeleton of the beast and put it on display at the Royal College of Surgeons, in London. That's when Du Chaillu vowed to devote the rest of his life to finding an actual specimen of the creature, a living one if possible.[20]

With funding from the National Academy of Natural Sciences, in Philadelphia, he mounted an expedition to West Africa, where he'd spent time as a boy when his father was a trader there. The late nineteenth century was a time when a very young man, armed with nothing but pluck, a modest bankroll, and the vaguest of maps, could strike out into the unknown and come back with enough specimens and stories to make him world-famous. He might even bring back a major new discovery, some exotic species hitherto unknown to science. In an age of grand and glorious voyages of discovery, Du Chaillu's expedition to Africa was one of the grandest of them all.

Only a few white men had ever touched the shores of "the Gaboon," as the small West African country was then known; few, if any, had ever penetrated more than a few miles into the interior, which was bisected by the equator—a steamy tangle later explorers called "the green hell." Even David Livingstone, who was mounting large-scale expeditions deep into the interior of southern Africa at the same time, never set foot in Gabon. But Du Chaillu, who had learned one of the local languages as a boy, plunged into the Dark Continent seemingly without fear. He traveled alone and on foot, not even carrying a tent, because he expected to be sustained by the native peoples he met along his way.

When he returned from Gabon, Du Chaillu published a book

about his exploits, which had the swashbuckling title *Explorations and Adventures in Equatorial Africa; with Accounts of the Manners and Customs of the People, and of the chase of the Gorilla, Crocodile, Leopard, Elephant, Hippopotamus and other Animals.* He maintained that he'd walked a total of about 8,000 miles on his trip. "I suffered fifty attacks of the African fever, taking, to cure myself, more than fourteen ounces of quinine," he wrote. "Of famine, long-continued exposures to the heavy tropical rains, and attacks of ferocious ants and venomous flies, it is not worthwhile to speak."[21]

His book was written with such breathless vividness that it electrified the world. But it also provoked widespread derision, with his preposterous tales of cannibals and a race of forest people so tiny they could be described as dwarves or pygmies. But the thing that excited the public more than anything else was his account of his first encounter with the legendary hairy ape-man of Africa:

> Suddenly, as we were yet creeping along, in a silence which made a heavy breath seem loud and distinct, the woods were at once filled with the tremendous barking roar of the gorilla. Then the underbrush swayed rapidly just ahead, and presently before us stood an immense male gorilla. He had gone through the jungle on his all-fours; but when he saw our party, he erected himself and looked us boldly in the face. He stood about a dozen yards from us, and was a sight I think I shall never forget. Nearly six feet high . . . with immense body, huge chest, and great muscular arms, with fiercely-glaring, large, deep gray eyes, and a hellish expression of face, which seemed to me like some nightmare vision: thus stood before us this king of the African forest.[22]

Although the book was greeted with disbelief by many, others found it so thrilling that it permanantly changed their lives. Years later, in 1933, an American filmmaker named Merian C. Cooper, who had come across an old copy of the book when he was a six-year-old boy in Florida, made a movie inspired by Du Chaillu's adventures. It was called *King Kong.*[23]

Henry Augustus Ward was now staring at a nineteen-year-old boy who seemed determined to outdo Paul Du Chaillu, one of the most famous explorers on the planet. Ward's amusement began to fade in the face of the unmitigated gall of this lad. He was serious—dead serious, apparently. Well, Ward thought, the Establishment was always in need of specimens from Africa, and they were not easy to come by. What if he were to finance young Hornaday's expedition in exchange for a share of the specimens he brought back from the field?

"All right," Ward said abruptly. "What if I were to allow you to take a leave of absence from your work here for this undertaking? What if I were to put up, say, half the money required to finance a collecting expedition? We'd have to write a contract, of course, laying out our understandings, and freeing the Establishment of liability—"

"*Done!*" Hornaday cried, momentarily letting loose the small boy, covered with mud and cockleburs, who had actually hatched the plot in the first place.[24]

Hornaday could hardly wait to dash off a letter to his relations back in Indiana, a place that already had come to seem like a sad backwater in the glow of his new reknown as a world-famous adventurer. With the same elaborate casualness he'd used in his encounter with Professor Ward, he wrote his Uncle Allen that he was mounting a collecting expedition for gorillas to West Africa, just like Paul Du Chaillu. It was several weeks after he posted the letter that his Uncle Allen, hero of the Civil War, an enormous man whose eyes had seen death, showed up at the door of his boarding house in Rochester. Uncle Allen was not smiling. In fact, he was quite determined to prevent his intrepid, moronic nephew from vanishing forever into the mists of Africa.

In his autobiography, Hornaday recalled how Uncle Allen told him, "I'm prepared to offer you a good position in a business office in Buffalo, run by an acquaintance of mine, at a starting salary of $75 a week." That was more than *eight times* what Will made as an apprentice taxidermist. But the thought of going gray sitting in a business office in Buffalo made him want to die.

"Thank you, uncle, but I'm sorry—I just can't do that."

Then Uncle Allen upped the ante, offering the boy a flat-out bribe.

"All right, I am prepared to offer you $500, outright, if you'll abandon this crazy plan to go to Africa. Honestly, Will—you'll get yourself killed over there."[25]

Will wavered, but still refused. Then, realizing that his Uncle Allen was here only because he cared about him, he gave ground. But not all of it.

"Well, Uncle, if you feel that way about it," he said, "I cannot go on, regardless of your feelings and judgement. I will not rob you of your $500, and I am willing to make my first venture abroad in some less dangerous place."[26]

With Uncle Allen's approval, Will and Professor Ward settled on the coast of Cuba and the Florida Everglades, because—though they were both still largely unexplored—these places were safer, and because Ward was in particular need of Atlantic seaboard maritime specimens. In October 1874, Will Hornaday sailed for the Everglades. He was not quite twenty years old.

CHAPTER 9

Yearning, Too Much, for Fame

When the sixteen-ton, three-masted mail schooner *Liberty* hove into Miami Harbor on a sparkling afternoon in early January 1875, with Will Hornaday at the rail, there was barely a Miami Harbor, or even a Miami, to be seen. The tiny neotropical settlement was not even incorporated as a town, and in fact, it wasn't much more than a remote postal stop for mail ships. Hornaday wrote in a letter to a friend that "there is no town here atall, three houses at the mouth of the river, and others at intervals of one and two miles, scattered along the shore of the Bay."[1]

Standing beside Hornaday at the rail was a dishevelled-looking young man, a bit older and a bit taller than Hornaday, wearing filthy clothes and a look of wonderment on his face. Every lucky man eventually stumbles upon a best friend, and the starlight of good fortune seemed to follow Hornaday wherever he went. "I shall always believe I was born under a lucky star as a compensation for not having been born rich,"[2] he would later say. A month earlier, in Key West Harbor, Hornaday had met Chester Jackson, a twenty-nine-year-old gallant from Racine, Wisconsin, who was taking a rambling winter trip through the South—Georgia, Alabama, Louisiana, and Florida—and had wound up in Key West, as so many adventurers do, because it was as far south as you could get in the United States. That's where Jackson had noticed an intense gentleman, his sleeves rolled up, sweat glistening on his brow, dressing out a freshly killed loggerhead turtle he'd bought from a fisherman on the docks. Loggerheads, one of the largest turtles in the world, have immense, heart-shaped, keeled shells and huge dark eyes filled with a kind of infinite sadness. They are like living submarines that can plunge to great depths and grow to eight feet long and weigh a thousand pounds or more (at least in those days, before the species was savaged to the edge of extinction). In his journal, Jackson later scribbled his first impressions of that first meeting:

> It was on a sunny morning when I wandered down to the fish market to see the great fish come in. . . . In the shade of the market near the wharf, a large Loggerhead laid on his back with an energetic young man taking off his carapace or breast plate. I thought him a fisherman at first, his working clothes (blue flannel shirt and light pants—straw hat, I believe) and occupation making me think so . . . in age he was about 20—Short in stature—roundly built—fine-shaped hands—head strongly set on a short neck— square shoulders—very dark hair—darkest brown eyes, bright, deep and quick—prominent nose, short upper lip that can easily turn into a sneer—firm mouth—with an expression over all of untiring energy—backed by a strong confidence in self and the desire to make the most of everything—he looked fully five years older than his age. A man's face with a boy's body, as it were.[3]

When Hornaday struggled to turn over the great, glistening, reddish-brown shell, he couldn't help but feel a pang of sorrow. Yet, if he didn't prepare this specimen for museum display, its delectible flesh would simply be used to make turtle soup, and its huge carapace, broad as a sled, would be thrown away. To the local fishermen, the sea seemed bountiful and infinite. In fact, there were virtually no bag limits or restrictions on fishing, or even any licenses required, to dip a net into an ocean that appeared to be as boundless as the sky. Bringing the sea turtle back to Rochester and "restoring" it to life for Professor Ward would at least bring people face to face with something that was, to Hornaday, more beautiful and perfect than a Mozart concerto.

Jackson watched the intense young man at a distance for awhile and then approached him. Jackson was curious about what he was doing, for one thing, but he was also "bursting for congenial company." Chatting while he worked, Hornaday told Jackson he was a collecting naturalist for Ward's Natural Science Establishment, in Rochester,

New York, and that he had delayed an expedition to Africa to undertake a specimen expedition into the Everglades, Cuba, and perhaps other places farther south. Maybe even to the Amazon. He asked if Jackson knew anything about a mail schooner called the *Liberty*, which was supposed to be headed north to Miami in a couple of days. Jackson, as it turned out, had already booked passage on the boat himself. Taking this serendipitous coincidence as a sign of traveller's luck, Jackson decided to abandon his plans (such as they were) and throw in his lot with young Hornaday, accompanying him for the rest of his expedition—possibly all the way to the Amazon. It seemed just too delicious a chance to pass up. Huck Finn had met his Tom Sawyer.[4]

When the two young adventurers arrived in the ragged settlement of Miami a couple of days later, Hornaday and Jackson pitched a tent on the sandy shore of Biscayne Bay and managed to scrounge a meal at a nearby farmhouse. They immediately set about getting ready to hunt specimens by sighting their rifles. They'd just met a local man, who walked around with a rifle casually slung under one arm, so the three of them set up targets at a distance of forty yards. Hornaday, armed with the trusty .40-caliber Maynard rifle that his half-brother David had given him, took aim and nailed four bull's-eyes, one right after another. Chester hit just one, and so did the local gun-toter. Hornaday had boasted to Professor Ward that he was a "crack shot," and that was proving to be true.[5]

In the following days, the two aspiring naturalists asked around to learn where they might go to find specimens, but everyone they met told them that even around this lonely outpost at the edge of the Everglades, the "river of grass," the flamingoes, spoonbills, scarlet ibis, magnificent frigatebirds, and other flamboyant avifauna had largely disappeared. Even in places where humanity had established only the most fragile foothold, nature seemed to be in full retreat. One day, Hornaday met a Seminole man who'd come into the settlement to trade, but he was disappointed to learn from him that most of the tribe had gone into the Everglades on a hunt, and their chief had instructed that no one be told the location of their wilderness camp. The man also declined to serve as guide into the swamp, as if it were a secret society to which the two young white men were not admitted.

Stymied in their attempt to penetrate the swamp, Hornaday and

Jackson rented a little flat-bottomed dinghy with oars for a dollar a week and crossed Biscayne Bay to the narrow spit of sand that would one day become the glittering high-rise metropolis of Miami Beach. In 1875, it was just a fragile dune and mangrove swamp flung between bay and ocean, where for the next couple of days, the two young men collected maritime specimens for Professor Ward. They found sponges, seashells, sea turtle eggs, about ten scorpions living in the sand not far from their tent, a leatherback turtle that they bought from another Seminole, and even the decomposing carcass of a manatee, one of the strange, bewhiskered "sea cows" thought to have given rise to the myth of mermaids. Rolling in the surf, the corpse was so rotten it could not be salvaged, but they managed to extract its skeleton for science. Still, picking up bones and shells on the beach was a far cry from hunting ape-men in Africa, as Hornaday had imagined himself doing.

By talking with a local family who lived near their camp, Hornaday learned that there were alligators in Arch Creek, one of many small, brackish, mangrove-tangled creeks draining out of the Everglades into the north end of Biscayne Bay. The family also told them something else: a mile back up the creek was one enormous alligator that had gotten that big by being fearsome, cunning, and elusive. For years, people had tried to bag the beast, but nobody had succeeded.

The two adventurers decided to move their camp up to the north end of the bay, and in fact, they pitched their tent directly on top of the odd natural limestone "arch" that spanned the water and gave the creek its name. The next morning, they stealthily rowed down Arch Creek for about a mile, dipping their oars into the water without a splash, then lifting them, dripping, back to the next stroke. They had just come around a bend when they spotted an enormous reptile sprawled on a mudbank, sunning, at a distance of about 150 yards. Its sheer size was startling—it appeared to be fourteen or fifteen feet in length, and fat as a hog. It would make a handsome museum specimen, for sure, if they could succeed in outwitting it.

From the bow of the boat, Will turned around and put one finger to his lips. Chester nodded, and they let the boat drift a little back downstream, slipping behind the bend and out of sight of the huge 'gator. They pulled alongside the bank and stopped, and Will pulled out his binoculars, and his Maynard .40-caliber. Then, with furtive oar-strokes, Chester began silently moving the boat forward and they crept back around the bend. The beast was still there, sprawled on the sandbar, facing them. Will brought him into focus with his glass . . . and then recoiled in shock. *It wasn't an alligator.* Its grey-green back, its long, sinister, tapered snout, and the protruding fourth tooth of its lower jaw made it clear that the beast was actually a crocodile.

A *crocodile!* But there were no crocodiles in the United States: this was a "fact" about which virtually all naturalists agreed. There were plenty of American alligators in Florida, *Alligator mississippiensis*, but crocodiles? None. There had been rumors that there might be some in Florida, but never any solid scientific proof. The only crocs in the Americas lived farther south, in Cuba, in Mexico, in Central America, and in certain places in South America like the fabled Orinoco River delta, in Venezuela.[6]

For a moment, Will Hornaday hardly dared to breathe. Had he and Chester just discovered the first crocodile in the United States— had they, perhaps, even discovered a whole new species? Was he, just like Du Chaillu, about to carve his first notch on the trophy-belt of scientific history? Just then, sensing some faint perturbation in its zone of safety, the immense reptile abruptly belly-paddled across the sandbar, plunged into the water and sank out of sight. For a moment, it was as if Will Hornaday had not even seen what he had just seen.

Basking on the sandbar, the croc had looked primitive, almost antediluvian, like an amphibious dinosaur. And, in fact, it would later become known that crocodiles are as old as dinosaurs, having arisen more than 220 million years ago, in the steamy swamps of the Triassic. Fairly early in this evolutionary saga, the physical design of the crocodile became so terrifyingly efficient, its hunting methods so crafty and so pitiless, that it actually evolved very little for the remainder of that unimaginably long span of time. Their size did change: early in their evolutionary history, ancient crocodillians called "archosaureans" grew so immense—fifty feet long, weighing eight tons—that they were capable of killing and consuming a dinosaur. And their means of locomotion changed somewhat: in ancient times, these fearsome monster lizards were able to walk upright, some of them on two legs, and could apparently "gallop" at high speeds, like the huge saltwater crocs of Australia do today. Crocodiles outwitted the dinosaurs in another way, too: when the great extinction event of 65 million years ago obliterated the dinosaurs and much of the rest of life on Earth, the crocodiles, waiting patiently in the murky water with only their eyes and nostrils exposed, survived.[7]

The skull of the present-day crocodile, with its distinctive tapering snout, still carries a basically archosaurean shape, making it a kind of living fossil, but one capable of crushing virtually anything that lives or breathes. Its phenomenal evolutionary success has to do with two things: stealth and savagery. Crocodiles are ambush hunters, able to remain perfectly still and almost perfectly invisible, adrift just beneath the water's surface until the moment they lunge. In fact, crocs spend most of their lives in a state of near-motionlessness, still as a log, adjusting their position with faint, quiet paddle-strokes. Then, with a ferocity unparalleled in the animal kingdom, they strike, and in a fraction of a second, they turn into the most ferocious reptiles on Earth. A rottweiler's bite force has been measured at 335 pounds per square inch; a great white shark, which can slice another shark in two, at 800 pounds per square inch. But nothing compares to a crocodile, whose bite force is more than 5,000 *pounds* per square inch. It is the most savage bite, by far, of any living creature on the planet.[8]

If Jackson and Hornaday were going to get anywhere close to the croc, they would have to match its furtiveness with their own. The next morning, they dressed the boat in branches and leaves so that it looked like a drifting sea-mat and very gently rowed it through the current toward the dragon's lair. He was on the mudbank again, sunning like a lizard king. But he wasn't fooled by their disguise: almost as soon as they drifted into view, he scrambled into the water and sank out of sight. Not for nothing had he gotten so old and huge.

The third morning, Hornaday and Jackson got up before first light and set in motion a new plan. Hornaday would take his .40 Maynard and creep along the far shore of the creek until he was opposite the croc's sandbar, and then he would hide in the mangroves. Jackson, also armed, would row the dinghy up the creek and stop just behind the bend. Then they'd both lay in wait, hoping that one or the other of them would get a chance at a shot. But when they arrived at their positions, the croc was not there, just the sunny sandbar and the gentle, peaceful current, slipping sweetly downstream. A long time passed; the soft dawn light faded away into the blank glare of full tropical day. Then, suddenly, an immense, gray, pebbly back surfaced in the middle of the stream. It paused there for a long time, motionless, until an inattentive observer would have mistaken it for nothing but a drifting log. But its stillness was not of inaction; it was of cunning. Its apparent lifelessness, so easily mistaken for lack of danger, was actually part of a pitiless plan. It was part of the reason its kind had outlived the dinosuars by 65 million years.

Then, gently, the log drifted slowly through the water towards the sandbar, stopped, seemed to change direction, and then began drifting back out to the center of the stream. Hornaday was an experienced hunter, but he was still only twenty years old. He could not wait any longer. He stood up, drew a bead on the old croc's head with the Maynard and fired. The croc seemed to explode in rage and pain, churning the water in a frenzy of froth, dove out of sight, then resurfaced, tail first, thrashing the surface of the creek. Hornaday got off a second shot, then yelled for Jackson.[9]

Chet, bring the boat up here! I got 'im once, but he's not down!

Jackson rowed furiously up the stream, then stopped, stood up in the boat, and tried to get off a shot. But his gun just clicked—a misfire. He rowed still closer to the thrashing croc, grabbed a long-handled fishing spear lying in the boat, and drove it into its back. The handle of the spear snapped off like a twig, and the croc headed downstream. Hornaday leaped from the bank into the bow of the boat and the two of them pursued the crazed monster downstream, Hornaday repeatedly firing whenever its body appeared above the surface. Finally, the beast's thrashing began to subside, and it rolled up against the muddy bank and succumbed, after all the many years of its life. (One Australian crocodile in captivity is thought to be 130 years old, so its life had no doubt been a long one.)

When Hornaday and Jackson were able to stretch the croc out to its full length on the shore, they discovered it was fourteen feet, two inches in length—but part of its tail had been bitten off, so it was likely closer to fifteen feet long. It was over five feet around at the belly. The animal was so huge that Hornaday had to dress it out in the swamp and bring back only the skin and skeleton because the body itself, which he estimated weighed over a thousand pounds, was too heavy to be dragged behind the boat. As Hornaday hoped, this great beast, which the two of them nicknamed "Ole Boss," would prove to be the first crocodile ever taken in Florida, and one of the largest crocs ever found in the state since that time. The day after they slew this monster, the adventurers returned to the swamp and shot a female, possibly Ole Boss's mate, which measured ten feet eight inches in length.

Flushed with success and heady with the idea that he might become the next Du Chaillu, Hornaday wrote his first scientific paper about the croc, for *American Naturalist*, when he returned to Rochester. In the paper, he proclaimed that he had not only discovered the first crocodile in Florida, but also that it was a brand-new species, which he called *Crocodylus acutus floridanus*. He based this claim on the fact that the skull and dorsal plates of "Ole Boss" were different than any known crocodile, with a snout midway between the narrow-beaked gavial and the broad-nosed alligator. But when the twenty-year-old naturalist's paper was published, it was greeted with something close to indifference. Few, if any, zoologists were convinced that young Hornaday had really notched a new species on the eighteen-member list of known crocodilians (which include alligators, crocodiles, caimans, and gavials). But Hornaday, as usual, was fiercely determined, pugnacious as a bulldog, and he stuck to his claim. Years later, when he had become a renowned naturalist, he continued to stick to this assertion through thirteen editions of his book *Hornaday's American Natural History*, a popular guide to the higher animals of North America, published from 1904 to 1931.[10]

In the twelfth edition, published in 1927, he placed the Florida crocodile as a subspecies of the American crocodile, describing it as native only to southern Florida and "the only crocodile which inhabits a country that is visited by killing frosts." Then he retold the story of the taking of "the alleged 'big 'gator' of Arch Creek," who was so crafty that he had permitted no one within rifleshot except the crafty author of the book. (Hornaday's taxonomic boast has long since been discarded; the beast is known to be an exceptionally large American crocodile.)

Even so, there was no disputing the fact that Hornaday and Jackson were the first to confirm the existence of crocodiles in North America, a zoological coup on its own. Hornaday returned to Rochester with the remains of Ole Boss and his mate packed in brine, then painstakingly mounted the big male, bitten-off tail and all. The mounting was later sold to the Smithsonian for $250, a sum that paid for the entire trip. Later, "Ole Boss" was exhibited by the Smithsonian at the Philadelphia Centennial Exposition of 1876 and created a sensation.

Many years earlier, when he was nine years old, Hornaday had killed a blue jay with a stone, and the stinging remorse he felt in that moment lingered for decades. But now, as a young naturalist intent on making his mark in the world, he'd grown increasingly numbed to the youthful sin-sorrow of the kill. Now "Ole Boss" was a primarily a jaunty feather in the cap of a young man who yearned, perhaps all too much, for fame.

CHAPTER 10

The Empress Josephine

The autumn after Hornaday returned from the Everglades and Cuba, Professor Ward sent his rising star to Chicago to help set up an exhibit at the Chicago Exposition of 1875. The exposition was a comparatively minor affair, dwarfed a few years later by Chicago's great World's Columbian Exposition of 1893, said to be the greatest fair ever mounted, with the world's first Ferris wheel, "Buffalo Bill's Wild West Show," and other modern wonders like a new food called the "hamburger," as well as electricity, which illuminated the entire 600-acre fairgrounds in such specactular fashion that it came to be called "The White City." Still, at the 1875 fair, Hornaday succeeded in mounting a handsome display of Ward's gemstone collection, mounted animals, and casts of ancient fossils, whose strangeness and significance was not fully understood at the time.[1]

On his way back home to Rochester, Hornaday stopped to visit his guardian, Ben Auten, in Battle Creek, Michigan. Auten was an officer of the Battle Creek Sanitarium, one of the world's most famous health resorts, whose regimen was based on principles advocated by John Harvey Kellogg—including frequent enemas, fresh air, sunshine, and a grain-based diet that later led to Kellogg's Corn Flakes. Battle Creek's notable patients had included Amelia Earhart, Henry Ford, and Mary Todd Lincoln. Hornaday's mother had spent the last few months of her life at the sanitarium before her death nine years earlier. While he was in Battle Creek, Auten invited the young naturalist to dinner at the home of an acquaintance. It was one of those seemingly chance events that would change his life forever. Also attending the dinner was a high school teacher named Josephine Chamberlain, who, like Hornaday, was twenty-one years old. When he saw her, it was as if his whole previous life melted away, and the only thing that remained was that moment:

> With an all-devouring look, my astonished eyes strove to take in that lovely and commanding personality. Never had I seen in the form of young womanhood anything quite comparable to her. I noted her ample height, her beautifully modelled form, and her wonderfully well-balanced head.... Miss Chamberlain's intellectual head and finely chiseled face, all perfectly modelled and poised, thrilled me.... She was a clear blonde, of a model fit for a figure of Diana, and her enunciation of pure English was a positive delight.... I was able to realize that her taste in dress was of the best, and that she wore her clothes in a jaunty and aristocratic air that in any country would make both men and women turn around and look.[2]

A quarter of a century later, in a letter to her, Hornaday remembered again that day:

> Several times recently I have found my thoughts going back to you as you were 24 years ago.... I remember you vividly in your best black silk gown at the never-to-be-forgotten dinner party of Emily Fellows—blessed Emily Fellows, whose hospitality gave me the opportunity to meet the finest Girl on earth.[3]

For her part, Josephine was a little taken aback by the presumption of this handsome young adventurer, and his forwardness, verging on rudeness, in bursting into her conversation whenever he pleased. He seemed to simply disregard the conventions of Victorian etiquette, looking directly into her eyes, even reaching out and touching her arm as he spoke. "Now *who* is this bold young man who dares to dispute my opinion on first acquaintance?" she wrote later, recalling this first meeting.[4]

He told her about his exploits in Cuba and the Everglades, and about slaying the king of the dragons, a brand-new species unknown to science. He told her that Professor Ward had asked him to go on a new collecting expedition, this time to the fabulous and menacing Orinoco River delta in South America. He couldn't help but mention the old saying, well known among seasoned adventurers like himself, that "when five men go up the Orinoco, only two return." Up the river, there were immense crocodiles, among the largest in the world; flesh-eating piranha, which could skeletonize a cow in seconds; and giant electric eels, which could produce a 650-volt shock that was enough to kill a man in a single jolt. Josephine listened to all this demurely, dropping her eyes frequently, as custom required, wondering how much of it might be true.

Hornaday did not leave the dinner without getting Josephine's mailing address and a promise to correspond with him from parts unknown. He would be sure to write back, he said—in the unlikely event, that is, that he survived the Orinoco.[5]

Actually, the South America trip had been mostly Chester Jackson's idea. After Jackson returned to the weary tedium of Wisconsin following his adventures in the Everglades, the two pals kept up a lively correspondence, and at one point—mostly in jest—Jackson suggested that the two of them, like Tom Sawyer and Huck Finn, keep going south, all the way down to the Amazon. It was, after all, Hornaday who had first implied that's where he was bound when they first met. Maybe they could even spend the winter down there, Jackson suggested, hunting and collecting for Professor Ward and having splendid adventures along the way.

Hornaday took him seriously. He thought maybe Professor Ward might actually go for it, especially in light of the fact that Ward had just returned from a trip abroad that proved to be a disappointment, because most of the European specimen dealers had only a paltry supply of museum-quality items. To procure the kind of specimens that he needed to fill his catalog, Ward would have to mount his own expeditions to some of the world's most remote and dangerous places, such as central Africa, southeast Asia, and of course the great river deltas of South America. Hornaday could not have picked a more propitious moment—especially after his recent triumph in the swamp—to propose that he and his new sidekick Jackson embark on a collecting trip to the Orinoco. Ward agreed to the trip and fronted them half the money. Jackson put up the rest. Still, it would be a shoestring operation all the way because the budget—as usual—would be so tight it squeaked.

By January, when Rochester was thigh-deep in snowdrifts, Jackson arrived in town, and he and Hornaday spent a couple of frantic, dizzy days getting outfitted for their big trip. They bought rubber blankets, wool blankets, a tent, ammunition, fishing tackle, ammonia for snake bites, alum, arsenic, quinine for malaria, a device for testing the strength of alcohol (for preserving specimens), a thermometer, New Bedford harpoons, field glasses, flasks of brandy, "court plaster" for cuts, various skinning knives and scrapers, two hatchets, forceps, a rock hammer, a couple thousand blank paper labels, and other supplies. Hornaday also had brought along a small collection of favorite weapons. There was his favorite of all, the trusty .40 Maynard rifle—the Excaliber that had slain the dragon. (Actually, it had two barrels, one .40 caliber and the other .45–.85 caliber.) He had another double-barreled, smoothbore gun, a breech-loading number 10. He had a Maynard shotgun, number 16. And he had a .32 caliber Smith & Wesson revolver, with cartridge belt and bag. He was like a regular Buffalo Bill, except better armed.[6]

Jackson had come armed with a strange double-barreled weapon that he'd had specially made for the trip. One barrel shot rifle bullets; the other, bird shot. The weapons added forty pounds of shot and ten pounds of Maynard bullets to their gear. This immense adventure kit, bursting with anticipation, was packed into a huge wooden crate specially built by carpenters at Ward's Natural Science Establishment. On the afternoon of January 21, 1876, the two swashbucklers and their crate boarded a train for New York City to catch a boat bound for Barbados and the rest of their lives. In his journal, Jackson later captured the emotion of this departure:

> Our feelings cannot be described—we were just intensely happy. Yet there was a shade of apprehension (we might never come back)—there was our faith in the success of the expedition—there was a wild freedom in it that made our pulses throb—we saw expeditions rich in conquests—and terrible animals—awful snakes—gorgeous birds—we saw ourselves swinging in our hammocks in the depths of the great woods—campfires—Indians—or paddling up the deep, dark rivers—we saw our safe return to home and friends wise in experience and chock-full of yarns of

adventure—We were happy—we leaned back in our car seat and talked and talked while the cars flitted through the villages carrying us swiftly to N.Y.[7]

Once they arrived in Manhattan, they got a shoebox of a hotel room and wandered down to the East River, where they admired the soaring, half-finished steel girders and struts of what would become the Brooklyn Bridge a few years later. They spotted their ship in the harbor, a dreadful, dirty-looking little three-masted bark, preposterously named the *Golden Fleece*, which was being loaded with corn, beans, and hay. The deck was crowded with piles of lumber, bundles of barrel staves, and horses, all bound for plantations in Barbados. The next day, they stopped at the Astor Library, silent as a mausoleum, to read up about the Orinoco and the Demerara, another river delta in British Guiana where Professor Ward wanted them to go. As if to demonstrate how ill prepared they were, they also stopped at a bookshop and bought a copy of a little book called *Spanish Made Easy*.

To the young men's delight, Professor Ward took the train down from Rochester and showed up at the harbor to see them off. He handed them a big bag of oranges, and just as the ship pulled away from the dock, shouted out, in a rare burst of feeling:

"I'd give one of my fingers to go with you!"

Even so, the trip did not get off to an auspicious start. As Jackson wrote in his journal, the morning of their departure was "a cold disagreeable day—chilly—cloudy—disheartening." When the *Golden Fleece* got out to sea, things got worse. The ship ran into a freezing North Atlantic gale, and the two would-be adventurers were driven below deck to their tiny quarters, where a small coal stove filled the air with noxious fumes and the ship pitched and heaved for days. Both of them got violently ill. Hornaday tried to nibble the tasteless crackers the sailors called hardtack, but he had no appetite. The winter gale was unrelenting and did not break for three days. Jackson wrote:

[H]ow the wind howled through the rigging—weird and awful—sometimes it would shriek through the blocks like a very maniac—the waves dashed over the sides—and made the ship stagger and groan beneath the great burden of water—in our berth we could feel the mighty sea gathering force—could hear it come rolling on—we held on to the edge of the berth to keep from being hurled to the floor—how our bones ached from being rolled backward and forward—the sailors ran on the deck to the hoarse cries of the captain—often we could hear the men at the pump—we might be leaking badly—we might be sinking —yet morning came at last—and oh! how grateful we were to see it.[8]

Four days out from the port of New York, the weather broke, the *Golden Fleece* plunged into the great, broad, blue avenue of the Gulf Stream, and the intrepid adventurers emerged from their seasick torture chamber down below. They stripped down to their shirtsleeves and basked in the neotropical sun. Ten days later, with moonlight on a still sea and the town clock booming midnight, the ship sailed into the harbor at Bridgetown, Barbados.

In the days and weeks that followed, Will and Chester made their way up the Orinoco and into other steamy river deltas. Hornaday later chronicled this trip in installments for a long travelogue called "Canoe and Rifle on the Orinoco," for a popular magazine called *Youth's Companion*, among whose other contributors included Jack London, Theodore Roosevelt, and Emily Dickinson.[9]

The great Orinoco River basin, the eighth-longest river in the world, was a muddy torrent more than three miles wide in places, crowded on both sides with nearly impenetrable jungle and swamp. It was overrun with life. Thousands of sea turtles, loggerheads, greens, hawksbills, and ridleys, some weighing 1,000 pounds, swam upriver at nesting season and swarmed onto the muddy beaches. There were flamboyant tropical birds in the trees—toucans and macaws—and wading birds on the shore, along with howler monkeys and the strange capybara, or water-hog, the world's largest rodent, as well as the Western hemisphere's biggest snake, the thirty-foot anaconda.[10] They rode the steamboat all the way up to Ciudad Bolivar, where they ventured out on hunting expeditions, at one point shooting a nearly twelve-foot crocodile which, though wounded, began slithering away into the river. Hornaday, afraid the beast would escape, grabbed the thing by the tail and it turned on him "with a deep guttural snarl like a dog" and lunged at him before Chester stilled its life with a well-placed bullet.[11]

"Bill, you fool! What in the name of heaven are you thinking?" Jackson yelled at him.

Hornaday was just thinking that he didn't want it to get away.

They continued on to the Demerara River delta, in Guyana, where they finally procured a manatee skeleton, though a whole specimen, skin and all, eluded them. They had been adventuring for more than six months and were both deeply tanned, and their clothes in tatters, when they boarded a steamship in Barbados in July 1876 and headed home. The trip had been wonderful fun, and the two vagabonds returned with an amazing array of specimens—crocodiles, electric eels, howler monkeys, sloth and puma, bats, birds, fish, and armadillos— but Hornaday was not satisfied. Years later, perhaps as a boast, he wrote to Theodore Roosevelt that South America was "the poorest country that I ever struck," and "the most unsatisfactory on Earth for a hunter-naturalist!"[12] Life was young, and he intended to do better in even more exotic places.

But now he was turning homeward, and his thoughts returned not to the adventures just past, but to the young woman from Battle Creek, Michigan, the Empress Josephine, whom he had mailed letters to from whatever port seemed civilized enough to get them to her. He wondered what she thought of him now, or if he was in her thoughts at all. He knew for certain that she was in his. In fact, by now he knew as surely as he'd ever known anything: he was giddily, utterly in love. In a letter to a friend filled with advice and confessions about his newfound joy, Hornaday later wrote:

Old fellow, I do wish you would fall dead in love with Miss ___ for you would immediately find yourself in another world entirely. There is absolutely nothing like it! For my part, I feel a calm and happy tranquillity all the while, all tasks are play, and I seem to tread on air. Because I *know* she's true. Well now, don't be afraid to love the girl for fear she can't be lassooed. My pard, that's the very way to win her. My word for it: only *love* her enough and she's yours. Like begets like, and if she won't capitulate without a seige, just lay siege, and sooner or later she must surrender.[13]

CHAPTER II

Man-Eaters of the Animallai Hills

One humid afternoon in late September 1877, the man the "coolies" called *sahib* came striding back into the expedition's hunting camp in the high-elevation teak forest of South India's Animallai Hills.[1] Sahib—a word variously translated as "trusted friend" or "owner"— had a .40-caliber Maynard rifle tucked into the crook of his arm and was wearing a tattered Norfolk jacket of rough outdoor fabric, with paired box pleats over the chest and back. Like many upper-class sportsmen of his day, he tended to dress up for shooting. Trailing behind him were his best man, Nangen, and his "half-caste" tracker, Pera Vera, whose skin was the color of ebony and who was wearing nothing but a loincloth, with his long, matted, jet-black hair drawn back and tied in a coil behind his head. In this wild country, especially with man-eaters afoot, it was foolhardy to go anywhere alone or unarmed.[2]

Suspended from a pole stretched between Pera Vera and Nangen's shoulders was a freshly killed axis deer, spotted as a fawn and with barrel-shaped antlers hanging almost to the ground. A murmur of excitement arose from the camp as the men approached; several women whooped with joy. Although axis deer, or "chital," were not uncommon on the Indian subcontinent, the expedition was—once again—running low on food, especially fresh meat. There was a woman in camp, the wife of one of the trackers, who had actually begun to cry with hunger for meat. In remote places, this cry of hunger had a name—in Africa, Du Chaillu reported, it was called *gouamba*. It was the longing of flesh for flesh, a hunger nothing else but meat would satisfy.[3]

As Pera Vera and Nangen unloaded the fat buck on the ground near the cooking fire, the *sahib* sat down on a camp stool and handed off his rifle, cartridge belt, and bag to Nangen. Then he began gingerly unfastening his boots. His feet and ankles were killing him. The warm, soggy air of the monsoon season, continuously wet feet, and all this walking had resulted in a half-dozen raw sores on each of his ankles. He had to dress them daily with court-plaster and cotton before he could even put on his hunting boots. Getting out of these boots, and getting a little heat from the fire, would help the burning and swelling go down.

Even so, despite these minor inconveniences, *sahib* Hornaday loved what he was doing with his life. Sometimes he found it hard to believe that Professor Ward had agreed to fund an expedition of two to three years in length, to some of the most delicious places on the planet. And to *hunt*, no less! Hunting and collecting were his favorite things in the world. One night a few months earlier, in a remote jungle camp in north India, lying in his hammock listening to his Hindi coolies chattering around the fire after spending the day skinning out an elephant, he wrote, "This is the jolliest life that ever was led."

On this perilous trek, Hornaday had spent the past year living in rough hunting camps like this one, sleeping on a cot, cooking over open fires, never going anywhere without his gun. By now, he barely remembered what a proper bed or the inside of a house even felt like. In addition to his earlier expeditions, on this trip he'd journeyed throughout India, from Benares to Bombay, hunting crocodiles in the Ganges and elephants along the Jumna, and soon he would depart for Ceylon, the Malay Peninsula, and Borneo, among the remotest places on the planet. He was by now Professor Ward's most competent and experienced hunter and specimen-collector, and likely one of the most experienced in the world. His natural temperament, brimming with bravado and an unassailable self-confidence, now was only magnified by the daily habit of ordering about trackers, cooks, porters, guides, and coolies. He had developed what military men called "command presence"—the bearing of a man to be reckoned with, a man to be taken seriously, a man to be feared. Given the fact that he wore a beard that was so thick and black it was more like fur than hair, and that his dark eyes were so fierce and combative that they tended to make other people look down, it was sometimes hard to believe William Temple Hornaday was only twenty-three years old.

For the previous seven weeks, Hornaday and his party had been hunting and collecting in the hill country of the province of Tamil Nadu, in the Western Ghats of South India. Owing to the elevation, which ranged from 2,000 feet to the 8,800-foot Anamudi, the highest peak in India south of the Himalayas, the days were warm but the nights cool, unlike the sweltering, malarial heat of the lowlands. Even so, it was monsoon season, and the air was always slightly damp.

"The Animallai Hills! How my nerves tingle and my pulse quickens as I write the name!" Hornaday wrote later, in the book he called *Two Years in the Jungle: The Experiences of a Hunter and Naturalist in India, Ceylon, the Malay Peninsula and Borneo*. Embedded in the title was one of the grinding contradictions of Hornaday's life: he was both a prominent conservationist and a professional killer. These hills, he went on, were a "Hunter's Paradise," and "no other locality in all the East Indies can boast of possessing such splendid open forests for hunting, and such a genial climate, combined with such a variety and abundance of large game."[4]

What he failed to mention in this rapturous passage was that when he'd arrived in India, a terrible famine was sweeping across the country like darkness at noon. During the two years of 1876 and 1877, it was later estimated that 10 million people died of starvation.[5] But it wasn't only the people who were perishing. The creatures of the forest were also on the grim edge of starvation. As if the people of India needed anything else to compound their misery, there was now something besides famine that stalked them in the darkness of the night, something that eyed them out of the shadows at twilight and at dawn. It was one of the most fearsome and pitiless predators on the planet, now grown desperate with hunger: the Bengal tiger. The big males, who could weigh over 500 pounds and whose terrifying roars could be heard from two miles away, could leap as much as thirty feet at a single bound and were so powerful they could drag the body of a young water buffalo weighing 500 pounds a quarter of a mile. Hunting alone along game trails and streambeds, they could kill and consume fifty pounds of meat a day. And now, emboldened by hunger, the tiger would pick up the scent of a human, perhaps a lone woman who had foolishly ventured too far afield in search of firewood. Then the tiger would begin to hunt her.

In India, the local people said there were three different kinds of tigers, Hornaday explained in his book.[6] First were the "game-killers"—animals who lived in the wild and hunted wild game, as nature intended. They were what Hornaday called "bold, honest hunters." Next were the "cattle-lifters"—tigers who had grown lazy and indolent after discovering that killing a dumb, slow hog or a bullock was much easier than taking down a nimble-footed axis deer or gazelle in the forest. The losses to poor farmers from these scavengers were staggering.

But by far the most frightening kind of tiger was one who had discovered the taste of human blood. There were various theories about what caused a tiger to "cross over" and become a man-eater. Hunters said that many of these animals were too old to hunt in the forest, or they had a painful wound, like a mouthful of infected porcupine quills or badly decaying teeth. Others said that it was because there was no longer enough game in the bush. Still others said the man-eaters were evil spirits, sent by the gods to exact retribution for some sin in this or a previous life.

But whatever the cause, a single man-eating tiger or tigress was enough to instill abject terror in a whole district. Generally, a man-eater would prowl through one area of several square miles, snatching a woman hanging clothes to dry one day, slipping into a village at dusk and making off with a child sitting on a doorstep the next, perhaps leaving nothing but a sad, tipped-over basket, an upended toy, or a bit of splintered bone. Other times, there would be a sighting of a huge, famous man-eater in one place, and by nightfall that same day, it would snatch a child out of a village five miles away.

In one case, in central India, a ravenous tigress caused the complete emptying of thirteen villages and threw out of cultivation fifteen square miles of farmland. The great Indian-born British big-game hunter Jim Corbett once killed a famous man-eating tigress called the Champawat Tigress, which alone was responsible for the deaths of 436 men, women, and children. "There is no more terrible thing," he wrote, "than to live and have one's being under the shadow of a man-eater."[7] The Champawat Tigress, who never killed in the same village twice and never revisited a kill, terrorized a region hundreds of square miles in size. She would carry off her victims at any time of day or night and consume them whole, eating their heads, hands, and sometimes even their clothing.

Most people, of course, were desperately frightened of tigers. But for Hornaday's purposes—that of securing specimens for Professor

Ward, and by extension for museums throughout the United States and Europe—he would have dearly loved to see a tiger. Unlike the farmers and villagers of India, William Temple Hornaday wanted to encounter a tiger, man-eating or otherwise—meet it face to face, at close range, with nothing but his trusty little .40-caliber Maynard rifle between them. "I had enough faith in the accuracy of my little Maynard rifle, and my own steadiness, to believe that between us we could floor a tiger if we ever got a fair chance," he wrote, with serene self-confidence.

It was quite a boast: the .40-caliber Maynard fired such small bullets that it took twenty-nine of them to make a pound. Four-bore big-game rifles could throw a four-ounce ball, eight times as heavy. And Henry Stanley, when he left for Africa to find Dr. David Livingstone a few years earlier in 1869, had reported taking with him "two muzzle-loading Holland half-pounders that carried an iron lead-coated explosive shell, containing a bursting charge of half an ounce of fine grain powder"[8]—armaments of almost preposterous destructiveness, meant to knock down an elephant, or perhaps two. By contrast, the Maynard rifle was practically a toy. The only way to stop a charging tiger with a weapon like the Maynard would be to hit a dead-on bulls-eye on the very first shot. A shot that wounded but did not kill would create an enraged 500-pound monster, a supreme carnivore, exploding out of the bush with its jaws wide open.[9]

In the midst of all this, there was one thing that brought William Hornaday almost unalloyed joy. It was that, just before he had left on this trip, he had returned to Battle Creek, Michigan, gone down on one knee, and asked the Empress Josephine to be his wife. She agreed, without hesitation (or at least, none that he noticed). It was a bold, almost reckless thing for her to do, because she knew well enough that her freshly minted fiancé would be gone for two or three years on an expedition that would be fraught with dangers of all sorts— charging elephants, venomous snakes, quicksand, illness, infections, assault, robbery, and drowning, to name just a few. Will was strong as a bullock, seemingly fearless, competent in any number of ways, and filled with a young man's conviction that he could overcome any peril. Even so, there was no getting around the fact that this expedition was dangerous in the extreme, and their engagement akin to getting betrothed to a soldier boy going off to the front. (Hornaday did not mention this to Josephine, but the whole expedition was so perilous that the Travellers Insurance Company had refused to underwrite it at all.)

In an ink-smudged, four-page letter from the Neilgherry Hills dated Monday, June 25, 1877, he wrote her: "Your letters, darling . . . never fail me either in frequency, length or sweetness. You see, I long since made up my mind that I would never marry a girl, or become engaged to one, who could not write a real good letter . . . eighteen months ago I passed a unanimous vote that Miss Chamberlain wrote the best letters I had ever received or read, and also that said Miss C. was the smartest girl of all I had ever known."[10]

He lived for her letters. It made all the difference in the world to him to know that every morning that he awoke in the Wainaad forest, or Mullaitivu, or the Neilgherry Hills, there was a beautiful young woman back in Battle Creek, Michigan, with a jaunty aristocratic air, who was thinking of him—pinning up her heavy hair, thinking of him; gathering up the supper dishes, thinking of him; cutting roses in the kitchen garden, thinking of him. And he was doing the same: marching off on a morning hunt on the slopes of Anamudi, thinking of her; preparing specimens by firelight in the bush of the Deccan plateau, thinking of her; lying in his hammock at night, listening to the hoarse croak of a hornbill or the distant trumpeting of elephants, thinking of her.

But, of course, everything was not as idyllic as his letters to Josephine sometimes made it seem. While he reveled in this rough life in exotic hunting camps, he had regularly been brought to his knees in India by tropical fevers of one kind or another. On this trip, he would get severely ill sixteen separate times, once crawling into a fleabag hotel room in Bombay, chugging quinine and drifting in and out of delirium for two weeks. More than one white adventurer had simply died in places like that. He'd grown so accustomed to these dreadful fevers that he could anticipate when the nausea would reach a gut-wrenching peak, and he would try to schedule his activities for the hours before the fever's terrible crescendo.

There were other times, often when he was ill, that he just felt low and lonely and a little bit lost. He badly missed his hunting companion and *doppelganger* Chester Jackson, who would have reveled in all this but was unable to come along on this grandest of grand adventures. Professor Ward was unwilling to pay his way, and this time Jackson could not afford to pay part of the passage himself.[11]

But one of the most worrisome developments lately was the fact that he and Professor Ward were more-or-less continuously squabbling. Hornaday had agreed, in a written contract signed before he left, to undertake the expedition on a shoestring budget and to devote all his time except Sundays "and other odd times" to the pursuit of specimens, and specifically those requested by Ward. To fill these orders, and to keep his enterprise afloat financially, Ward seemed to want Hornaday to produce several museums' worth of specimens, in no time and at no cost, regardless of risk or hardship. Ward seemed to have no real idea how difficult and dangerous it was to procure specimens out in the bush. You couldn't just pick a tiger off a tree! In a series of letters to Jackson, back home in Wisconsin, Hornaday complained bitterly about Ward's demands:

> Gospel truth. He *never* thanks anyone, or praises or compliments me in the least, and I am told others under him fare exactly the same. Why, he says right out, that every improvement he makes in my character is so much money in his pocket, and it is to his interest to try & make something out of me. He told me that himself.[12]

Just beneath the surface of this letter, one can hear the yearning of a boy for a father's uncritical love, for someone who will praise and support him, not just exploit his money-making potential or treat him as some kind of sadistic nineteenth-century character-building experiment. There were moments when the lost thirteen-year-old boy, still hungry for love, showed through.

There were other, darker worries that surfaced on this trip. Despite the abundance of game in the Animallai Hills, there were many places in India—in fact, most places—that had been virtually "hunted out." At one point, Hornaday had participated in a grand hunt in the imperial British style, with shooters riding in howdahs on the back of elephants and twenty-four servants either preparing meals or beating the bush for game, but all they'd taken, in days of hunting, was a single black deer and a couple of gazelles. The massive loss of large mammals that he would witness later in the Montana Territory of the United States was already appallingly apparent on much of the Indian subcontinent. Historians might later call this period of the late nineteenth (and early twentieth century) the "Progressive Era," but biologists would come to call it the "Age of Extinction."

In his book, which was published in 1885 and made Hornaday justly and suddenly famous, he described the remote jungles, swamps, and forests of East Asia and Borneo with deep feeling and precise zoological detail. (Of the crocodillian called the gavial, for example, he wrote that it had "very slender and elongated jaws, with an expanded end, quite like the handle of a frying-pan, smooth and compact, set with twenty-seven teeth on the upper jaw and twenty five in the lower.") But if his love of the natural world was all-consuming, what were his relations with the *human* world? How did he feel about and act toward all the dark-skinned people who carried the gear, set up the camps, cooked the food, and cared for the pack animals on this expedition? If a man's character can be seen most clearly in the way he treats people who cannot do him any favors, how did Hornaday treat the lowly porters, cooks, and coolies?

In his book, he spoke admiringly of the pluck and courage of his two assistants, Pera Vera and Nangen. Later in his trip, when a Chinese half-caste assistant named Eng Quee became lost in a swamp in Borneo, Hornaday led a rescue party into the snake-infested darkness and thigh-deep bogwater to rescue him. He wrote respectfully of the Malay people's "sobriety, their quiet, dignified manner under all circumstances and their entire disinclination to loud-mouthed brawling," though he also found them phenomenally lazy. "Procrastination is the evil genius of the Malay, and the exasperation of whoever looks to him for help in time of need."

The most pressing human concern on his trip through India was, of course, the famine. In response to what had clearly become a national crisis, Hornaday rode down out of the mountains from his airy, high-elevation camp one day to the Animallai River and the desolate plain below. There he encountered a heartbreaking sight. He came upon a small child, about four years old, entirely naked, aimlessly hobbling around through the sandy mud of a dried-up pond. His feet and legs were swollen with "famine dropsy," as if he had elephantiasis, so that his ankles were as big around as his thighs. He was so weak he could only walk a few inches at a time. The little boy's "sunken cheeks, hollow eyes, and protruding ribs told of starvation, and it was plain to see the helpless waif would soon die, unless cared for." While Hornaday was trying to decide how best to help the boy, a grown man, naked except for a dirty loincloth, stepped out from behind a bush. He, too, was in the last stages of starvation, "indeed a living skeleton, literally skin and bone. He was nearly six feet high, but I could have picked him up in my arms and carried him like a child."

Hornaday instructed his coolies to pick up the little boy and the man and carry them to the relief camp at Animallai. When they got there, Hornaday was informed that both of the little boy's parents had died, and there was no one else in the world to care for him. Hornaday placed him in the care of a doctor at the camp, who found him a bed in a hospital shed and promised that the boy would have "every attention." What actually happened to the child, however, Hornaday never did find out. Neither did he cancel or postpone his collecting expedition to be of further service to the suffering people of India.

But it was when he encountered the Dyak headhunters of Borneo that he became so enamored of their way of life that one wonders if, like Margaret Mead among the South Sea islanders, he was blinded by his own adoration. The Dyaks, he maintained, were kind, happy, thrifty, honest, and scrupulously faithful in paying their debts. They respected women and treated them as equals. They lived in huge communal longhouses, but they seemed to get along famously. Stealing, he said, was simply unheard of. "Where else but among the Dyaks will a traveller dare to trust a cart-load of boxes and packages, none of them securely fastened . . . in the centre of a village of fifty strange natives with no one to watch for thieves?" In fact, Hornaday wrote, "in human sympathy, and charity, the Dyaks are not outranked by any people living, so far as I know."[13]

There was, of course, the small matter of head-hunting. Since time immemorial, Hornaday reported, it was the custom of the various Dyak tribes to cut off the heads of conquered enemies and keep the cleaned skulls as trophies of war. A warrior's hearth was often festooned with heads, hanging from the rafters like so many coconuts. Often a Dyak girl would scorn a suitor who had not taken a head. A warrior's grief at the death of his wife or child "could only be assuaged with a fresh head, taken by himself, of course, and the death of a chief often involved a regular head-hunting expedition."[14] Even so, Hornaday laid most of the blame for this festival of bloodletting on the "instigation and encouragement of the reprobate Malays, who so nearly ruined the country." Overall, he concluded, the customs and character of these half-naked natives were far more praiseworthy than the hypocrisy, venality and deceit of the "civilized" citizens of the West.

In short, Hornaday's attitude and behavior toward native peoples showed a profound empathy and—within limits—an admirable loving-kindness.

There were two main ways to hunt tigers in India. The most common method was to hunt them from a howdah, a small compartment mounted on the back of an elephant. Another way was to hunt them from a machan, a platform of bamboo poles about fifteen or twenty feet off the ground that is erected near a tiger's recent kill. The most dangerous and foolhardy way, rarely practiced, and the way reponsible for nine-tenths of all deaths of men hunting tigers, was to hunt them on foot.

Hornaday wanted to hunt a tiger on foot. And one day, the young hunter got his chance. It was September 27, 1877. He was having one of his periodic fever spells and had felt low for a couple of days. On the days that he'd been able to hunt, he'd gotten no game at all, and now that the fat axis deer had been eaten, there was—once again— no meat left in camp. Now, because of the regularity of the fever, he knew he was going to have an attack at about two in the afternoon. It was still morning, so he calculated that he would have a few pain-free hours to hunt, and perhaps bring back some venison, before he was incapacitated with nausea. Most of the men were away from camp, so he took with him Pera Vera; Nangen, a "quiet but courageous fellow";[15] and a small boy.

Hornaday had the Maynard rifle tucked under one arm, with Pera Vera carrying the 16-gauge Maynard shotgun, loaded with bird shot for jungle fowl. They walked through the forest all morning, at one point encountering a small herd of axis deer feeding in a glade. But Hornaday was too exhausted to undertake a stalk, so they let them go. It was almost noon and they were circling back around toward camp when suddenly they heard "a fearful growling and roaring" in the bush a few hundred yards ahead. Instantly on the alert, Hornaday dropped to one knee and raised his weapon.

"Tiger, Vera?" Hornaday whispered.[16]

"No, sahib, panther. Shall we go for it?"

"Of course!"

They crept through the dry forest, communicating to each other only with hand signals and trying not to step on twigs or dry leaves, getting closer and closer to the sound. Every so often, they would hear a roaring growl, enough to raise the hair on one's neck; then it would stop. Then, distantly, perhaps half a mile away, they heard trumpeting and the noisy breaking of branches.

"*Elephants,*" Vera said, in a harsh whisper.

They crept on, increasingly uneasy about the fact that they could not see the panther, although they seemed to be getting very close to the place where it seemed to have been. They came to a small nullah, or streambed, and there in the sandy wash, clear as day, was the trail of a tiger. It wasn't a panther at all. Pera Vera and Nangen knelt to examine the enormous pugmarks in the wet sand.

"Fresh," Vera said. "Very fresh."

Hornaday also knelt down to take a close look at the tracks.

"Fresh," he repeated, although he later confessed in his journal that he wasn't certain if they were fresh or not.

Now Vera, the second tracker, began looking fearfully at Hornaday's small rifle, something that was fine for deer but extremely questionable for anything larger. As if to emphasize his point, Vera stuck his little finger into the muzzle of the gun; it fit snugly.

"Sahib, would you really dare to fire this small rifle at a big tiger?"

"Why, sure," Hornaday whispered. "Just show me one and you'll see!"

The party began tracking the tiger's trail along the sandy creek bottom, with Vera in the lead, Hornaday following with his Maynard in his shooting hand, and Nangen and the boy following, as silent as shadows. The creek bed was about eight feet below the level of a dry, open thorn forest, forty feet wide, and almost dry except for muddy puddles here and there. The tiger's tracks told the story of its movement up the stream, in places seeming to lollygag along, stopping here to play in a puddle, there to investigate this or that or to rake his claws through the sand. Silently, the hunting party followed this meandering trail for about a mile until they came upon a dense clump of bamboo, growing out of the bend in the creek.

Suddenly Vera stopped short, grabbed Hornaday's arm, and

pointed through the bamboo thicket. He had a habit of doing this when pointing out game, and Hornaday could tell how big the game was by how fiercely he grabbed his arm. Now his grip was like a C-clamp.

There was the tiger, only thirty yards away. It was the first tiger Hornaday had ever seen in the wild, and he was absolutely splendid. "His long, jet-black stripes seemed to stand out in relief, like bands of black velvet, while the black-and-white markings upon his head were most beautiful," Hornaday wrote later. He was also huge—"Great Caesar!" he thought. "He's as big as an ox!"[17]

The hunters were lucky: they were downwind from the big cat, and so far, the tiger had not seen or heard them. The tiger reached the other bank of the streambed, sniffed it idly, then turned back, shade and sunlight dappling its velvety stripes. Quietly and carefully, Hornaday stepped in front of Vera, lifted a spare cartridge and put it between his teeth, raised his rifle, and waited. Just as the tiger crossed to the middle of the stream, he seemed to sense or smell the hunters, gave an angry, irritated growl, and turned its huge face directly at them through the bamboo thicket. The animal was so enormous, it could have covered the distance between them in a couple of bounds. Hornaday calmly aimed his little rifle squarely at the tiger's left eye, squeezed off a shot, and without waiting to see what happened next, shoved the other cartridge into the chamber. When he got the big cat in his sights again, it was still in the middle of the streambed, but now he was woozily circling around and around in the same spot, confused, apparently badly wounded. When the enormous face came around again, so big it looked like a black-and-orange planet, Hornaday fired at his neck, probing for the spine, and the tiger instantly dropped in the sand. He immediately shoved in a fresh cartridge, and they all just stood there, waiting for a long time, with the rifle at full cock. Then, very carefully, the hunting party approached the fallen monarch up the streambed. Hornaday knew well enough that this was an extremely dangerous situation—in fact, many tiger-hunting fatalities, or "accidents," as they were called in India, occurred after the animal appeared to be dead. But this great beast, magnificent as he was, had now breathed his last.

For a hunter, the great moment of triumph was laying a hand on the fallen foe, and the more fearsome the enemy, the greater the triumph. With a kind of awe bordering on reverence—more reverence, in fact, than he'd ever felt in church—Hornaday knelt beside the sprawled tiger and stroked the glossy sides, still warm; pulled back the lips to see the terrible incisors, the last thing many a terrified animal, or perhaps even a child, ever saw; pulled open a heavy eyelid to look into the eye that had so recently gazed fearlessly at every foe; and handled the huge, heavy paws, now with retracted claws, which had made those meandering pugmarks in the sand and which, minutes earlier, could have disemboweled him in an instant.

The tiger was very likely the greatest prize of Hornaday's entire hunting career, which would span decades. Hornaday could not help but feel a sense of pride at his own skill and the courage of his men (including, amazingly enough, the small boy). After all, they were completely unarmed, and they had recently seen Hornaday miss an axis deer at a similar distance; yet when they faced down this god of the jungle at such close quarters, they didn't bolt.

When they laid the tiger out on the sand and took measurements, it turned out to be nine feet, eight inches from the nose to the tip of the tail; three feet, seven inches high at the shoulder; and four feet, two inches in girth at the belly. They reckoned that it weighed 495 pounds. There was no evidence that this magnificent animal was a man-eater—in fact, owing to what appeared to be its near-perfect health, it probably was not. But the cat, as it turned out, was the biggest Bengal tiger ever killed in India up to that time, and the record was not broken for another fifteen years. As word got out about the size and circumstances of the kill, big-game hunters and government officials throughout India marveled at Hornaday's feat. In recognition of his achievement, officials of the Madras district government rewarded him with a bounty of 100 rupees instead of the usual 35. The villagers in the area also were awed by the boldness and skill of Hornaday's kill. He must be, they said, a *sadhu* (saint). A few years later, this great animal, whom Hornaday called "Old Stripes," was mounted and put on display in the museum of natural history at Cornell University, where its cold predatory gaze chilled the blood of generations of prey animals for years to come.[18]

CHAPTER 12

Darwin's Firestorm

One of the larger purposes behind the flurry of orders coming in to Ward's Natural Science Establishment in the late 1870s, and the pressing need for Hornaday's expedition to the Malay and Borneo, was the keen competition among unversities and museums to prove or disprove, by means of comparative anatomy, the world-rattling theory of Charles Darwin. The theory was so simple that T. H. Huxley later exclaimed, "How stupid of me not to have thought of it!"[1] Plainly stated, Darwin's idea was that species do not remain fixed and stable over time—they change through a process called *natural selection*, which favors organisms better adapted to their surroundings. (Darwin himself did not use the term *evolution* until the sixth edition of his book, preferring instead the term *descent with modification*.)

Darwin had been working on his theory for more than twenty years, in his small, cluttered office at Down House, in Kent, but had never published anything about it. Then, in the early summer of 1858, he received a long letter and a draft of a scientific paper from a young British naturalist named Alfred Russel Wallace. Wallace, at the time, was on an eight-year-long collecting expedition to the Malay Peninsula and Borneo (exploring some of the very same areas that Hornaday would visit two decades later). In what he later described as a "flash of insight," Wallace had hit upon almost precisely the same ideas as Darwin had—in fact, Darwin later wrote, Wallace's paper was so similar, "I never saw a more striking coincidence."[2]

Darwin and Wallace eventually decided that they should give a joint presentation about their theory, so that they could both fairly claim credit. The theory was unveiled to the world on July 1, 1858, at a meeting of the British scientific group called the Linnean Society. The meeting was attended by about thirty people; the Darwin-Wallace paper—now considered by many to be the greatest scientific paper ever written—was greeted with no comment at all. One attendee, Reverend Samuel Haughton of Dublin, later wrote that "all that was new in [it] was old, and what was true was false."[3] Neither author was in attendance. Wallace was in Malaya, and Darwin was burying his youngest son, who had just died of scarlet fever.

But when Darwin's book *On the Origin of Species* was published the next year, in 1859, it lit a firestorm of controversy in the life sciences, as well as in the letters to the editor of almost every popular periodical. Even Darwin himself felt deeply conflicted about his book, saying that revealing the theory was "like confessing a murder." Cartoonists found Darwin all too easy to lampoon, with his vaguely simian features and overhanging Neanderthal brow. He was forever being depicted with a man's head attached to the body of an ape. In his book, Darwin had barely mentioned how his theory might change man's kinship with the great apes, but people had been quick to connect the dots, and the resulting controversies rained down out of pulpits and lecture halls in a hail of fire and brimstone.

Museums and unversities began to compete to build ever more complete collections of natural history specimens and thus bring some facts into the debate about whether species remained fixed and stable over time, and whether—God save us—humans might share a common ancestor with the apes. It was an alarming and preposterous idea, and it was not only churchmen and politicians who were skeptical. The great naturalist Louis Agassiz, of Harvard, had always been steadfastly opposed to Darwin's ideas and hoped that his museum's collections—including the specimens gathered by Hornaday for Professor Ward, especially those of the higher primates—would demonstrate the falsity of the "Darwinian theory."

The same year Darwin's book was published, Paul Du Chaillu emerged from the equatorial jungles of the Gabon with the bodies of creatures as otherworldly as corpses from an alien spacecraft. They were covered in black hair, had elongated arms, handlike feet, black, smashed-in faces, and overhanging brows. Even so, a fair-minded observer would have had to admit there was something more than vaguely human about them. Was it really true that these hairy "ape-men" were the missing link between apes and humans, as the Darwin-Wallace theory seemed to suggest? The theory was one thing, but how did it hold up in the face of these creatures? The public, thronging to museums and menageries, was terribly curious to see for themselves. Hence, Professor Ward's great interest in sending William Hornaday to the island of Borneo, which was said to be home to more apes and monkeys than any other place on the planet, especially the odd, long-haired, reddish ape known as the "orangutan."

On his way to the penultimate destination of Borneo, Hornaday collected and hunted on the spice island of Ceylon (now Sri Lanka), following blunt instructions from Professor Ward: "Plunder Ceylon. Rake the island over as with a fine-toothed comb; catch everything you can, and send me the best of it."[4] Hornaday also spent a couple of months on the Malay Peninsula, following in the footsteps of Wallace, whose famous book *The Malay Archipelago* (published a couple of years earlier, in 1869) he had read. Hornaday was in awe of Wallace's scientific acumen—Hornaday himself had admitted, at a fairly early age, that "I will never amount to much, scientifically." Wallace, by contrast, had discerned that in the Malay Archipelago, there was a distinct dividing line—later known as the Wallace Line—in which animals on one side of the line were more closely related to Australian species, and on the other side, to the species of Asia. It was a breath-taking insight that, like the idea of evolution, required an almost god-like perspective spanning vast panoramas of time and space.

Wallace was also an indefatigable specimen collector, at a time when simply discovering and enumerating the earth's species, like finding all the Christmas presents under the tree, was one of the principal tasks of science. In 1852, while returning from a four-year exploration of the Rio Negro, in Brazil, his ship caught fire and his entire specimen collection, all neatly tagged and cataloged, was de-stroyed. So he simply started over. In the Malay Archipelago, between 1854 and 1862, he collected more than 125,000 specimens, of which 80,000 were beetles (and 1,000 of these were species that were new to science).[5]

Hornaday also was a tireless collector—a perfect hired hand for Professor Ward's indefatigable ambitions. From time to time, when he found himself in a port city large enough to accommodate his wishes, Hornaday sent shipments back to Rochester in enormous wooden crates, sometimes twelve or fifteen at a time—great oaken treasure chests of wonders from remote worlds: The iridescendent skins of hummingbirds, fragile as parchment, the size of large postage stamps. A bonneted macque. A tapir, the horse-rhinoceros that looks more like a pig. Tiny, bug-eyed lorises. Skins and skeletons of improbable "mouse deer." Fantastic birds, from hornbills to argus pheasants.

If Hornaday lacked the scientific genius of an Alfred Russel Wallace, he was still an acutely observant naturalist, always recording what he saw in amazed and meticulous detail like a curious boy. At one point, he wrote, a villager brought him "a beautiful little tarsier (*Tarsius spectrum*), alive and unhurt. Although it is a monkey, it jumps like a kangaroo, which it is enabled to do by means of its very long hind legs. . . . The structure of its hands is very peculiar. Each long slender finger terminates in a flat round disc which acts like a sucker of an octopus, and enables the little animal to hold on to a limb by the side pressure of its hands and without grasping, as all the other monkeys do."[6]

Hornaday arrived in Borneo in August 1878. By then, he had been travelling for more than two years. He was twenty-four years old, bearded and deeply tanned, strong and lean as a rail, his belt cinched up two or three notches since the time he left Rochester. His body had been repeatedly wracked by malarial fevers and other tropical diseases, and he'd grown as accustomed as the natives to rough camp life, questionable food, half-rations (or even no rations), the gloomy miasmas of the monsoon season, and the vagaries of good hunting and bad. Like a gunslinger from the Old West, he always carried a weapon, whether a long rifle, a shotgun, or a pistol, and although he'd always been a great shot, now he was even better.

Among his many other useful and unusual accomplishments, he had at one point managed to skin and skeletonize an elephant in the deep jungle of India, seventy yards from a tiger's lair, while suffering from malarial fever. At the same time, he put down a mutiny among the coolies and skinners of his party. All of that took extraordinary fortitude, physical stamina, and the command presence of a general. He was no longer the boastful boy that he had been on that night a few years earlier at the dinner party in Battle Creek, when he first met Josephine and took such pleasure in embellishing the dangers of his upcoming expedition just to see her face flush and her dark eyes dart out at him, full of questioning and concern. Now he didn't have to embellish anything. He'd faced down a Bengal tiger at thirty paces and conquered him with a tiny rifle. He'd been rushed by elephants; had close encounters with crocodiles, gavials, and monstrous snakes; nearly drowned; fallen into quicksand; had repeatedly run out of money and food; and had for weeks at a time been forced to hunt just to survive. Something else had been happening to Will Hornaday, too, though he did not even know it: he was getting famous.

At least he was getting famous back in Rochester. Although Professor Ward had objected at first to how much time Hornaday seemed to be spending writing long, descriptive letters—even though, as part of their original agreement, Hornaday had been given permission to write a book about his adventures, so long as it didn't interfere with his collecting—Ward eventually realized that this epistolary travelogue would be of great interest to the public, but more importantly, would be good publicity for Ward's Natural Science Establishment. So every time one of Hornaday's dog-eared letters arrived from somewhere in the far-off bush, sometimes spattered with mud or blood, Ward would pass it along to the *Rochester Democrat Chronicle* for publication. Some of these letters found their way into the *New York Times*. Scratching out his letters with a steel-nibbed pen dipped in ink by the light of a tallow candle in some rough-hewn jungle camp, Hornaday thought he was writing only to Professor Ward. He did not realize that he was actually writing for a growing and enthusiastic fan base.

In 1878, the interior of Borneo was virtually impenetrable. "The heart of Africa," Hornaday wrote, "is not nearly so inaccessible as the heart of Borneo."[7] The third-largest island in the world, it was covered by an unbroken, mountainous, cloud-shrouded jungle. Ancient seamen called it "the land below the wind" because it was so remote from the trade winds, sheltered in a tropical backwater of sea islands where few Westerners ever ventured. Straddling the equator in the South China Sea, it was ringed by the narrow, crooked peninsula of Malay and the spice island of Sumatra; the archipelago of Java and the Lesser Sunda Islands; and the islands of Sulawesi and New

Guinea. Rumors about what might lie in its interior, including a race of men with tails, "beckon to the explorer with whispered promises of undiscovered wonders," Hornaday wrote.[8]

To a farm boy from Iowa barely out of his teens, it all seemed almost unimaginably exotic—and almost as far away from home as it was possible for him to get, in every way. For Hornaday, Borneo represented the pinnacle of his adventures as a collector.

On his way to Borneo, Hornaday stopped in Singapore to gather information and supplies, and he was lucky enough to make the acquaintance of a good-natured Englishman named A. R. Haughton Esq.—a high-ranking official of the British raja of the Territory of Sarawak, on the north coast of Borneo. Haughton told Hornaday that, although local hunters prized the orang for its meat, it had not yet been exterminated in the raja's territory, and the valleys of the Sadong and Btang Lupar rivers were teeming with wildlife—including, no doubt, orangs.

Overjoyed by his prospects, he sat down that first night in his tiny hotel room and wrote Professor Ward a letter of thanks:

> At last, after much tribulation, the promised land is reached, and naturally enough my first letter is to the man who got me here.... I have reached "the height of my ambition"... but for my good luck in falling with you and casting my lot with Ward's Natural Science Establishment I might at present moment be a long, long ways from Borneo after all.[9]

But orangs proved harder to find than he'd hoped. He and his two assistants, Pera Vera and Eng Quee, his Chinese servant, took a government schooner twenty miles up the Sadong River and were introduced to the Malay headman of the village, and then to a party of sea Dyaks, whom Hornaday asked in turn about where to find orangs. Most of them dressed in nothing but bark loincloths, with old bits of colored cloth wrapped around their heads like turbans. Yes, there were orangs in the forest, the men said, but they didn't really know where—they moved around through the trees. So, accompanied by a guide, Hornaday and his men spent a week tramping through the swampy jungle near the banks of the Sadong, often thigh-deep in water, without success.

Hornaday had almost given up hope of finding any orangs when two Dyaks arrived at the village and told him that they'd seen two orangs on their way down the Simujan River. Hastily, Hornaday put together a small collecting party in two dugout canoes, with Eng Quee, Pera Vera, and three Malays to serve guides and oarsmen.

Eight miles up this dark tidal river, Hornaday's party put ashore at a Dyak village, the first one he had ever seen.[10] It consisted not of a collection of houses, but of a single immense longhouse about 190 feet long, 30 feet wide, and elevated about 10 feet off the ground. The floor of the longhouse was made of narrow strips of *nibong* palm, tightly lashed together like a bamboo mat; it was springy and comfortable to the touch. Sixteen families lived in the communal house, which had a windowless wall at the back, where the families lived, and a huge, open-air platform at the front. When Hornaday and his party climbed up the notched log that served as a ladder to this stilt house, they were immediately surrounded by throngs of filthy, merry children who stared with huge eyes at the "orang-putei," or white man, and the "orang-China," or Chinese man. Women produced fresh palm mats, and they sat down on them by a smoldering fire that had been built in the middle of the porch, on a bed of dirt.

Pera Vera and Eng Quee were chatting with the Dyaks in Malay when Hornaday's eyes drifted up into the gloomy recesses of the ceiling. There, suspended from a rafter like so many grapefruit, were a bundle of about twenty blackened human heads. They were grimy with smoke and soot from the fire, and so much of the flesh had disintegrated that each one was bound with rattan to keep the lower jaw in place. After he came to feel more comfortable with the Dyaks, he learned, through his Malay interpreter, that human heads were symbols of power and prestige, and that the pursuit of them had led to a state of almost continuous warfare among neighboring tribes. Headhunting had officially been outlawed in Borneo, but it was impossible to stamp it out in these remote regions.[11]

Hornaday did not have any particular problem with the ancient custom of headhunting, and in fact, when he later came to live with these people for a month, he grew to admire them very much indeed. Wallace also had a favorable impression of the Dyaks: "The more I see of uncivilized people, the better I think of human nature on the whole," he wrote.[12] They were the happiest people Hornaday had ever known. Though they were almost wholly without religion, he found that they were highly moral. They were strictly honest, did not

covet, and did not steal, even from Chinese or Malays who had mis-
treated them. Adultery was unheard of. Marriage was celebrated and
respected, even though the marriage ceremony was so simple and so
casual it almost seemed like child's play—sometimes just the waving
of a fowl above the heads of the betrothed.

A couple of days later, just after dawn, Hornaday's small collecting
party moved silently up the Simujan River in two dugouts.[13] The river
had dwindled by now to a width of only twenty feet, although the
current was stiff and a dense submerged forest of water palms blan-
keted either side. Hornaday looked up from his dugout and spotted
a couple of disorderly nests of branches and leaves, in a small tree,
about twenty feet off the ground.

"*Mias—Orang-utan*," the Malay boatman whispered. "*Man of the
forest.*"[14] Orangs, which spent almost their entire lives in trees, traveled
through the forest like nomads, building crude sleeping-nests wherever they found themselves each night and then abandoning them the
next morning. As Hornaday's party slipped down the Simujan, they
began to see more and more of these abandoned nests, like arboreal
litter, always about twenty feet above the ground or the water. Now
they were in the true heart of Borneo, the place where the "old man of
the forest" lived. Suddenly, they saw it: a live orangutan in a tree, about
a hundred yards ahead.

"A last . . . a real live Orang utan. How my heart throbbed! But he
twigged us as quickly as we did him & hid himself in the thick leaves
of a huge creeper that encicled the trunk of the tree. We paddled up as
fast as possible but couldn't see a thing until we got right opposite the
tree, when we saw a huge, red hairy arm encircling the trunk."

The dugout hung up in the dense thickets of water palm, so Hornaday and a Malay boatman jumped out of the boat and plunged
through neck-deep water in pursuit of the orang as he flitted from tree
to tree. Eventually, Hornaday brought down his first specimen of the
hairy ape-man. He was four feet tall, and seven feet three inches from
fingertip to fingertip. (Human beings, by contrast, measure almost
exactly the same from head to toe and fingertip to fingertip.) "What
an ever-lasting double-geared hug, he could have given a fellow with
those tremendous long arms!" Hornaday wrote. Before the day was
out, they had taken two more; and after five days, after the Dyaks

brought in a couple more, they had nine orangs to dress and prepare meticulously for museum mounting. By the time he was through, Hornaday's party had collected forty-three specimens of orangutan, including one of the largest specimens ever taken by a naturalist, an immense male they named "Rajah," whose outstretched arms measured seven feet, ten and three-quarter inches across.

But whatever happened to the remorse that Hornaday once felt as a nine-year-old boy back in Iowa, when he took the life of a blue jay? Now he was taking the lives of creatures that appeared to be distant relations of man, whose females suckled their eerily humanoid young and carried them astride their hips "precisely as do the coolie-women of Hindostan."[15] Later in life, when he had become a crusading conservationist fighting for stricter game laws and bag limits of all kinds, his enemies threw back at him the forty-three dead orangutans. Yes, these "specimens" had all found their way into museums and collections around the world, all in the name of science, but why had he taken so many? In a letter to Professor Ward early in the hunt, he sounded like a boastful boy, blinded by the thrill of the game: ""I shall not leave here with less than 25 good Orangs, and I expect to have even more than that. Senior Piccari got 24, and have I not vowed to snow every naturalist completely under?"[16]

As a careful and observant naturalist, Hornaday did meticulously weigh, measure, and study each one of the series of specimens, and in the process, he contradicted an assertion that Alfred Russel Wallace had made in his own book. From Wallace's examination of seventeen freshly killed orangs, as well as reports from other naturalists, Wallace concluded that "up to this time we have not the least reliable evidence of the existence of orangs in Borneo more than 4 feet 2 inches high." But no fewer than seven of Hornaday's specimens exceeded this height; in this way, his collection contributed to the body of knowledge about this elusive species.[17]

After all these measurements and observations, Hornaday could not help but express a profound fellow-feeling for these mournful old men of the treetops. "Let such an [sic] one (if, indeed, one exists today) who is prejudiced against the Darwinian views, go to Borneo," he wrote. "Let him there watch from day to day this strangely human form in all its various phases of existence. Let him see the orang climb, walk, build its nest, eat, drink, and fight like a human rough. Let him see the female suckle her young and carry it astride her hip. . . . Let him witness their human-like emotions of affection, satisfaction, pain, and rage." Let him witness all this, he said, and feel "how much more potent has been this lesson" than all the theories and abstractions in books. Humans and the great apes were indeed kin.[18]

Even so, there was no escaping the fact that there was a heartrend-ing contradiction at the core of what Hornaday was doing here in Borneo—he was killing what he professed to love. Like Audubon, he had had to make a dark bargain with death to bring these creatures to the attention of the public, who would never see them in the wild. Still, over the months he spent in Borneo, he observed their behavior in the wild with such acuteness that he later published an article in the *Proceedings of the American Association for the Advancement of Science*, "On the Species of Bornean Orangs, with Notes on Their Habits," which animal behaviorists such as Robert Yerkes cited for decades afterwards.[19] But the contradiction was there nonetheless, like a bone lodged in the throat.

At the beginning of his long journey back home, Hornaday stopped for a couple of weeks in Singapore and, by one of those lucky strokes of which his life was so full, he was introduced to the Scots-American industrialist Andrew Carnegie, who was on a year-long, round-the-world grand tour of his own.

It was the morning of January 10, 1879, when he and Hornaday met. Carnegie, seated in the elegant drawing room of the U.S. con-sul's house, was wearing a sumptuous high-waisted morning coat and had a tidily trimmed beard; although he was only forty-four years old, his hair was markedly receding. But what was most striking about Carnegie was his diminutive size: he was barely five feet tall and weighed no more than 100 pounds. His friend Mark Twain once said of him: "Mr. Carnegie is no smaller than Napoleon, but for some reason or other, he looks smaller than he really is. He looks incredibly small, almost unthinkably small."[20] It was said that Carnegie favored high-heeled boots and top hats to add a few inches to his stature.

By contrast, Will Hornaday—who had always been self-conscious about his size—looked like a veritable giant. Wearing his Norfolk hunting jacket, with a little orang youngster he called "Old Man" on his lap, he and the steel magnate, with his melodious brogue, chat-ted like old friends. These two diminutive, preposterously bold, complex, and contradictory men took an immediate liking to each other. They had more than a little in common. Carnegie had once written of himself that "whatever I engage in, I push inordinately";[21] words that could as easily have been written about Hornaday. The young naturalist was returning from his epic journey, with one of the largest collections of natural history specimens ever amassed by one man. Carnegie, for his part, was in the process of putting together his own epic haul, becoming not just one of the richest men in America, but one of the richest men who ever lived.

Although Carnegie was known as a brutal businessman and strike-breaker, a man who gave his steelworkers only one day off per year, his manner on that January morning in Singapore was congenial and unpretentious. He was, Hornaday later wrote, "an ideal American. . . . I should call him a model millionare." For his part, Carnegie later wrote of his encounter with the brash young American naturalist that "the recital of Mister Hornaday's adventures are extremely interesting, and I predict that some day a book from him will have a great run."[22]

In fact, that book, *Two Years in the Jungle*, would become one of the best-selling adventure travel books of the nineteenth century. It was reviewed, almost entirely favorably, by more than fifty newspapers, literary magazines, and scientific journals, including the august *Science* and *Nature*. Because of Hornaday's boyish zest, his breezy, vernacular style, his wide-ranging knowledge of natural history and zoology, his "Mark Twain–ish humor," and the outlandish escapades he described, one reviewer described *Two Years* as "one of the best books of travel and adventure ever published."[23] On the day he died, almost fifty years later, the tenth edition was still in print.

Hornaday's friendship with Carnegie would prove long-lasting, genuine, and also strategically important. As the years went by and Hornaday plunged ever deeper into his bitter "war for wildlife," seeming to manufacture new enemies at every turn, he repeatedly turned to Carnegie for help. And every time he did so, Carnegie responded. He was determined to give away as much of his fortune as possible before he died, and helping to fund Mr. Hornaday's war was something he felt was urgent.

Hornaday returned by ship to San Francisco, and then he took a train to his old school in Iowa, where he was treated like a conquering hero. He gave a series of lectures about his adventures and discoveries.

But he could hardly wait to get to Battle Creek to see his bride-to-be, Josephine. She was overjoyed to see him, having lived by letter for almost three years. Strong-willed, dignified, and intelligent, Josephine was a perfect match for this small, fierce, impetuous man. On September 11, 1879, Josephine Chamberlain and William Temple Hornaday were married in the Seventh-day Adventist Church in Battle Creek, Michigan.[24] It was a sweet and harmonious union that would last his lifetime, and it would become increasingly precious to him as his war for wildlife became more tempestuous, more public, and more punishing.

Although he did not mention Josephine by name in the text of his book, Hornaday did fondly allude to her in the concluding chapter:

> Early in February [1879] I turned my face homeward, by way of China and Japan, and reached Rochester safe and well, just two years and nine months from the time of my departure. From first to last, I had been remarkably prospered, quite as if the prayers and good wishes of my friends had enlisted the services of a special guardian angel to accompany me at every step, in addition to the one I left behind me, whose charming missives of news, hopeful encouragement, and unfaltering affection followed me everywhere—one by every mail, without a single break—without which I would have been lonesome indeed.[25]

It's fascinating to note that this endless stream of letters, which kept Hornaday afloat in dark and dangerous waters, was almost the only written record that Josephine left of her life. Although William Temple Hornaday would leave a voluminous record of his own life, published and unpublished—in addition to his nearly two dozen books, there is an immense archive of his papers at the Library of Congress, the Smithsonian, and elsewhere—the only published letter that Josephine appears to have written was one which appeared in 1903 in the *New York Times*. In it, she complained that there was no shelter at certain streetcar transfer points in the city, forcing women and children to stand in the rain sometimes. No matter how sophisticated and intelligent she may have been, she seems to have largely vanished from the written record like disappearing ink, as most other women of her day did.

On his way home to Rochester, Hornaday stopped for seventeen days in Michigan to rediscover his fiancée after such a long absence. These few days with Josephine, he wrote to Chester Jackson, were "the pleasantest of all my life so far."[26] As if there were any further doubt of his feelings, on the day he received the first copies of his book while working at the National Museum, he was so excited that he tore off his canvas taxidermist's apron and rushed home to show one to Josephine. He wanted to surprise her with the dedication, which she knew nothing about. It read:

TO
MY GOOD WIFE
JOSEPHINE
WHOSE PRESENCE BOTH WHEN SEEN AND UNSEEN
HAS EVER BEEN THE SUNSHINE OF MY LIFE
THIS BOOK
IS AFFECTIONATELY DEDICATED[27]

CHAPTER 13

"A Thief in the Night"

In March 1887, Hornaday had returned from his heartbreaking bison trip to the Montana Territory so recently that his hunting boots, tucked in a back hall of his house in Washington, were still slathered with Montana mud. The mud would wash off. But the sorrow and sense of desolation evoked by what he had seen in the West was seared into his soul.

He had seen how astoundingly fast it could happen: a noble beast like the American bison decimated from herds of 10 or 15 million, down to less than 1,000, in twenty years. *Twenty years!* The worst instincts of humanity, put to work in the most efficient way possible, could achieve dark wonders in a virtual instant. Without armies of wildlife protectors, without a network of laws and the manpower to enforce them, and without some safe reserve, some last stand against annihilation like a zoological park—without that, he feared, all was lost.

It was out of this abject despair that the idea first came to him—suddenly, boldly, and fully formed, like "a thief in the night,"[1] he would later write. There should be—there *must* be—a national zoological park in the nation's capital, a place where breeding pairs of bison and other vanishing species could make a final stand against extinction and where ordinary people could come face to face with the whole marvelous phantasmagoria of nonhuman life. No one really knew if captive breeding of endangered species had any reasonable chance of success, but the war for wildlife was going so badly, in so many places, Hornaday felt that he absolutely must try. And *now*.

It seems a curiosity that, in his voluminous writings, Hornaday never dwelled on this in any great detail, but the zoo epiphany was evidence of a profound inner transformation. In seizing upon this last hope for the preservation of the wild, one could argue that Hornaday had reached the third and final stage of the sorrowful story of humanity's contact with wilderness. In the first stage, indigenous peoples and early explorers existed in a state of perpetual immersion in the wild, from which they drew material and spiritual sustenance without causing it lasting harm. In the second stage, civilization began to control, exploit, and "conquer" the wilderness, through exploration and settlement, military and scientific conquest, and ultimately in a fantastic bloodbath of excess, the decimation of species, and the collapse of indigenous cultures. In the final stage, civilizations awoke to a sense of overwhelming cultural remorse, the birth of conservation, and the impulse to save wildlife by whatever means before it was too late.[2]

Hornaday was a man whose sprawling life, with its gnawing contradictions and transformations, straddled all three of these epochs of human contact with wilderness. As a young man, he was an explorer and adventurer into the nearly Edenic wildness of Borneo, Malaya, and the Orinoco, witnessing firsthand the last days of the first stage. As a taxidermist and specimen collector for Ward's, he eagerly participated in the second stage, including its bloody excesses. And as his life ripened and darkened and he began to see what was happening to planet Earth more clearly, he was now ready to become one of the country's most ardent defenders of everything that was being lost. The young specimen collector was a far different man than the one who dreamed of a great zoo in the nation's capital and who was now furiously writing, night after night, his raging polemic *The Extermination of the American Bison*—a book that laid out, in all its heart-wrenching particulars, the national crime then occurring in the hinterlands of the West.

Yet it was also Hornaday's nature to be obstinate almost to the point of absurdity. When attacked, he circled the wagons, denying the inner doubts that had clearly led to what amounted to a dramatic conversion experience. Later in life, at a time when the fire-breathing conservationist was coming under increasing attack for having killed those forty-three orangutans, he wrote a friend, "I am not a repentant sinner in regard to my previous career as a killer and preserver of wild animals, but I am positively the most defiant devil that ever came to town. I am ready and anxious to match records for my whole 76 years with any sportsman who wishes to back his record against mine for square dealing with wild animals."[3]

To Hornaday, his whole life was of one piece comprising the four strategic tasks he had set before himself to pull the buffalo back from extinction, if it still could be done. The first had been the writing of his angry book; the second, the creation of a political organization to be called the American Bison Society, which would harness the public's outrage; the third, the creation of his monumental mounted bison group. Now came the fourth, the founding of a national zoo in Washington to serve as the home of a small captive bison herd, and perhaps even the first experiments in captive breeding.

He did not waste a moment getting to work.

As soon as he had the idea for the zoo, Hornaday sat down and wrote a letter to the secretary of the Smithsonian Institution, who was also his boss, Professor Baird, a man he liked and respected immensely. Although Baird had recently been very ill and was often absent from the office, he dropped the letter by Baird's office anyway. Only a few hours later, Baird's assistant, Dr. G. Brown Goode, assistant secretary of the Smithsonian, showed up at Hornaday's office door. He was enthusiastic about Hornaday's big idea but cautioned him that Baird was a very sick man, and the idea would have to be put aside for the present. "Later on, I'll take it up with you," he said, somewhat mysteriously.[4]

Hornaday dearly hoped that Professor Baird would recover soon because he seemed the perfect man to champion the idea through the complex hierarchy of the Smithsonian and Congress, which would have to approve both the idea and the funding. Baird was a nineteenth-century scientific generalist at a time when a single man could straddle most of the different disciplines of science comfortably. At Dickinson College, he had taught natural history, chemistry, mathematics, and physiology; his published writings covered geology, minerology, botany, iconography, zoology, and anthropology as well. At the age of seventeen, he'd written to John James Audubon and described two kinds of flycatchers that proved to be new to science. Later he had been instrumental in creating the U.S. Commission of Fish and Fisheries, and as fish commissioner, he had studied the decline in coastal fisheries in the southern New England states. Baird had begun to see in the seas what Hornaday had seen on the land: a vast, steady, and alarming decline in wild populations.[5]

Unfortunately, only a couple of months after Hornaday sent his letter, Baird died. Professor Goode took over until a permanent successor could be appointed. Hornaday described Goode as "a progressive and daring museum-builder, a most lovable man, ready to try any good idea once." Goode made good on his promise to "take it up later on," and in the fall of 1887, he and Hornaday "threw in together on the development of the idea [of the national zoo], and we worked like beavers, with no ambition beyond the successful accomplishment of a Big Thing."[6]

Brown proposed that they start "a little tryout zoo" on the Smithsonian grounds to test the public's interest. In one stroke, Brown created a "Department of Living Animals" at the National Museum, with Hornaday as curator. Now, in addition to stuffing and mounting skins as realistically as possible, Hornaday would be providing food, water, and habitats for real, living animals on the mall in Washington.

Professor Goode was also appointed acting U.S. fish commissioner, temporarily taking over another of Baird's duties, and one of the first things he did was direct the new curator of living animals, William Temple Hornaday, to ride a Fish Commission railroad car across the American West to collect specimens of American mammals, birds, and reptiles for the "little tryout zoo."

A Fish Commission employee would be in charge of distributing 800 pails of young fish, mainly carp, to ranchmen across the West as the train made its way toward the Pacific. As the fish tanks emptied, Hornaday could use them to begin bedding down the future residents of the National Zoo.[7]

(It may seem curious that the Fish Commission was distributing carp, of all things, a fish often considered a nuisance. But in a department bulletin from 1874, Baird made what he considered an important distinction between the related "junk" species such as suckers and chubbs, and the common or German carp, or *Cyprinus carpio*, which has been cultivated as a food fish for centuries. Its flesh was "firm, flaky, and in some varieties almost equal to the European trout," according to Baird. These fish were not meant to be introduced to water already stocked with good native species, but only for ponds and streams where no better fish could be raised. Even so, it was an early foray into ill-advised introductions of invasive species into places nature had not intended them to be.)[8]

Travelling west through the Dakotas and the Montana and Washington territories, Hornaday bought or was given a cinnamon bear, a white-tailed deer, a Columbia black-tailed deer, five prairie dogs, a Cross fox, a mule deer, two badgers, a red fox, and two spotted lynx. The fifteen animals, all species indigenous to the United States or its territories, were reasonably well behaved once they were bedded in the converted fish tanks. The lone exception was a big badger with a fat, flattened body and huge paddle-like paws, which slept in a tank directly beneath Hornaday's berth. Every night about bedtime, the badger began attempting to dig his way out of the railroad car, scratching away at the glass of the tank with such determination that Hornaday had to get up and slap the tank with a wooden lath to frighten it into submission.[9]

One day when the train stopped in Cheyenne, Wyoming, hundreds of people swarmed around the railroad car, which was stopped on a siding, "just as hungry to see some wild-western beast as if none ever had existed outside that car." It brought home to Hornaday with the force of a hammer blow the grave peril facing the natural world. But that was not the only experience that did so. In Salt Lake City, stacked and ready to be loaded onto a railcar, he saw the skins of 140 little spotted mule deer fawns, and he was told matter-of-factly that they were to be made into men's vests.[10] In Denver, when he saw seventy mountain goat skins stacked in the same way, he decided to buy them (for fifty cents apiece) for use as part of the "extermination exhibit" that he was planning at the National Museum. It would become part of his great propaganda war in the battle for wildlife.

At the beginning, the grandly designated "Department of Living Animals of the National Museum" was a ramshackle affair, really just a collection of small wire pens and paddocks in the western shadow of the Smithsonian castle, which sat on the edge of the broad pedestrian walkway known as the "national mall." At first, the fifteen animals Hornaday had collected on his rail trip out west, including four prairie dogs, were the sum total of the animal population of the National Zoo.

But that changed rapidly. From the very start, the public was fascinated by the zoo, and people began showing up to see the animals in great numbers, just as the people of Wyoming had showed up to peer at the badgers, foxes, and deer in the railcar on a siding in Cheyenne. People began bringing animals as gifts, like the magi bearing frankincense and myrrh. One of the first benefactors of the Department of Living Animals, in fact, was the president of the United States, Grover Cleveland. Cleveland had been given a golden eagle as a Christmas present, and rather than return it to the sender, as was customary, he gave it to Hornaday for the new zoo. A benefactor in Texas contributed two black bears and a jaguar. Then Hornaday bought a grizzly bear cub from the Crow Indian Reservation in Montana. And so on and so on, until between the early winter of 1887 and the early spring of 1888, the zoo had grown from 15 to 172 animals. In fact, it had grown so rapidly that it was bursting at the seams, in need of space, accomodations, funding, and staff.[11]

Of all the new residents at the Department of Living Animals, the rarest and most wonderful were four American bison, contributed by a rancher in Nebraska. In December 1887, Hornaday wrote Professor Goode a letter to propose formally that the institution begin attempting to preserve the buffalo by breeding them in captivity, something he'd been thinking about ever since the death of Sandy:

> In view of the fact that thus far, this government has done nothing to preserve alive any specimens of the American Bison, the most striking and conspicuous species on this continent, I have the honor to propose that the Smithsonian Institution or the National Museum, one or both, take immediate steps to procure . . . the nucleus of a herd of live buffaloes . . . which may, in a small measure, atone for the national disgrace that attaches to the heartless and senseless extermination of the species in a wild state.[12]

The four bison, consisting of a breeding pair and two of their calves, one male and one female, were a gift from Dr. Valentine T. McGillicuddy, a legendary frontier surgeon who was also the Indian agent of the Sioux Reservation in the Dakota Territory.[13] The animals had been captured in the Black Hills, which was sacred land to the Sioux. In fact, during a vision quest, the Oglala Sioux medicine man Black Elk, who had fought Custer at the Battle of Little Bighorn, had ascended the great stone monolith called Harney Peak, at the center of the Black Hills, and declared that it was "the center of the universe." He'd been only a nine-year-old boy at the time, but what he learned there that day shaped the rest of his life. From Harney Peak, Black Elk saw "more than I can tell and understood more than I saw," he later told John C. Neihardt for a famous book called *Black Elk Speaks*. "For I was seeing in a sacred manner the shapes of all things in the spirit, and the shape of all things as they must live together like one being."[14] In some supernatural sense, it was almost as if McGillicuddy's gift of a breeding pair of buffalo had been sent by Black Elk and the Sioux, from the center of the universe, to populate the new zoo in the country's capital.

In September 1888, Dr. Samuel Pierpont Langley was appointed to succeed the deceased Baird as secretary of the Smithsonian. Hornaday greeted this news warily, describing Langley in his autobiography as "an austere physicist from Pittsburgh."[15] Langley took an office up in the tower of the Smithsonian castle so that he could peer down on the goings-on below, including the somewhat unsightly shanties and cages of Hornaday's little proto-zoo. A celebrated inventor, Langley was one of the leading innovators in the quest to solve "the problem of flight," as it was then called. As the new head of the institution, his primary interest was in establishing an astrophysical laboratory at the Smithsonian. He had no great interest in this motley collection of cages and all their braying, barking, shrieking inhabitants down there.

Goode suggested to Langley that, given the great interest in the "tryout zoo," the Smithsonian begin scouting out a bigger, better location for the *real* zoo, the National Zoo of the United States. Goode suggested Rock Creek Park, an area of picturesque hill and dale, mostly forested, beside a small rocky river very close to downtown Washington. Hornaday loved the idea—it would provide visitors with a feel for the wild places where the wild things roamed. Langley seemed to assent to this, if only by lack of objection.

But as the weeks and months went by, Hornaday grew increasingly disenchanted with the Smithsonian's new secretary. Langley was, Hornaday wrote, a preeningly proud, deeply private man, a "seasoned bachelor of lonely habits, a domineering temper, and the congeniality of an iceberg...his 'no' was like the snap of a steel trap."[16]

Hornaday, himself a proud, quirky, and sometimes difficult man, had met his match in Samuel Langley. But this time he was outranked.

It's quite possible that Hornaday found Langley hostile to his zoo plans because the secretary was simply not very interested in them. His mind was elsewhere. Langley was a brilliant, self-taught astronomer who as a boy had designed and built advanced telescopes with which he'd mapped the Sun and the Galilean moons of Jupiter. But what fired his passion more than anything else was the great race to build a heavier-than-air flying machine, a feat more than one respected student of aerodynamics said was not possible. Over a period of sixteen years, Langley built repeated iterations of a craft he called an "aerodrome," which grew ever more elaborate, more expensive, and more ungainly.[17] Most of the money was provided by the government; Langley got the funding at least partly because of all his prestigious academic degrees and appointments, which now included being the administrator of the Smithsonian. Langley launched his awkward-looking airships off a houseboat floating in the Potomac River. For the first few launches, Langley was unwise enough to allow the press to be present, who duly noted that the "flights" lasted only a few moments and ended in spectacular crashes into the river. The reporters' pens began to drip poison. The papers started calling these seemingly ridiculous experiments "Langley's Folly," and questioning the expenditure of taxpayer money on something that would very likely prove a bust. Langley, wounded, withdrew into himself.

Meanwhile, Hornaday and Goode kept trying to push the idea of a genuine National Zoo in Congress, which would have to approve and fund the project. Recognizing that Congress served at the behest of the public, Hornaday began his campaign by going directly to the press, giving a series of newspaper interviews in which he pointed out that the United States was the only great country without a national zoo, and that having one might be the only way to save the buffalo from annihilation.[18]

Newspaper editorial pages around the country picked up on Hornaday's tone of alarm, so that the whole idea of a national zoo seemed to take on a life of its own. In the spring of 1888, the *New York Public Opinion* summed up the popular mood regarding the zoo:

> With all our great game animals being swept out of existence by modern breech-loaders, a magnificent site within two miles of the

Executive Mansion, a huge surplus in the Treasury, gifts of live animals pouring into the Smithsonian, the public clamoring for a National Zoo, and a competent naturalist ready and anxious to build it up, what reason is there why the bill should not be passed and work begun at once?[19]

When the time came to begin pushing in earnest for the first round of funding for the zoo, Goode and Hornaday were able to enlist the support of two key senators, James Beck of Kentucky and William Allison of Iowa. A bill for an enabling act was drafted and introduced in the Senate on May 2, 1888. It called for the then-extravagant sum of $200,000 to buy 166 acres of Rock Creek Park as a site for the zoo. Langley now agreed to let Hornaday spend part of his official hours trying to sell the idea to Congress, a task for which Hornaday, more than any other man in Washington, was eminently qualified. Hornaday made a detailed relief map of the proposed park, complete with tiny trees and enclosures for the animals, to use as a visual aid for his public relations campaign.

Hornaday tucked his relief map under his arm when he went to testify before the House Committee on Appropriations, which was considering the zoological park bill.[20] A little awed by the grand drawing room behind the Speaker's stand where the hearing took place, Hornaday nevertheless made an "eloquent appeal" for the zoo, according to a story in the *Washington Post*. Most of the discussion that followed Hornaday's presentation was positive, though several representatives argued that the proposed zoo would be too expensive and benefit only the people of Washington. One House member, Mississippi Democrat Thomas Stockdale, told a reporter that the zoo "would be of no use to the poor who come to Washington to visit the last of the buffaloes." The whole idea, he said, "does not sound like republicanism. It echoes like royalty." When it came to a vote, the zoo bill was voted down, by a vote of 36 in favor, 56 against, with one abstention.

Still, Hornaday was not too terribly worried about this initial defeat because he'd been given a brief tutorial in Washington politics by House member "Fighting Joe" Wheeler, an old Confederate cavalry hero. Wheeler explained that the Democrats had opposed the zoo bill as a part of a complex political ploy, and they'd more than likely pass the amendment the next year. The failure of the zoo amendment, in other words, had absolutely nothing to do with bison, elk, or moose, and everything to do with power politics in Washington. Fighting Joe was teaching Will Hornaday about the way battles were fought in the capital: rarely was anything what it seemed.

Before the opening of the next session, in December of 1888, "Buffalo Bill" Cody made an extravagant offer: he wanted to give the Department of Living Animals eighteen more buffalo, the third-largest captive herd in existence. But Hornaday had to turn Cody down because there was simply not enough room in the zoo's cramped, temporary quarters. It was a kind of melancholy public relations coup, which Hornaday used to maximum advantage in the press.

For the next session of Congress, a bill for the establishment of a zoological park was introduced in both the House and the Senate at about the same time. Hornaday and his compatriots had enlisted the help of a canny Philadelphia lawyer named Thomas Donaldson.[21] Hornaday also was riding a tide of good publicity: most newspapers supported the idea of a National Zoo, even in places like San Francisco and Denver, where the paper's readers would probably never even get to see it. More than a bit surprisingly, among the powerful people who stepped up to support the bill was Langley. In a letter read before the House of Representatives, the Smithsonian head said that a zoological park was needed to serve as "a city of refuge for vanishing races" of animals.

Ultimately, when the measure came to a vote in the House, it sailed through on a vote of 131 to 98. It looked as though Hornaday's vision was going to be realized in record time, and with almost no opposition. But of course, Washington had a few more tricks up its sleeve for Hornaday.

On July 4, 1889, a Zoological Park Commission was created with Hornaday as superintendent and Professor Langley as chairman. Hornaday got the happy task of going down to Rock Creek Park on a series of sunny afternoons to stake out the boundaries of the hoped-for zoo, marker flags snapping merrily in the summer breeze. Here was where the bison enclosure would go, here the deer park, here the monkey house.

He had a new office at the Smithsonian with a temporary sign that said, "Zoological Park Commission" hung on his door. Langley gave him free rein to begin creating the zoo, even though Goode did not want him to give up his work as chief taxidermist, especially because he was working on several different habitat groups at the time. Although Hornaday was still a relatively young man—only thirty-four years old—he had attained a position of great power and importance in the world of Washington, and of wildlife conservation. In fact, one newspaper reporter, commenting on his qualifications for his new job as zookeeper-in-chief, wrote that Hornaday was "young, energetic, and thoroughly informed of the work expected of him ... there is probably no other man in America, and few in any other part of the world, whose knowledge of animal life and habits is more extensive than his."

But the fights and disputes over the zoo's border began almost immediately; and the survey, platting, and negotiations over twelve separate parcels of land that needed to be bought were so contentious that it made Hornaday's head hurt. The theater of war in the battle to save the animals had shifted from the Montana Territory, where the enemies were the hide-hunters, railroads, settlers, and thrill-killers, to the halls of Congress, where the enemies were mind-bogglingly complicated power politics and hidden agendas of all kinds.

Even after Hornaday finally secured title to the last piece of property needed for the zoo, he still needed to secure funding for the project for its first year. Now a bit more seasoned and cynical player in Washington power politics, Hornaday went back to Congress to ask for $92,000 to cover the cost of the current year's operations. It was a startling sum—Dr. Goode was aghast, and Professor Langley, generally about as emotional as a barnacle, was severely shocked. Goode gave Hornaday some sage counsel about the ways of Washington.[22]

"In Washington, the development of a new institution always moves slowly at first," he told Hornaday. "By no possibility can you get more than $25,000 now. If you ask for so large a sum as $92,000, you may get nothing. I strongly advise that the amount be made $25,000."[23]

Goode, no doubt, did not quite understand that Will Hornaday was the man who had approached his first job as a fifteen-year-old by asking, "What can you do for me?" Boldly was the only way he knew how to operate. Besides, he had worked out the numbers, and the zoo needed $92,000 to pay all its bills for one year, so he decided to ask for $92,000. To Hornaday's surprise, the funding request sailed through the Senate. But in the House, it came up against the scowling countenance of Joseph "Uncle Joe" Cannon, one of the craftiest and most dominating congressmen ever to serve as Speaker of the House, and a man who had fought the zoo almost every step of the way. Hornaday took his map and argued his case once again for a national zoo to preserve the bison, to assuage the nation's guilt at their near-extermination, and to educate the public. When he was done, he took questions from the congressmen. Not all of them were friendly, but after an hour of sparring, he felt that he had defended his case adequately.

He looked over at Uncle Joe Cannon sitting in his gaudy chair at the head of the chamber. Cannon uncrossed his legs and seemed to look sourly at the carpet.

"Wel-l," Cannon said, in disgust, "I suppose we'll have to pass this damned bill!" And they did.

It was April 1, 1890, and as Hornaday later described it, the first bill marked the actual creation of the Washington Zoological Park, and this second bill served as its "swaddling clothes." Once President Benjamin Harrison signed the act, the money became available. The temporary Zoological Park Commission was dissolved, and a new National Zoological Park was created, with Smithsonian secretary Samuel Langley at the top of the flowchart of power.

And that, Hornaday later wrote, is when "some mighty unpleasant things" began to happen.[24]

CHAPTER 14

A Dream Deferred

Samuel Langley was "a hard man and devilish difficult to get on with," Hornaday wrote, and in fact, according to Hornaday's telling of the story, ever since Langley's ascension to the job of secretary of the Smithsonian, he had instituted a "quiet reign of terror."[1] Still, Hornaday had found that in the face of conflict or disagreement, Langley was at least frank and fair. Hornaday was willing to put up with him because he was devoted to the glittering vision of a national zoo. But the back-channel whispers at the Smithonian were that "getting along with Secretary Langley is like trying to sleep with a porcupine," and that Hornaday was the only person on staff who was not afraid of him.[2]

Within days of the passage of the Act of Congress that finally created the National Zoo, and which placed the whole enterprise under the thumb of Secretary Langley, Hornaday received a letter from Langley that he found both odd and menacing. The letter included the following "Resolution":

RESOLVED, That all correspondence of this institution with any person or society shall be conducted by the Secretary, and no assistant or employee shall write or receive any official letter or communication pertaining to the affairs of the institution, except under the authority and by the direction of the Secretary; and all such correspondence shall be duly registered and recorded in such manner as the Secretary shall direct.

The whole idea for a national zoo had been Hornaday's to begin with. He and Dr. G. Brown Goode had worked tirelessly and without ego to flesh out the endless details and sell it to Congress; then they'd fought like hellcats to procure the first two rounds of funding. As superintendent of the Zoological Park Commission, Hornaday had envisioned himself as a kind of Noah, overseeing all the breeding pairs of animals from a great ark shipwrecked in Rock Creek Park. Now with this preposterous "Resolution," he was knocked down to the role of a mere "employee," or even a child, someone vaguely untrustworthy who needed to be supervised and controlled lest he do something brash, foolish, or even illegal. To Langley, the resolution might have seemed a legitimate clarification of Hornaday's subordinate role; but to the proud Hornaday, it felt like an insufferable comeuppance.

This new resolution, with its implied suspicion and complete reordering of Hornaday's universe, worried him in the extreme. He decided to pay a visit to the secretary. That was Hornaday's nature. He did not know how to simply accept his fate, like a condemned man on the gallows; all he knew how to do was fight like mad to fashion his *own* fate. According to Hornaday's later account, Langley received him in his vast upstairs office in the Smithsonian tower "with set mouth and hostile eye . . . the secretarial atmosphere was charged with electricity."[3]

The whole preliminary plan for the national zoo, which had been worked out in painstaking detail over the course of several years with apparent cordiality, now was completely scrapped. Hornaday had laid out plans for huge, natural enclosures, taking advantage of Rock Creek Park's stony outcrops and ancient trees so that zoogoers could catch glimpses of the animals in something like their natural habitat. It was a revolutionary model for a zoo, and later it would be imitated around the world. But to this notion, Langley said coldly, "I have no intention of doing that," with his mouth so tightly set he seemed to be nipping off the ends of words.

Referring to one choice piece of the proposed grounds, Langley told Hornaday: *No portion of that property will be given up to animals—all of it will be kept as the private grounds of the park administration.*

Open to visitors?

No. It will not be open to visitors.

Multiple entrances?

There will be no entrance down the Adams Mill Road.

A scenic bridge across Rock Creek?

There will be no bridge across the river, except on the Quarry Road.[4]

All these supposedly controversial details had been specified in Hornaday's original plan—and approved by Langley.

Slap after slap, rebuff after rebuff, Langley seemed determined not so much to create a great zoo as to make sure that *he* was in charge of it—down to the tiniest detail. But all the foregoing paled in comparison to Langley's final revelation. He told Hornaday that he had appointed a committee of three men from the National Museum, who would take charge of the development of the zoological park and "control" Hornaday's activities, because Langley "had no time" to control them himself. Hornaday knew very well that two of these men—Major John Wesley Powell and Frederick True, curator of mammals at the Smithsonian and Hornaday's former boss—were "hostiles," who could simply overrule the other committee member, Dr. Goode, who was a friend. The committee was effectively stacked against him. And furthermore, Langley went on—as if this were not enough—Hornaday's job as superintendent would be only "provisional." Once a suitable director of the National Zoo was found, the committee would be dissolved, and Hornaday would serve as the new director's assistant.

Assistant!

Hornaday was being demoted from chief visionary and director of the national zoo to cage-cleaner and janitor. William Temple Hornaday was a man who had been born on a farm in the middle of nowhere, without wealth or any particular advantages in life, and he had battled his way to a position of power and prominence in the nation's capital by means of grit, determination, and the glittering zeal of a visionary. He was a fighter down to his fingernails, but this kind of fighting—Washington fighting—was utterly confounding to him. Was the enemy Langley, or was there a person or persons behind him who had set this up? If so, why? And what was the best way to fight back? It was as if he were being stabbed in the back, but when he turned to see who was wielding the knife, they had disappeared.

A couple of days later, after he'd regathered his composure, Hornaday went back upstairs to see Langley in his office.

I'd like to respectfully propose, Secretary Langley, that you postpone convening this committee for six months, Hornaday said. *Just give me a "trial run" conducting the affairs of the park as superintendent. The moment I make my first mistake, I'll resign. But I have been doing this job quite successfully up to this point, and I'm confident I can demonstrate to you that I'll be able to continue.*

No, Mr. Hornaday, I simply do not feel that you have adequate executive experience for the job, Langley said stiffly. *I have talked this over with Major Powell, and he agrees with me.*

Executive experience? But I'm only asking to be allowed to continue doing what I have been doing. I think this committee is just an unnecessary and cumbersome layer of bureaucracy. Why can't it simply be postponed until I can prove myself to your satisfaction?

No, sir, Langley said, growing icier as he got angrier. *Major Powell's opinion is final.* It was as if he was transferring the blame to John Wesley Powell, one of the two "hostiles" on the committee, even though Langley himself was the secretary of the Smithsonian and could overrule anything Powell wanted. Powell, who had lost an arm at Shiloh fighting for the Union, had later become the first man to explore the Colorado River through the Grand Canyon. But that didn't mean he knew anything about running a zoo.

But sir, Hornaday protested, *I can't conceive how the existence of this committee would further the ultimate goal of creating a superb zoological park in Washington. It would only make my job more complicated and difficult!*

No, Mister Hornaday! Langley shouted, now thoroughly enraged, stamping his right foot on the carpet underneath his desk. *I will not!*

For Hornaday, that petulant foot-stamp and Langley's belittling rebuff were enough to decide his future course of action. When Hornaday got home from work that day, he told Josephine, his life partner and confidante, everything that had happened. He asked her if she felt he should even continue at his job at the National Museum.

"Never!" she snapped. "What's the use of going on if you can find no satisfaction in the work and have no real success? What would you have at the finish? Failure!"

Hornaday told her that he really felt the only course open to him was to resign. Maybe they could move up to Buffalo and get into the real estate business with his old friend George Hedley.

"By all means I would resign—and at once," Josephine said, eyes flashing like an enraged tigress. "We can sell this house and move to

Buffalo within a month. I'm sorry your dream of a great National Zoo has been so spoiled. But now it will never come true—*never!*"

So the next day, firmly, calmly and cheerfully, Hornaday sent Langley a letter of resignation by interoffice mail. Langley's acceptance came back by return mail, a special delivery of ice. A couple of days later, when Hornaday happened across Langley in the hall, he greeted the secretary and smiled. But Langley silently glared back at him.

It was a sudden, hugely disappointing turn of events. When Hornaday's resignation became public, it created a stir in official Washington. The newspapers tended to side with Hornaday in the fight, with one reporter for the *Washington Critic* describing his resignation as "a great loss to the government."

William Temple Hornaday was only thirty-six years old, with the best part of his life still ahead of him. He had a life companion, Josephine, who was wise and calm, sophisticated and intelligent, and who was willing to follow him anywhere. That in itself was very nearly enough. "It is good to be loved and missed and longed for by the Finest woman on earth," he had written in one of his hundreds, perhaps thousands, of letters to her. "Never was a man more fortunate or more blessed in one woman than I am in you, and I grudge every moment that you are away from me. . . . I have grown as fond of you, and so dependent on your companionship, that when away from you I feel like a wild goose lost in the fog."[5]

Hornaday had resigned, he said to friends and in his private writings, due to the "great Langley disillusionment" and "the death of my plans for a really great Zoological Park."[6] He couldn't help it: bitterness seeped into every word he said about it, like an ink stain. Luckily, he had an open doorway to a new and different life, so he and Josephine stepped through it. They moved to Buffalo, New York, a place where his hunting friend George Hedley was prospering in the real estate business. Hedley had tried repeatedly to lure Hornaday up to Buffalo with the promise of material gain far in excess of anything a zookeeper or taxidermist could command. But Hornaday was adamant: fighting the war for wildlife was his life's passion and the source of its meaning. A bucket of gold did not make much difference to him.

But now, everything had changed. Now he had no income at all, other than modest book royalties, and no other immediate propects.

He gladly accepted Hedley's offer to become secretary of the Union Land Exchange in Buffalo, and he and Josephine moved to the city in the summer of 1890. The company's business consisted of buying large tracts of land around Buffalo, subdividing it, and selling these smaller subdivisions to other developers. Hornaday was not unqualified for his new job: he had spent more time than he cared to recall wrangling with landowners and lawyers over buying, surveying, and platting land for the zoo.

Becoming a real estate developer was an odd transformation for a conservationist, a wrenching U-turn in many ways. But Buffalo was booming, there seemed to be an insatiable demand for new housing, and for the first couple of years, the Union Land Exchange boomed along with Buffalo. Niagara Falls was now being harnessed to provide electric power, and the town lit up with that nineteenth-century wonder, the electric lightbulb. In 1892, Hornaday had a handsome house built for himself and Josephine on Humboldt Parkway at a cost of $8,000 (about $250,000 in today's dollars).[7]

Then came 1893. A financial panic swept through the post–Civil War economy, and the gross national product fell about 4 percent in a single year, and 6 percent the next year. By 1894, unemployment soared to more than 18 percent.[8] The panic deepened into one of the worst depressions in U.S. history. After years of doing a "roaring trade," between March 1893 and July 1894, the Union Land Exchange did not make a single sale. By contrast, Hornaday's previous life as a wildlife warrior and zookeeper, with all its turbulence and uncertainty, seemed tame.[9]

To support himself and Josephine, Hornaday turned to writing articles about natural history for popular magazines. He began to dabble in local politics, but eventually he grew so disgusted with the incompetence and venality of other politicians that he began to wonder whether he might just return to Borneo to live among the Dyak head-hunters, who were so good-hearted, decent, and moral.

But eventually, his efforts to retreat from the war for wildlife were overwhelmed by his growing alarm that the war was being lost, and fast. He began shouting from the rooftops again, ill-tempered and unsociable, pouring out his concerns in articles and letters to the editor. By 1896, he had almost entirely lost interest in his not-very-successful career as a businessman and was champing at the bit to resume the great fight for the the wild animals. The task was too urgent, the price for inaction too great.

Then, one day in 1896, out of the blue, a letter landed in his mailbox. It was from the board of directors of the newly formed New York Zoological Society, a committee of men whose names he knew, and whom he also knew were "men of the kind who never do small things." The letter explained that the board intended to build a New York zoological park, something befitting one of the greatest cities in the world, and the members were inquiring as to whether he might be interested in the job of director. His first reaction was: "No! Positively not! I am forever done with 'scientists' and zoological parks!" But in fairly short order, he realized that this was the chance of a lifetime and accepted the job with gratitude. The starshine of good fortune had fallen on William Temple Hornaday once again.

Looking back on the series of events that led him to become the first director of what would later become the world-renowned Bronx Zoo, Hornaday reflected later in life that his resignation from the National Zoo was "one of the wisest acts of my life. . . . I have been so pleased with its results that I now look back upon Professor Langley as a cantankerous instrument chosen by the hand of Fortune to pilot me to the theatre of my real life work, while his fell into the Potomac."[10]

Hornaday can be forgiven his bitter fit of pique—but if he were to pay a visit to the National Zoo today, more than a century after his falling-out with Samuel Langley, he would probably be pleased by what he found. In contrast to Langley's cramped, controlling vision of a kind of Alcatraz for animals, the 163-acre National Zoological Park now attempts to display its more than two thousand animals and birds in large, naturalistic enclosures that at least somewhat resemble their natural habitat—a style imitated in zoos around the world. Behind the scenes, the zoo also conducts extensive scientific research in captive breeding and conservation biology. Long after both men's deaths, Hornaday's vision is the one that ultimately won out.

CHAPTER 15

Scandal at the Zoo

When William and Josephine Hornaday moved from Buffalo to Stamford, Connecticut, in 1896, the country was in the throes of a Gilded Age zoo-building craze. City after city announced plans to create zoological parks, most of them modeled after Hornaday's original design for the National Zoo—Boston, Buffalo, Cincinnati, Pittsburgh, San Francisco, and St. Louis all laid-out gaudy dreams, often adorned with Italianate piazzas, fountains, and lavish, formal lawns and gardens, as a diadem on each city's crown of ambition and an echo of some imagined Eden.[1] A couple of months before he was offered the job in New York, Hornaday had turned down a similar offer to build a zoo in Pittsburgh.[2] The great World's Columbian Exposition of 1893, in Chicago, had shown every other American city the outer limits of the possible and given them a high-water mark to match.[3]

And yet New York, the biggest, brawniest, messiest city on the continent, had only the Central Park menagerie—a motley collection of outdoor cages inhabited by a few sorrowful dromedaries, bears, and monkeys, all perennially infected with fleas.[4] The Central Park zoo was popular with the teeming masses—the pipefitters, carpenters, dishwashers, clerks, and waitresses who swarmed the Lower East Side in uncountable numbers, most living in squalid tenements without indoor plumbing and speaking a babel of different languages. In 1894, according to one historian, New York City had over 1.8 million residents, of whom 1.4 million had been born abroad or had at least one foreign-born parent.[5] The editor of the *Saturday Evening Post* called New York "a great foreign city with an American quarter."[6] Rudyard Kipling put it more harshly, calling the city "a despotism of the alien, by the alien, for the alien, tempered with occasional insurrections of decent folk."[7]

At the same time, less than a mile uptown, a whole different class of people were conducting lives so foreign to the Central Park zoo-goers that they might have been orbiting a different sun. A great stillness hung over their world, punctuated by polite sounds like the distant clink of serving dishes in the butler's pantry or the whirr of carriage wheels up a long gravel drive. It was a world of Park Avenue mansions, country estates on the Hudson, gentlemen's clubs, and sumptuous private railroad cars. And in 1895, the idea of creating a world-class zoo in New York—something entirely different from the flea-bitten sideshow in Central Park—began to take shape in the rarefied air of this upper-class world.

Theodore Roosevelt—a man who seemed to be everywhere, doing everything, and who was very much a part of this influential world—had a hand in it. Along with two young aristocratic brothers, Madison and DeForest Grant, Roosevelt formed a committee of the Boone and Crockett Club in 1895 to look into creating a New York Zoological Society and a splendid New York zoo.[8] The committee chose as its chairman Professor Henry Fairfield Osborn, the celebrated paleontologist at the American Museum of Natural History, who was a childhood friend of Roosevelt. Among many other accomplishments, he had first described and named *Tyrannosaurus rex*.[9]

Henry Fairfield Osborn, Madison Grant, and William Temple Hornaday, the zoo's new director, would emerge as a kind of triumvirate of energy, vision, and determination, who together began willing the New York zoo into being. And what they envisioned was breathtaking: The biggest zoo in the world, spread over something like 300 acres, which would make it four times larger (at least geographically) than the Berlin Zoo, the world's largest. It would not be a zoo like the private reserves of European noblemen, beautiful but inaccessible to the average man, or the zoos of Europe, which were small urban affairs. It would be a sprawling showpiece for New York and the New World, filled with huge naturalistic enclosures that would suggest the immensity and majesty of America.

Hornaday insisted the New York zoo, unlike most European

zoos, should be free most days of the week, so that the "Man-Without-A-Quarter" would not be shut out.[10] European zoos, he felt, were too much the playground of the leisure classes. He wanted to bring wildlife to the millions, not just those that *had* millions. Even so, Hornaday was quite clear about who buttered his bread, and he worked tirelessly to curry favor—and funds—from the well-to-do classes, to such an extent that one society magazine later wrote that "Not to be in the New York Zoological Society is not to be in society."[11]

Unlike Hornaday, both Grant and Osborne were patricians to the bone, having been born into the closest thing to an aristocracy the United States ever had. Madison Grant grew up spending summers and many weekends at his grandfather's Long Island estate, Oatlands, with its turreted mansion and massive stone fireplaces, and surrounded by elegant flower gardens, stables, and a tropical conservatory.[12] Grant's love of nature began here, by collecting fish and reptiles. "I began by collecting turtles as a boy and never recovered from the prediliction," he once wrote to Osborn. Grant's mother was descended from the first Dutch colonists who settled New York, and his father's relations included a signer of the Declaration of Independence. Grant went on to graduate from Yale and Columbia Law School, but—a sure sign of his pedigree—never needed to hold a job at all.

Henry Fairfield Osborn also was born into a wealthy New York family, and he grew up roaming the grounds of Castle Rock, his family's palatial estate on the Hudson. His father had made his fortune in railroads, but Osborn was always more interested in natural history, and after graduating from Princeton, he became head of the Department of Vertebrate Paleontology at the American Museum of Natural History, eventually becoming the museum's president.[13] He was, like Grant, a member of all the most exclusive men's clubs—the Metropolitan, the Century, the University, and of course the Boone and Crockett Club, Teddy Roosevelt's cabal of big-game hunters whose membership was limited to a hundred. Both these men shared a passion for conservation, and—like Roosevelt and other exemplars of their class—loved hunting in exotic places like East Africa and Alaska. Grant, who never married, sometimes spent four months of the year on lavish hunts.[14]

When Grant, Osborn, and the other committee members began searching for someone to serve as the actual hands-on director of the future zoo, the name of William Temple Hornaday came up at once. Hornaday was one of the few men in the country who had ever been involved in the building of a world-class zoo, however briefly. He was also a nationally known naturalist, author, specimen collector, and advocate of wildlife conservation. He was a hunter, though now a reformed one. (One unsympathetic historian has referred to him as "a classic example of the repentant hunter" who, "with all the zeal of the convert, set about atoning for his early sins.")[15]

But if Grant and Osborn were born to fine china, good genes, and overbred horses, Hornaday was born to a clapboard farmhouse in Indiana, no particular genes or connections at all, and the love of a good honest street fight. He'd achieved what he had in life by sheer will, natural ability, and good luck. Next to his pair of patrician Medicis, Hornaday later confessed to always feeling inferior, fearing that Osborn and Grant viewed him as merely "a Philistine from the jungles of Buffalo."[16] Grant was by nature and breeding a behind-the-scenes man who preferred to work by having a Macanudo and a drink at the Century Club with some influential friend. Not only would there be no news account of such encounters, there would be no written record at all beyond a charge to Grant's private account at the club. Hornaday, by contrast, preferred to fight his fights in the open, often very loudly, on a level that the common man could understand and in a way that attracted a great deal of attention. He did not mind getting a bloody nose. In fact, his nose would be bloody for most of the next thirty years.

William Temple Hornaday's first assignment after he was hired as director of the still-imaginary New York zoo was a delicious one: to scout out a location of about 300 acres, not too far outside Manhattan, to be the site of New York's most spectacular new attraction. After surveying all the undeveloped land on the city's margins, he went for a ramble one sunny afternoon in February 1896, all alone, in what was then known as South Bronx Park, along Pelham Avenue.

"At that time," Hornaday recalled later, the park "was an unbroken wilderness, to the eye almost as wild and unkempt as the heart of the Adirondacks." When he first saw it, he experienced a sense of "almost paralyzing astonishment and profound gratitude. It seemed incredible that such *virgin forest* . . . had been spared in the City of

New York in 1896!"[17] In a two-hour hike on that winter afternoon, Hornaday imagined it all: Here were the great outdoor flying cages for immense raptors; here the stately houses for primates, small deer, antelope, large birds, lions, elephants, reptiles. Here, the bear dens for the giant brown and Kodiak bears from Alaska, and grizzlies from the American West. Here, the immense open-air enclosures for hoofed and horned herd animals, including bison, six or eight times as spacious as anything in Europe. When he reported his find to Grant and Osborn, they were both delighted, and eventually— after much political wrangling and backstabbing—the city handed over 264 acres to the newly formed New York Zoological Society.

Hornaday's second assignment was even more enjoyable than the first: in April 1896, he and Josephine were dispatched on a tour of fifteen European zoos, including the renowned Berlin Zoo, where Carl Hagenbeck had pioneered the use of moats and barless enclosures to enhance the zoogoing experience. Hornaday's task was to learn what these venerable zoos had done right and what they had done wrong.[18]

Over the next three years, Hornaday was the on-site supervisor of the construction of America's premier zoo. He reported to work each morning promptly at 8 a.m., worked until sundown, then went home to write his books and direct the movement of his troops in the broader war for wildlife, shepherding legislation through Congress and lending a prominent national voice to little-known local battles. His energy, his punctuality, and his attention to detail were legendary. He argued with the zoo's architects over tiny details, insisted that not a single tree be cut without his permission, directed the purchase, shipping, and care of animals, mediated employee disputes, and acted as chief spokesperson to the press.

For several of these frenetic years, Hornaday was working out of a modest office at 69 Wall Street and living in a rented house on East 30th Street, in midtown Manhattan, while Josephine stayed in Buffalo trying to sell the house on Humboldt Parkway. They bridged the 300 miles that separated them with a constant flurry of letters, often sent every day. Despite the prominence of Hornaday's new position, his letters to Josephine make clear that the young couple was almost continuously worried about money. "I have now just $175 left and *got* to have a new suit of clothes before the 12th," Hornaday complained. " I cannot appear before the Academy of Sciences on that night without it. My trousers are simply *done*, and they show it." There were newsy updates on doings at the infant zoo, like the death of a baby eland, and the beautiful great anteater bought off a steamer from Venezuela for $40 and "temporarily quartered in my office til next Monday, when the new Keeper's shed will be ready."[19]

Yet his letters always seemed to end on the same note: in adoration and longing for Josephine. "What a perfect *sun* you have been to my existence, ever since I found you!" he wrote in May 1902. "Dear heart, without you the world would be dark indeed, not only to me but to many others. So bright and good a woman as you should be endowed with the strength of an Amazon and the longevity of Methuselah. The women who bless the world the most should live the longest."

His letters also show a side of Hornaday that could be short-tempered and even a little cruel. "My last letter is for a definite purpose—to end everything between C. J. and me & to keep him from coming to my office and lounging around as he was in the habit of doing," he snapped in one letter. "Henceforth we are total strangers. I was a fool to ever begin to treat him decently after all he has done to disgrace himself. He is a skunk and I mean to keep him at a *skunk's distance*." Hornaday was also not above occasional cattiness about prominent people he'd been getting to know. The famous naturalist and writer John Burroughs, he wrote to Josephine, was "a real, true *cad*! He speaks meanly of his wife because she is not his mental equal—he, with the Giant Intellect that barely keeps him and his poor wife alive in a *shanty!*"[20]

As the zoo's opening day approached, railroad cars filled with exotic animals came pouring into the Bronx: an immense Alaskan brown bear from north of the Arctic Circle, an African Black Rhino, elephants, kudu, waterbuck, Grevy's zebras, a lumbering elephant tortoise, tapirs, capybaras, kangaroos, harpy eagles, red-crested turaco, impeyan pheasants, ostriches, and cassowaries. A sixteen-foot python escaped and was recaptured its first night in the zoo. And for a short time, a small group of queasy orangutans had to be quartered in the Hornadays' living room, where Josephine (who had by now moved to New York) patiently fed them a teaspoon of Fletcher's castoria each day to settle their stomachs.[21]

On the afternoon of Wednesday, November 8, 1899, a cold, overcast day with a knifing wind, the New York Zoological Park officially opened. A huge crowd of about 2,000 people turned out, with attendees ranging from the Park Avenue peerage, including J. P. Morgan, a generous patron of the zoo, to a few of the short-order cooks and scullery maids who'd gotten off work to come to the opening and who would soon desert the Central Park menagerie in favor of this magnificent animal park, even though it was farther out of town.[22]

Director Hornaday wore a cap mounted with a gold eagle, and his assistant curators were all arrayed in gray and green uniforms, like soldiers on parade. Hornaday, Professor Osborn, Madison Grant, and other dignitaries were seated at a bunting-draped podium when Osborn stood to make a few brief remarks. "Unlike the small closed zoological gardens of Europe, this is a free Park, projected upon a scale larger than has ever been attempted before," he began. After extolling the splendors of the new park, he promised even grander exhibitions in the future. In an innocent-sounding line that would eerily foreshadow one of the new zoo's darkest days to come, he added that "later we shall find a place upon the buffalo range for the Indian and his teepee."[23] Then Hornaday officially opened the zoo's gates to "the millions." The zoo would not be fully finished for another seven years, but when it opened that November afternoon, it already boasted a stately collection of (still incomplete) Beaux-Arts pavilions grouped around a circular sea-lion pool, with 22 exhibits featuring 843 animals of 157 different species.

From the very beginning, the zoo was a smash hit. In 1900, its first full year of operation, it drew a half million visitors. Within three years, there were a million visitors a year; and by 1914, more than 2 million.[24] By 1909, there were 5,000 birds, mammals, and reptiles in the collection, making New York's zoo the largest in the world not only geographically, but also in terms of the number of specimens. Under the exacting direction of Hornaday, Grant, and Osborn, the zoo had become, one distinguished foreign critic wrote, "at once the envy and the despair of all European makers of zoological gardens."[25]

Even so, what happened at the newly opened New York Zoological Park for eighteen days in the autumn of 1906 would stain Hornaday's reputation permanently—and, more darkly, the reputation of Madison Grant as well. It was as if, beneath the sumptuous neoclassical gardens and lawns of the zoo, there was a poisoned river murmuring in the darkness, and for those few days in September, it emerged, alarmingly, into the light.

The episode began in seeming innocence—or at least, what passed for innocence in that long-ago time. In 1904, a flamboyant explorer, missionary, and perennially impoverished entrepeneur named Samuel Phillips Verner was hired to bring back about a dozen African pygmies for an "ethnographic exhibit" at the St. Louis World's Fair. Hoping to legitimize the fledgling science of anthropology, Dr. William McGee aspired to display "representatives of all the world's races, ranging from the smallest pygmies to the most gigantic peoples, from the darkest blacks to the dominant whites." The exhibit was to be called the University of Man.[26]

It is helpful to remember that turn-of-the-century America was a place where such a "University" was not entirely unthinkable. The great Apache warrior Geronimo, billed as the "Human Tyger" even though he was approaching eighty and a prisoner of war under constant armed guard, was also on display at the St. Louis Fair.[27] And in 1897—to name just one other example—Arctic explorer Robert Peary returned from Greenland with six Eskimos, who were put on display (for twenty-five cents a look) at the American Museum of Natural History. Within eight months, four had died of tuberculosis, and renowned anthropologist Franz Boas had their skeletons stripped of flesh, bleached, and added to the museum's collections. Yet this episode provoked hardly a murmur of outrage in the press.[28]

Verner disappeared into the interior of Africa and, after two months of searching, succeeded in buying a twenty-one-year-old Congolese pygmy named Ota Benga from slave traders, in what was then called the Congo Free State. The total purchase price was a pound of salt and a bolt of cloth. Verner probably saved Ota's life: not only was the murderous Force Publique of King Leopold of Belgium rampaging through the Congo, and Ota's wife and children had already been murdered, but Ota was also being held captive by the slave-trading Bashilele tribe, who were inclined to eat their prisoners. He was in danger of being murdered or eaten when the blue-eyed *muzungu*, or white man, offered to buy him from the Bashilele. This may well explain why, when Verner asked Ota if he wished to accompany him across the ocean, he agreed. Even though Ota no doubt failed to fully understand what he was getting into, he seems to have come along willingly.[29]

Verner brought Benga, seven other pygmies, and a young Congolese man to St. Louis, having promised to return the eight pygmies to their African homes when the fair ended. The nine Africans proved to be one of the most popular attractions at the fair, where the crowds gawked, jeered, and at one point threw mud pies. Visitors were especially eager to see Benga's teeth, which had been filed to sharp points in his early youth. Verner and others encouraged the impression that this crude cosmetic dentistry had been carried out because Benga was a cannibal—in fact, the "only genuine African cannibal in America," according to one newspaper account. Benga learned to charge a nickel for showing visitors his terrible teeth. At one point, visitors to the fair got so excited by the sight of this "man-eating savage" that the First Illinois Regiment had to be called to control the mob.[30]

From St. Louis, Ota Benga and the eight other Africans traveled with Verner to New Orleans just in time for Mardi Gras, before finally returning to Africa. Benga briefly lived among his old tribe, the Batwa, but increasingly he seemed to feel alienated and uncomfortable even among his own people. Benga married a Batwa woman, but she died of snakebite. Eventually, when Verner returned to America, Ota Benga asked to go with him (according to Verner's account, he actually threatened to drown himself if he was not permitted to go).[31]

Samuel Verner, with his stiff collars, his preening pomposity, and his puffed-up resume, arrived in New York in August 1906, with the small African "cannibal" Ota Benga. The two of them seemed to have developed a genuine friendship. Benga called Verner by the African name Fwela. But by then Verner was growing increasingly desperate about his own personal financial situation, and he arranged for Benga to stay in a spare room at the American Museum of Natural History in New York City so that he could begin negotiating with the museum's curator, Henry Bumpus, over the acquisition of Verner's spoils from Africa, which included everything from a gigantic beetle to a chimpanzee. (Verner also asked for a job, but Bumpus, skeptical of his credentials, turned him down. Eventually Verner—the great explorer—found a job as a night-shift ticket-taker on the subway, scribbling articles about Africa when work was slow.)[32]

Benga seemed to enjoy his stay at the museum, sometimes wandering around the grounds wearing a bark loincloth to entertain visitors. But eventually he began to grow homesick for his African homeland—even though, by now, he did not quite belong there, either. Samuel Verner began looking for a more permanent place for Benga to live, and he finally brought him to the New York Zoological

Park, where William Temple Hornaday was now the imperious and well-known director. Hornaday agreed to buy the chimpanzee from Verner for $275, and also agreed to let Ota stay at the zoo temporarily. The agreement between the two men was that Ota "belonged" to Verner, who could return and take him back at any time.[33]

Hornaday, like Verner, seems to have genuinely liked the little African, who stood just under five feet tall though he was fully grown. He welcomed him to the zoo and, at first, he simply let him walk the grounds (usually wearing Western clothes), encouraging the keepers to allow Ota access to many of the animals. Ota grew especially fond of an orangutan named Dohong, "the presiding genius of the Monkey House," who had been taught to ride a tricycle, wear pants and a shirt, and eat with a knife and fork. (Dohong's antics made it clear that the distinction between a "zoo" and a "circus" was not entirely clear in those days.) The zookeepers opened Dohong's cage doors whenever Ota wished, and they encouraged Ota to set up his hammock in an adjoining, empty Monkey House cage that was shared by the orang and several chimps. The keepers set up a target made of straw in the cage, gave Ota his bow and arrows, and encouraged him to try a bit of target practice.[34]

In other words, Ota's transit from outside to inside the cage was such a stealthy, seemingly casual progression that later Hornaday and everyone else involved could maintain that it wasn't even deliberately planned. (In his private letters to Josephine, there is a passing suggestion that this exhibit might even have been years in the making. In a letter dated May 27, 1902, on New York Zoological Society letterhead, Hornaday wrote: "To speak first of important things.... I will tell you that the hunt for a dusky maiden of Congolese ancestry has just been begun.")[35]

Yet Ota Benga's confinement had been foreshadowed, not just in Professor Osborn's comments about "an Indian in a teepee" at the zoo's opening ceremonies, but in something Hornaday had written ten years earlier. He had imagined what he conceived of as the "ultimate" zoo exhibit—the pseudoscientific display of "American aborigines" in their natural habitat. It would be both educational and unforgettable, "*at once* getting hold of the Public," by "illustrating the house life of aborigines of North America." Such an exhibit could "be made a very picturesque, striking, and popular feature, at very moderate cost; and it would be 'something new under the sun.'" Left unsaid was the presumption that an exhibit like that would require real, living aborigines to be kept in some kind of confinement. Despite Hornaday's disdain for the cheap theatrics of P. T. Barnum, Barnum would have loved it.

Pleased by this new, if temporary, acquisition, Hornaday wrote a short article for the *Zoological Society Bulletin* called "An African Pigmy," with a photo on the front page of Ota holding a chimp named Polly. "On September 9, a genuine African pigmy, belonging to the sub-race commonly miscalled 'dwarfs,' was employed in the Zoo-logical Park," he began in a dispassionate, scientific-sounding way. A handwritten version of the piece describes the pygmies as "the small-est racial division of the human genus, and probably the lowest in cultural development," but Hornaday struck these lines from the pub-lished piece.[36]

In fact, Ota Benga had become an "employee" of the zoo several days earlier, and the press had quickly gotten wind of this. On Satur-day, September 8, 1906, the first headline appeared, in the *New York Times*: "Bushman Shares a Cage with Bronx Park Apes."[37] The story explained that the tiny "Bushman," wearing nothing but a bark loin-cloth and accompanied by an orangutan named Dohong, was locked in the cage except when his keeper let him out, and that throngs of curiosity-seekers had begun to crowd around his enclosure. "Ist dass ein Mensch?" asked one German visitor. "Is it a man?"[38] The exhibit "had for many visitors more than a provocation to laughter," the *Times* reported. "There were laughs enough in it too, but there was some-thing about it which made the serious-minded grave."[39]

The next day, Sunday, September 9, Director Hornaday had a sign installed outside the enclosure at the Monkey House:

The African Pygmy, "Ota Benga."
Age, 28 years.
Height, 4 feet 11 inches.
Brought from the Kasai River, Congo Free State,
South Central Africa, by Dr. Samuel P. Verner
Weight 103 pounds
Exhibited each afternoon during September.[40]

The sign was meant to be subdued, scientific, and nonjudgmen-tal, like every other sign in the park, but by now Hornaday found he had a mob scene on his hands. Having read in the papers about the "pygmy in the zoo"—or, better yet, the "cannibal in the zoo"—thousands had made their way out to the Bronx to see him for themselves. "The Bushman didn't seem to mind it, and the sight plainly pleased the crowd," the *Times* reported that day. "Few expressed audible objection to the sight of a human being in a cage. There was always a crowd before the cage, most of the time roaring with laughter, and from almost every corner of the garden could be heard the question:

'Where is the Pygmy?'

And the answer was, 'In the monkey house.'"[41]

But already there were rumbles of outrage. The Reverend R. S. MacArthur, a white preacher, thundered: "The person responsible for this exhibition degrades himself as much as he does the African.... We send out missionaries to Africa to Christianize the people, and then we bring one here to brutalize him." That Sunday, a committee of Clergymen from the Colored Baptist Ministers Conference called the exhibit "an outrage" and announced that they would appeal to the mayor of New York, which chartered the zoo, to put a stop to the "degrading exhibition." The delegation's leader, the Reverend James Gordon, said that "our race, we think, is depressed enough, without exhibiting one of us with the apes. We think we are worthy of being considered human beings, with souls."[42] But the ministers were angriest about the fact that the exhibit seemed to insinuate that Ota Benga was the "missing link" between apes and humans, thus adding credence to the godless theories of Charles Darwin.

"This is a Christian country ... and the exhibition evidently aims to be a demonstration of the Darwinian theory of evolution," Gordon fumed. "The Darwinian theory is absolutely opposed to Christianity, and a public demonstration in its favor should not be permitted."

By Monday, September 10, Hornaday waded in, defensive and angry. He seemed hurt that he was being misunderstood. In response to MacArthur's remarks about "brutalizing" Ota Benga, Hornaday said:

> This is the most ridiculous thing I have ever heard of. As for the boy being exhibited in a cage, it was done simply for the convenience of the thousands of people who wanted to see him. We have no platform that we could place him on, and this big open air cage was the best place we could find to put him where every-

body could see him. Why, we are taking excellent care of the little fellow and he is great favorite with everybody connected with the zoo. He has one of the best rooms in the primate house.[43]

Not then, nor at any time later in his long life, did Hornaday publicly apologize for the exhibition, nor did he ever quite seem to understand why it could be considered offensive. But as the situation escalated into something akin to a slow-motion riot, Hornaday was the public face of the New York Zoological Society, trying to explain the zoo's intentions and fending off body blows from the public, the press, and the preachers.

The role of Madison Grant in all this was, as usual, a backstage affair. After the preachers were turned away by Mayor George B. McLellan Jr., who refused to help them, they marched into Grant's law office. But when they asked to be given custody of Ota Benga, in order to free him, Grant told them that the zoo was only holding him in trust for Dr. Verner and had no authority to hand him over. This, the preachers said afterwards, was "no satisfactory reply," although it was perfectly in character for Grant: a muffled "go away" from behind a walnut-paneled door.[44]

Nevertheless, the next day, Grant ordered that Ota Benga no longer be displayed in a cage, although he was still "employed" by the zoo (as Hornaday put it) and still slept in the primate house at night. But by now the news had spread through the city. On Sunday, September 16, 40,000 people came to the zoo, and, according to the *Times*, "nearly every man, woman, and child of this crowd made for the monkey house to see the star attraction in the park—the wild man from Africa. They chased him about the grounds all day, howling, jeering, and yelling. Some of them poked him in the ribs, others tripped him up, all laughed at him."[45] Ota threw a tantrum, tried to bite one keeper, and at one point even brandished a stolen knife. Hornaday, alarmed by all this, tried to contact Verner to get him to take Ota Benga away, complaining that "the boy ... does quite what he pleases, and it is utterly impossible to control him."[46]

Although Madison Grant may not have been the public face of this affair, his deeper convictions about race were glaringly on display—and would later become well known to the world. He was not just insensitive to the issue of race; some historians would later call him "the nation's most influential racist."[47]

To men like Madison Grant, the tidal wave of unkempt immigrants who filled the streets of New York—and now the Beaux-Arts
pavillions and gardens of the New York Zoo—was deeply alarming.
These people were a threat to his class and, he felt, a danger to the
nation. Grant was a deep believer in the theory of eugenics, a word
coined by Darwin's eccentric and erudite half-cousin, Sir Francis Dal-
ton, in 1883. Simply put, eugenics meant the program of improving
the human race through controlled breeding, much as horse breeders
refine a bloodline of thoroughbreds. The idea caught hold in America
and spawned a new generation of "scientific racists" who came to believe that to invigorate humankind, the dominant Teutonic or Nordic
races should be selected for breeding, while the weak, the infirm, the
feebleminded, and those of degenerate races such as Jews and blacks
should either be encouraged not to reproduce or forcibly sterilized.
Eugenicists believed that "charity" was misguided because it enabled
the weak to survive, therefore diminishing the vigor of the race.[48]

The most famous book about eugenics to emerge from America,
published in 1916, was *The Passing of the Great Race*. Its author was
none other than Madison Grant. The book attempted to explain all of
Western history in terms of racial theory, showing how great nations
crumbled and fell when their strength was sapped by interbreeding
with the "mongrel races," and other nations rose on the majestic power
of racial purity. Grant actually argued in his book that Negroes were
so much less developed than Nordics that they belonged to a separate species—possibly even a separate subgenera. The book became
enormously influential, going through four editions in the United
States and many translations, including a translation into German.
Years later, at the Nuremberg trials, it emerged that Grant's book had
found its way into the hands of Adolf Hitler himself.

"Entertaining, passionate, erudite—*The Passing of the Great Race*
did for scientific racism what *The Communist Manifesto* did for scientific socialism," writes historian Jonathan Peter Spiro in a biography of Madison Grant. "Fortunately for Marx and Grant, they both
died before they could see the horrors that resulted when a regime
embraced their philosophy and tried to remake society in its name."[49]

Spiro points out that, to Grant, the cause of conservation and his
battle to preserve the purity of the race were both intertwined and
both deeply personal. He was trying to save an old, threatened world,
a world as safe for the pale patricians of the Upper East Side as for the

monk seal and the eider duck. Surveying the hordes coming ashore at Ellis Island, Spiro writes, Grant "had to accept the fact that yet another mammal—the blue-eyed, long-headed Teutons—needed to be added to the list of endangered North American species. After all, it is one thing to learn that the bison are headed for extinction; it is quite another to learn that you yourself are similarly doomed." Even so, his conclusions were so repellent that when Grant died in 1937, his family fed his personal papers into a fire.[50]

While there is no evidence that Hornaday was a "scientific racist" like Grant, there is no question that he was (by modern lights) shockingly insensitive to matters of race. In *Our Vanishing Wild Life*, he wrote that "toward wildlife the Italian laborer is a human mongoose ... wherever they settle, their tendency is to root out the native American and take his place and his income,"[51] a charge as unfocused and dangerous as a blast of buckshot. When some Piegan Indians stole a buffalo that he'd killed in Montana, he called them "a gang of coyotes in human form."[52] And his explanation for why he was now exhibiting Ota Benga in a cage did not quite suffice. "I do not wish to offend my colored brothers' feelings or the feelings of anyone, for that matter," Hornaday told the press. "I am giving the exhibitions purely as an ethnological exhibit. It is my duty to interest visitors to the park, and what I have done in exhibiting Benga is in pursuance of this. I am a believer in the Darwinian theory."[53]

In other words, Ota Benga was a vivid display of human evolutionary progress as described by Darwin—the steady progression from "lower" to "higher" living forms. Hornaday was not alone in these beliefs, of course. The *New York Evening Post* pointed out, helpfully, that Benga was not actually at the bottom rung of human development. Because he wasn't coal-black, there were darker-skinned blacks who were lower.[54]

(In an interview with a newspaper in Bridgeport, Connecticut, twenty years later, Hornaday further clarified his views about the hierarchy of sentient life, including animals. "There is not the slightest doubt that the highest races of animals have more intelligence than the lowest races of man.... The highest animals are far better developed, more consistent, worthier and even more spiritual than the lowest men." Furthermore, Hornaday added, "if there is a direct, personal, high interest in the lives of human beings, I have every reason to believe that the same interest extends to animal beings. If all humans have souls, some animals have souls."[55] In further defense of four-legged beings, Hornaday added in one of his books, *Minds and Manners of Wild Animals*: "If every man devoted to his affairs and to the affairs of his city and state the same measure of intelligence and honest industry that every warm-blooded wild animal devotes to its affairs, the people of this world would abound in good health, prosperity, peace and happiness.")[56]

But the clamor, and the outrage, persisted. On September 11, Hornaday seemed to amend his earlier position, telling the *New York Times*, "[I]f Ota Benga is in a cage, he is only there to look after the animals. If there is a notice on the cage, it is only put there to avoid answering the many questions that are asked about him. He is absolutely free. The only restriction that is put upon him is to prevent him from getting away from the keepers. This is done for his own safety."[57] The director also disavowed the Darwinian connection. "I hope my colored bretheren [*sic*] will not take the absurd position that I am giving the exhibition to show the close analogy of the African savage to the apes. Benga is in the primate house because that was the most comfortable place we could find for him."

Nevertheless, Hornaday ultimately bowed to public pressure. After eighteen days, he had Benga removed from public display, although the little man—now a star, but one attempting to hide—continued to live at the zoo. Afterward, Hornaday was dismissive of the whole drama, calling what had happened an "absurd matter. . . . The whole episode is good comic-opera material, and nothing more. When the history of the Zoological Park is written, this incident will form its most amusing passage."[58]

The furor gradually died down. Toward the end of 1906, Benga was released into the custody of the Reverend Gordon, superintendent of a church-sponsored New York orphanage called the Howard Colored Orphan Asylum. But the public's frenzy of interest in this "cannibal" from darkest Africa continued unabated. In January 1910, Gordon arranged for Benga to be relocated to Lynchburg, Virginia, away from the unpleasant glare of the big city. (It was, of course, a crashing irony that Gordon's idea of where to send Benga for greater peace and safety was to move him to the South.) Tutored by black Lynchburg poet Anne Spencer, his English improved, and he sometimes attended elementary school at the local Baptist Seminary.[59]

Ota Benga also liked to frequent the woods around Lynchburg

to fish, hunt, and gather wild honey. Often he was accompanied by a small gang of white boys, aged five to eleven, many of them children of the town's most prominent citizens. Despite some worries that Benga might be a subversive influence on the boys, the youngsters loved these forays into the forest with the little African. In an interview nearly eighty years later, one of them recalled that when Benga strung a long bow that was as long as he was tall, it sounded "like Beethoven." Another described Benga as a hero, a genuine pal, a "close relative." It was the children, more than anyone, who saw him not as the Other, but simply as a human being, no matter how small or dark.[60]

Benga showed the boys how to imitate the calls that would attract quail and wild turkey. He showed them that bee stings suffered in the hunt for honey, rather than being painful, were actually hilarious, the pygmy equivalent of slipping on a banana peel. Back in the town, Benga learned to make compromises with the society that he was living in. His name was Americanized to "Otto Bingo." The pointed teeth that once had been used to stigmatize him as a cannibal were now capped by a dentist, so his smile looked cheerful rather than horrifying. He wore trousers, shirts, and shoes, though somewhat uncomfortably. On certain moonlit nights, often accompanied by his band of boys, Ota Benga would return to the forest dressed only in a bark loincloth. There he would light a ceremonial fire, dance the ceremonial dances, and sing the ceremonial songs that were to be performed only on such occasions. He told the boys that this was how he had danced and sung in Africa. As Peter Matthiessen writes of such ancient tribal practices in *African Silences:* "All songs are implicitly sacred. 'The forest gives us this song,' the people say. 'The forest *is* this song.' "[61]

But outside of Lynchburg, the Great War was raging and Ota knew it, from having heard people talking. He knew that the war had even spread to the Congo, to his beloved African forest. He understood that it would be impossible to return home. He confided to the boys, sometimes with tears in his eyes, that he wanted to go home. But now he couldn't go home. Even Samuel Verner, the man he knew as Fwela, the man who had rescued him and promised one day to take him back to Africa, had disappeared, pursuing schemes and business ventures that had led mostly to poverty and despair. Benga could not afford a steamship ticket back home, even if it were possible for him to go there. And once he arrived back on the Kasai River, in the Congo, he might well discover that he no longer belonged there, either. He had become a man without a country, a forest without a song.

Increasingly despondent, on March 20, 1916, in the late afternoon, he walked into the woods outside Lynchburg. He built a ceremonial fire. He knelt in front of it and broke off the caps that covered his pointed teeth. Then he took out a revolver he had stolen earlier that day, pointed it at his heart, and pulled the trigger. His small body was found there the next day, sprawled beside the fire-pit. He was later buried in an unmarked grave, in the black section of the Old City Cemetery.

PART THREE

Wildlife Warrior

CHAPTER 16

The Dark Shadow

On a sunny March morning in 1910, an excitable and self-involved columnist from the *New York World* who went by the pen name of Kate Carew was sent by her editor over to the Bronx Zoo, to see if spring was stirring among the animals. It was not an assignment Carew particularly relished. In fact, she confided to her readers, the prospect of making a trip to the malodorous zoo made her feel "so mortified—my dears, I could have sat right down and had a good cry." She decided to begin by interviewing "the Sultan of the Zoo, that renowned naturalist, author, explorer and hunter, William T. Hornaday."[1]

When Carew was ushered into Hornaday's high-ceilinged office, adorned with trophy heads of a mountain sheep and a ten-point whitetail buck, as well as a small arsenal of wall-mounted rifles and shotguns, "the sun shone through Director Hornaday's window and bathed him where he sat at his desk, a thickset man with large, fine, kind eyes, a long nose of mixed architecture and a black and white beard arranged in stripes. . . . The cut of that beard and his olive coloring, and the heavy blackness of his brows and eyes—perhaps something in their form, too, give him a Latin look."

Carew went on to report that she had indeed found "the sweet trouble of spring" stirring up the animals at the zoo, and that the distinguished director Hornaday had laughed delightedly when she told him that she'd noticed one of the grizzly bears acting like a kitten. "Oh, yes," he said. "He's beginning to feel the spring." The warmth and friskiness in the air caused enormous changes in the animals' behavior, Hornaday explained—the bears, for instance, often started tearing things up in their excitement. When Carew told Hornaday a funny story about her cat, he laughed knowingly again. "I can easily imagine a cat doing all that," he said. "Cat psychology is very complex and mysterious, and cats have a sense of humor, too—their methods of play show that to an observant eye."

This was the kind of fawning publicity Hornaday had grown acustomed to—and why the opprobrium of the Ota Benga incident had come as such a shock.

Newspaper photos of Hornaday taken around this time show a distinguished-looking man seemingly settling into a contented middle age. He's dressed like a Wall Street banker, wearing a conservative pinstriped suit with a waistcoat and watch fob and a high, stiff "turnover" collar, and a tidily trimmed graying beard. He does not appear to be entirely comfortable stuffily starched and buttoned up in his Sunday best. Years earlier, when he was on his great collecting expedition in India and Borneo, he'd written his new love, Josphine, that "if you should actually *see* me as I come from hunting when out in the jungles, I fear you would refuse to even look upon me again. I don't know what it is, but dirt and old clothes stick to me naturally, and become me but too well. It shows a depraved taste, I know, but it does my heart good to wipe everything on my pants."[2]

Despite his distinguished appearance in the photograph, and his smart suit, it's the eyes that give him away: dark and ferocious, they seem to be filled with unearthly, unsettling luminescence. They are not "civilized" at all. They are the eyes of a man determined to change the world. (One newspaper feature writer who came to visit said that Hornaday had "very big black eyes . . . they look like none you ever saw before; they seem to smolder and smoke like charred embers in a fire.")[3]

In 1906, he was awarded an honorary doctor of science degree from the University of Pittsburgh (and later from Yale), so he was now "Dr. Hornaday," with the letters ScD appended to his growing trophy case of degrees, appointments, and publications. By now, Hornaday had begun to achieve national renown as an author, adventurer, naturalist, and defender of wildlife. One day, the *New York World-Telegram* sent over famed newspaperman A. J. Liebling just to do a story about Hornaday's birthday (though Hornaday turned out to be much more interested in talking about the plight of the white rhinoceros).[4]

Yet all his newfound fame was little comfort. As director of the New York Zoological Park, Hornaday had frequent contact with zoologists, zookeepers, collectors, and curators around the country and around the world. Combined with his own personal travels to some of the globe's remotest outposts, as a peripatetic hunter, collector, and student of natural history, he had an almost unparalleled view of the status of birds and wildlife across the home planet. And what he had begun to see now, at the dawning of a new century, scared him to the depths of his being.

In his modest office at the New York zoological park, Hornaday later wrote in his unpublished autobiography, he went into "executive session," trying to come to grips with this terrible fear. Everything he knew and had learned, everywhere he had been, forced him to the conclusion that the birds and game of the United States were being destroyed faster than they could reproduce. The natural balance had been tipped. It was as if a vast, wide-rimmed bowl were emptying faster than it was filling up, and the outcome of this imbalance was as inexorable as gravity. If the slaughter was not stopped, a vast wave of extinction would sweep across the world.

It infuriated Hornaday that the ornithologists of the day—the people who avowedly loved the birds the most—seemed to be much more interested in "studying the skins, nests, eggs, and migrations of birds than in the preservation of the birds themselves."[5] Yet meanwhile, all around him, he saw evidence that dozens of bird species were in grave peril, if they were not already lost. What was the use of studying them if they would vanish forever soon? Almost nothing in the avian world could compare to the almost incalculable legions of the passenger pigeon, which had darkened the skies when he was a boy. Ornithologist Alexander Wilson had once estimated a flock of passenger pigeons at 2,230,272,000 birds—that's 2 *billion*—which he called "an almost inconceivable multitude, and yet probably far below the actual amount."[6] And yet the passenger pigeon had now almost vanished. And the heath hen, just to name one other imperiled species, had become extinct everywhere except for one remnant colony on Martha's Vineyard. (The last passenger pigeon on Earth, named Martha, died in 1914 at the Cincinnati Zoo; the last heath hen perished in the spring of 1933.)

Even in Washington, Hornaday found "absolutely no man-power functioning through the federal government for any form or phase of wild life protection, save traces in the Yellowstone Park."[7] (Yellowstone, the world's first national park, was established by an act of Congress in 1872, but because there was no effective enforcement of game laws, hunting, trapping, and pillaging of timber and minerals were so widespread that the park had to be taken over by the U.S. Army in 1886, as if it were a war-torn country of its own. Yellowstone remained under military occupation for the next thirty years.)[8]

"On the whole," Hornaday later wrote, looking back on the situation in the early twentieth century, "the evil conditions surrounding the wild life of America were so bad that it is difficult to imagine how they could have been any worse" (though, of course, they did get worse). Not only was the approaching darkness going unnoticed by almost everyone, but no one had mapped out a comprehensive battle plan proposing the thoroughgoing reforms that would be required to even slow down, much less halt, the destruction. For now, Hornaday wrote, "there was nothing to do but plunge in and try to salvage the situation, piece by piece, and from day to day."[9]

Even the new conservation organizations often seemed impotent. One day, while searching through the annual reports of the American Ornithologists' Union "looking to hook up with some group of bird men," Hornaday found a notice from 1894 of the union's Bird Protection Committee asking "to be discharged, the need for such a committee being no longer urgent; of late its functions having been merely advisory, and its services not often required."[10]

The whole house was burning down, and the firemen were asking to be discharged because they couldn't even smell the smoke!

Most of Hornaday's waking hours were consumed with the task of building and managing the New York Zoological Park, and he was delighted with his job, but there were days when his official duties seemed almost beside the point. Outside the tidy perimeters of the park, a great war was going on, arguably the greatest and most important war in human history, and vast armies were massing against all the nonhuman life on the planet. What good would it do to keep a few lonely examples of vanished species behind bars in New York if night had fallen on the rest of the world?

Hornaday was itching to get into the fight for wildlife, but he was disgusted by the timidity and impotence of the American Ornithological Union and other such groups. Fortunately, the bylaws of the

New York Zoological Society offered him a justification to enter the fray. When the society was created in 1895, Grant and Osborn set down as its second declared object six ringing words: its essential purpose, among others, was "THE PRESERVATION OF OUR NATIVE ANIMALS." (Hornaday wrote these words in his autobiography all in capital letters, like a shout from the Almighty.) Later, partly at Hornaday's urging, the original wording was broadened to "THE WILD ANIMAL LIFE OF THE WORLD."[11]

To become a champion and a crusader for all the wild animal life of the world was the noblest calling imaginable—a task big enough for Hornaday's outsized ambition and personality.

It was a clarion call to action, and William Temple Hornaday intended to take up the fight. The board of directors, of course, had hired him to run the zoo. That was his day job. But he volunteered for the additional job of running a war because he felt that he had no choice. He solemnly assured the board that his official duties at the zoo would come first and that he would pursue the broader mandate of wildlife protection on his own time, without a dime of further compensation.

"I have taken up this matter," he wrote his friend Charles Bessey, the famed botanist and his former professor, "solely because no one else has done so in a manner to suit me, and I think the time is ripe for a grand crusade for the better protection of our birds and quadrupeds in the districts they are so rapidly disappearing."[12] Later, in his autobiography, written at the age of eighty, he did not express a moment's regret about embarking on this "grand crusade." In fact, "had I elected to remain passive, I could have shirked the whole thirty-four years of it; but my sense of duty would not permit it."[13]

Over the next several decades, Hornaday seemed to be living a multitude of lives at once, running the New York zoo at the same time he was conducting a global war for wildlife on multiple fronts simultaneously. He fought the seal hunters on the Pribilof Islands, who seemed determined to drive the Alaskan fur seal to extinction. He waded into the battle against the gun manufacturers, fighting to reduce the absurd lethality of the new repeating shotguns that seemed to be turning sportsmanlike hunting into mass murder. He fought the millinery feather trade and its cunning lobbyists in Washington, who were hunting the world's most exquisite birds to extinction just to adorn women's hats. He fought for bag limits and shorter seasons on birds and game. He fought for the establishment of wild-life reserves and ranges across the West and elsewhere. In fact, wher-ever he found the enemies of wildlife, he fought them, in a stream of books and articles, in congressional testimony, and in speeches and public appearances without end. And when he went after the en-emies of wildlife, he did it like an avenging angel of the Lord.

Some historians of the period have argued that Mr. Hornaday could actually have achieved a good deal more for the cause of conser-vation were he not "the most defiant devil who ever came to town," not so ferociously combative, not so unwilling to make alliances with con-servation groups with which he disagreed—chief among them the gun lobbies and hunting groups. It's easy enough to say such things today, long after the smoke has cleared from those battlefields. But during his lifetime, Hornaday faced a phalanx of implacable foes who were enormously well funded, had access to political and legislative power, and very often had the weight of public opinion on their side as well. But in the killing-fields of the Montana Territory, Hornaday had seen firsthand what happened when market hunting, sport gun-ning, thrill-killing, and plain lawlessness were allowed to run riot, as it had all across the country.

Throughout all this, Hornaday remained a devoted spouse, writ-ing a prodigious stream of letters to "the Empress Josephine," who remained by his side come what may. He opened one letter to her: "Really, there is no reason on earth why I should write you just now, unless it is the fear that if it is not done now, you may miss a letter tomorrow morning."[14]

Josephine's love was something Hornaday came to depend on, like milk and honey in the wilderness, especially when his public battles grew increasingly bitter and he came to feel increasingly alone. Their only child, a daughter named Helen, also became an ardent defender of her father's good name and his privacy, rarely speaking out in public but praising and comforting him in her private letters—much as her mother did. There were times when he felt betrayed, often by those who were allegedly his friends. There were times when his enemies attacked him with poisonous lies or nasty innuendo, and having be-come such a public man, he had to fight back publicly, even when it was awkward and embarrassing to answer an untruth. His response to all these attacks was to be forever on the attack, never to back down or apologize, to respond to a withering hail of incoming fire with relentless fusillades of his own. As the nineteenth century turned into the twentieth, his whole life gradually became one of more-or-less continuous war.

The year before he was appointed director of the New York zoo, Hornaday had begun closely examining the battlefield situation in the "war for wildlife," and what he found was alarming. The enemy had taken the high ground with vastly greater arms and manpower; and the defense was scattered, demoralized, and sorely lacking in armaments and ammunition. There were laws on the books in many states to protect songbirds, gamebirds, and other game, but they were essentially worthless because there was no funding or public interest in actually enforcing them. Many of these hunting laws had been essentially dictated by hunters themselves, to maximize their kills. But even where the game laws offered some protection, there was very little money to pay salaried wardens, and unsalaried wardens were very often useless. If there was no enforcement, there might as well be no game laws at all.

The first task in his "grand crusade," Hornaday believed, would be to be to "scare America into a state of wakefulness and anxiety, by sounding out alarms."[15] This, of course, was not a scientific intent, not an open-minded search for truth; it was a propagandistic intent, from a man absolutely convinced of his rightness.

As a way of beginning the crusade and creating a simple "baseline" of data about populations of birds and game, he decided to survey several hundred knowledgable people around the country. He would ask them four basic questions: Are birds decreasing in number in your locality? About how many are there now in comparison with the number fifteen years ago? What agency (or class of men) has been most destructive to the birds of your locality? What important birds or quadrupeds are becoming extinct in your state?[16]

Hornaday's survey drew responses from nearly two hundred observers, representing all but three of the states and territories in the nation. He received what he considered a "satisfactory" number of responses from thirty-six states, so he only included these in his final report. Many who responded were ornithologists, naturalists, or simply astute observers of the state of nature in their areas, and many of their answers were lengthy and detailed. It was clear that they had responded to Hornaday's questions with deep seriousness, perhaps welcoming the inquiry from someone who shared their alarm about what was happening.

Hornaday's report, *The Destruction of Our Birds and Mammals: A Report on the Results of an Inquiry*,"[17] was published by the New York Zoological Society in its second annual report in 1898. He opened the survey with an unabashed call to arms: "Unless man is willing to accept a place on the list of predatory animals which have no other thought than the wolfish instinct to slay every living species save their own, he is bound by the unwritten laws of civilization to protect from annihilation the beasts and birds that still beautify the earth."[18]

Of all the states reporting in his survey, he went on to say, the average decrease in bird life during the previous fifteen years was *nearly half* (that is, 46 percent). The highest declines were in Florida (77 percent); with an estimated 75 percent decline in birds in Connecticut, Montana, and the Indian territories. Three states—North Carolina, Oregon, and California—appeared to be in balance, with no noticeable decline at all, and four Western states—Kansas, Wyoming, Utah, and Washington—reported a slight increase over the fifteen-year span.[19]

According to a tabulation of the survey's responses, the villains included "pot hunters" (those who hunted for food), "sportsmen," boys, egg collectors, and Italians, "who kill all sorts of birds for food."[20] But Hornaday set aside a special ring in hell for the plume hunters and for the women who wore their wares. "One of the strangest anomalies of modern civilization is the spectacle of modern woman—the refined and tender-hearted, the merciful and compassionate—suddenly transformed into a creature heedlessly destructive of bird life, and in practise as bloodthirsty as the most sanguinary birds of prey."[21]

(But even Hornaday himself did not entirely rise above all the pernicious beliefs of his day. In his report, he mentions that "the fact has been clearly established by the researches of the U.S. Biological Survey that of all our hawks and owls, only the sharp-shinned hawk, Cooper's hawk, and the goshawk have a debit balance against them, and deserve destruction."[22] He based these erroneous conclusions on studies showing that the contents of the stomachs of many of these birds contained large numbers of songbirds, and sometimes domestic poultry.)

In his report, Hornaday also described, with a kind of raging incredulity, a peculiarly ignorant form of small-town American sport known as the "side-hunt." It was, Hornaday wrote, essentially "a game of murder," in which a large group of men and boys—sometimes 100 or more—divided into two teams, armed themselves to the teeth, and then, for a given period of time, shot every living thing in sight to earn points. In one side-hunt, for instance, a fox was worth 500 points, a mink 150, a heron 100, and so on. At the end of the hunt, scores were totaled up to see which side had "won." Hornaday reported that on Thanksgiving Day, 1897, fourteen boys in a side-hunt in Sedan, Indiana, bagged fifty English sparrows, eight chipping sparrows, five bluejays, twenty-seven nuthatches, seventeen downy woodpeckers, fourteen hairy woodpeckers, twelve red-bellied woodpeckers, and two flying squirrels.[23]

When Hornaday got word that a social club in Rome, New York, was staging a merry three-day side-hunt in November 1902, he fired off an angry protest to the local newspaper. The paper printed Hornaday's broadside, along with an editorial that took the side of . . . the hunters. "If any wild creature of any sort remains alive in the vicinity of Rome on November 5th, it will not be the fault of the 'Noble Three Hundred,'" the editors fired back.[24]

Yet when Hornaday's report describing such attitudes and their consequences was published, it was largely met with disbelief. Two of Hornaday's own bird-loving friends quietly scoffed that it was "greatly exaggerated." A review of the report in the *Auk*, a publication of the American Ornithologists' Union, concluded that "game and plume birds are unquestionably on the high road to extermination, and certain species of our small birds are decreasing, but the general destruction in the latter class is probably not nearly so great as Mr. Hornaday's figures imply."[25]

If his report were greeted with this kind of skepticism by bird-lovers, how would it be greeted by the general public? As it turned out, with a yawn, if it was greeted at all. At least William Dutcher, the gallant president of the National Audubon Societies (later Society), had two thousand copies of the report printed and sent out to state legislators around the country.

The numbers in the survey were just the sort of firebombs that Hornaday loved to lob at the sleeping public, and he made wide use of them, hoping to stoke the public's fury at what was happening. "We need all the ammunition that we can possibly get," Hornaday wrote to a colleague, Dr. Theodore Palmer of the U.S. Biological Survey, "and everything that we get, we will use over and over again."[26] Hornaday's use of facts and figures as propaganda tools rather than instruments of scientific understanding was something for which he was criticized throughout his life. But such was his fear and rage at what was happening to wildlife that he felt that nothing but fire and brimstone would capture the public's attention. Madison Grant, one of the founders of the Zoological Society, eventually forbade Hornaday from printing "yellow pamphlets" on society stationary.

More than a century after the fact, it's difficult to say whether Hornaday's numbers were inflated for the purpose of "scaring America"; but—as he always did—Hornaday defended the numbers in his survey until the end of his life. At that time, he wrote in his autobiography, "it was clearly evident (1) that the wild life of the nation . . . was being very generally and very [viciously] attacked by deadly enemies, (2) that some of it was in desperate straits, (3) that it was NOWHERE being given the humane and courageous protection that its rights demanded, and (4) that it would be a herculean task to save about a hundred important species from quick extermination."[27]

Warming to his task, Hornaday went on to say that, in 1898, "while there had been a lot of talk about game protection, the American spirit of protection and square-dealing with game was so weak and puerile that not one single species of game was being conserved on an adequate and permanent basis. I challenge history to disprove this sweeping statement." (Later, in a version of his unpublished autobiography, this "sweeping statement" was crossed out, as though Hornaday had stepped back, ever so slightly, from the fight.)[28]

To the public at large, and many ornithologists in particular, his survey might have seemed alarmist. But Hornaday had, after all, witnessed something that few people in New York society had ever seen—the near-extermination of a noble species in an astonishingly short period of time. And he was damn well determined never to let it happen again.

CHAPTER 17

Empire of the Buffalo

A few days after the first frost of October 1907, as the wind across the Great Plains stirred the tallgrass prairie in fifty-mile waves, a steam locomotive pulling two Arms Palace horse cars chugged into the station in the tiny cowtown of Cache, Oklahoma, not far from the Wichita Mountains. An enormous crowd had gathered in the station—mud-spattered cowboys; ranchers; and hundreds of Plains Indians, with their spotted ponies and open wagons known as "Indian hacks," the women wearing their brightest ceremonial blankets, many with papooses on their backs. Some had been waiting for days. They were waiting for something that they had hardly dared could ever really happen, something that had been foretold in dreams and prophecies.[1]

Standing apart and seemingly above the crowd was the great warrior Quanah Parker, the last chief of the Comanches, a statuesque and silent figure with a fierce, impenetrable face, eyes narrowed to slits, and black hair twisted into a pair of braids extending down below his waist. Parker had been born nearby, in the Wichitas, six decades earlier, and his life was the stuff of legend. His father had been the feared Comanche war chief Peta Nocona; his grandfather, Iron Jacket, was said to be able to blow away bullets with his breath. But Quanah was born with one foot in the white man's world: his mother was a white woman named Cynthia Ann Parker who'd been kidnapped by a Comanche war party when she was nine years old and renamed Nautdah, or "Someone Found."[2] She came of age among the Comanche, learned their language, married a Comanche, and had three children. When she was kidnapped back into the white world at the age of thirty-three, by Texas Rangers, she was so completely Comanche she had forgotten how to speak Engish, or at least she refused to do so. When the Rangers attacked a Comanche buffalo camp along the Pease River, killing Peta Nocoma and eleven others, she'd been taken captive—a squaw so covered with dirt and buffalo grease that it was only after she'd been cleaned up that the officers noticed she had pale blue eyes.[3]

Only two Comanche horsemen escaped the Rangers that day: Nautdah's son Quanah, who was only twelve years old, and his younger brother. Newly orphaned and straddling two worlds as a mixed-blood "half breed," Quanah Parker quickly became a dauntless hunter, superb horseman, and cunning tactician. He burned with hatred for the whites who had killed his father and kidnapped his mother and sister. As he grew older, he began staging ever more daring raids, with larger and larger war parties, farther and farther into the white man's land. He stole horses and pillaged towns, killing and terrorizing with such fearlessness that he became known as the greatest war chief of the Comanches.[4]

Parker was especially outraged at the massacre of the buffalo because without them, the Comanches would be unable to survive. In 1874, he led a war party of 250 Comanche, Cheyenne, Arapahoe, and Kiowa braves in an attack on a white trading post at Adobe Walls, in the Texas panhandle, which supplied the 300-odd buffalo hunters fast at work exterminating the once-enormous southern herd. Parker had managed to electrify much of the Comanche nation and neighboring tribes, partly because of his own reputation and partly because a medicine man named Isa-tai swore that his protective magic, or *puha*, was so powerful that it would repel the white men's bullets. Yet despite Quanah's fearless leadership, astounding horsemanship, and courage under fire, the Indians were vastly outgunned. What became known as the Second Battle of Adobe Walls ended inconclusively; but spiritually, it was a devastating defeat. Even the tribes' greatest warrior and its most revered medicine man could not defeat the buffalo-butchering whites. Quanah Parker, who had never lost a battle with the white man, became the last chief to enter the reservation when he and a weary band of 400 entered Fort Sill in 1875. He could see what was happening to the buffalo, and to his people, and had come to realize that to resist any further was futile.[5]

—⟋⟋⟍—

Two decades later, in a far-off world, one of the earliest and most popular exhibits at the newly opened New York Zoological Park was a twenty-acre naturalistic enclosure with a small herd of several dozen bison. It was Director Hornaday's attempt to suggest the epic tableaus of the Western territories and the enormous emptiness of places like the Staked Plain of Texas and New Mexico, which the Spanish conquistadore Coronado had described as "plains so vast, that I did not find their limit anywhere I went, with no more land marks than if we had been swallowed up by the sea."[6]

Very few people in the East had actually seen a live buffalo, much less a landscape that looked like Coronado's endless ocean of grass. But perhaps partly because the buffalo in the New York Zoological Park were so far away from their native habitat, Hornaday struggled to keep them alive in the early days. He'd been attracted to the site on the Bronx River partly because the lush grass would provide natural forage for the buffalo, deer, antelope, and other ungulates, but it turned out that the bison had trouble digesting the grass, and several became painfully bloated and nearly died. Although Hornaday had the native grass burned off and even removed the topsoil, it was several years before the problem of forage was solved and the herd began to thrive in its ersatz prairie in the Bronx.[7]

But even if captive breeding did turn out to be possible, Hornaday wrote, "in view of the well-known fact that no large species of quadruped can be bred and perpetuated for centuries in the confinement of zoological gardens, even large ones such as the New York Zoological Park . . . the only way to insure the perpetuation of the bison species permanently is to create large herds" in natural reserves, perhaps in the West.[8] He began trying to find such a location, a protected buffalo Eden in which a small nucleus herd could thrive, reproduce, and eventually bring the species back from the brink.

At the same time, Hornaday was taking the first steps toward forming some kind of political organization that would harness the power of public outrage, as well as the gold in the nation's treasury, to save the bison. From almost the time they first met in the half-completed buffalo display at the National Museum in 1887, Hornaday and Theodore Roosevelt had been talking about this. But their inchoate ideas had been tabled mainly because both men were too busy to attend to them. Hornaday was running the New York Zoological Park, writing books, and conducting a war; and Roosevelt had thrown his energies into another conservation organization, the Boone and Crockett Club, but now he was too busy even for that. In 1901, with the assasination of President William McKinley, Vice President Roosevelt had taken up residence at a palatial new home at 1600 Pennsylvania Avenue.

It was an eccentric young naturalist and former *New York Times* reporter named Ernest Harold Baynes who helped kick-start the creation of an organization that would come to be called the American Bison Society.[9] In 1904, Baynes was living in a rented cottage on a vast game reserve in New Hampshire where the owner, railroad magnate Austin Corbin, kept 160 head of bison. Baynes became enthralled with the history, biology, and majesty of the American bison, and he began writing and lecturing on the subject. Like Hornaday, Baynes had come to see that the bison's existence in the wild was in grave peril. He came to believe that the only way to save them from extinction was to create some sort of national organization that would (among other things) put private herds like Corbin's under government control.[10] Baynes wrote to President Roosevelt suggesting this idea, and Roosevelt wrote back enthusiastically, even agreeing to become honorary president of such an organization, provided that the other slate of officers met with his approval. When Baynes approached Hornaday, he too responded enthusiastically, and after a flurry of correspondence between the two men, on the evening of December 8, 1905, in the reception room of the Lion House at the half-finished New York Zoological Park, the first official meeting of the American Bison Society was held. Two hundred invitations had been sent out, but only fourteen people showed up. There were thirteen men (including Baynes and Hornaday) and one woman in attendance at that first meeting. Later, Hornaday was elected president, with Roosevelt as honorary president and Baynes as secretary.

The group quickly set about raising money, expanding its membership, clanging the bell about the perilous state of the buffalo, and trying to find a place to establish a free-roaming, semi-wild herd that would ultimately lead to the return of the American bison.[11] Baynes was indefatigable, one summer giving more than 150 lectures about the buffalo in small towns from New Hampshire to Nebraska. One of the most popular parts of his talk consisted of slides of bison calves in harness, pulling a wagon. He claimed to drive the only team of harness-broken bison in the world. But Martin Garretson, a later secretary of the American Bison Society, was skeptical of Baynes's theatrics. In his book *The American Bison*, he wrote, "The general opinion expressed in the rural community in that neighborhood was: 'Baynes hitches 'em up, and they take him where they d— please.'"[12]

Hornaday, meanwhile, was growing annoyed with what he felt was Baynes' amateurishness, and he moved to take control of the organization.[12] He intensified his efforts to find a bison range, first trying, and failing, to establish one in New York State's Adirondacks. Then he began looking into the possibility of establishing a bison range on the Flathead Indian Reservation in northwest Montana, but that also failed. Hornaday then began focusing on the Wichita Mountains of southwestern Oklahoma. In 1901, shortly before his death, President McKinley had designated a large tract of land in the Wichitas as a national forest. Hornaday knew that this land had been among the richest grazing grounds of the great southern herd and that Oklahoma, with its light snowfall, would provide a relatively mild climate for bison to overwinter. The Wichitas were also something of a natural curiosity, with low, eerie, dome-shaped mountains of red granite, a thick forest of black-jack and post-oak, and an odd confluence of East and West. They were one of the few places where the Eastern bluebird might cross paths with the Western bluebird, and the Eastern meadowlark might overhear the warbling of its kin, the Western meadowlark.[13]

In February 1905, through the federal Lacey Act, Congress authorized President Roosevelt to create a game reserve in the Wichitas—the first big-game reserve in the United States, in fact— and Roosevelt had the unmitigated joy of creating, with one stroke of the pen, a 60,800-acre sanctuary for big-game animals. In his comments about the Wichita National Forest and Game Reserve, Roosevelt spoke of deer, elk, and antelope, but he did not specifically mention buffalo. But back in New York, Hornaday was already mentally trying to figure out where to build the buffalo fences and calculating how much it would cost.[14]

One other thing about the Wichitas that Hornaday probably did not know: the mountains had long been considered sacred to the Comanche and other plains people. According to prophetic revelations revered by the Kiowa, it was into Mount Scott, the highest of the granite domes, that the buffalo had disappeared, and from which they would reappear one day, pouring forth like rivers of living water.[15]

In April 1905, the popular young "cowboy president," Teddy Roosevelt, arranged a four-day hunting holiday into the Oklahoma Territory, coursing for wolves near Sheridan's Fort Sill. Like everything else he did, this lark was accompanied by huge publicity and mobs of onlookers. As his train, the "Roosevelt Special," stopped at stations on its way west from Washington, enormous crowds turned out, and when it arrived in Frederick, Oklahoma, on April 5, a throng of 6,000 people crowded into a specially built grandstand to see him. Besides looking forward to "four days' fun under God's blue heaven," hunting game birds and "prairie wolves" (coyotes), Roosevelt had a couple of other things in mind. For one thing, he wanted to look over the Wichita reserve as a possible home for the nation's first reintroduced free-ranging bison herd. Going out there to look the place over, Roosevelt, in a sense, was acting as an "advance scout" for Hornaday.[16]

The other thing Roosevelt wanted to do on this trip was get to know Quanah Parker a bit better and see him on his home ground. A month earlier, in March, Quanah had ridden in an open car, wearing buckskins and a war bonnet, in Roosevelt's inaugural parade. When Roosevelt and Parker first met, the two men seemed to feel a profound kinship. Roosevelt loved Parker's reverence for the buffalo, his dauntless courage, and his almost mystical presence, in which his every utterance seemed to have some sacred import. Parker, for his part, could sense that Roosevelt shared his reverence for the glories of the grassland and all its inhabitants.[17]

Roosevelt asked Parker what he could do for the Indian chief, and Parker told the president that he wanted the last of the tribe's grazing lands in Oklahoma to be preserved. When Roosevelt told Parker about the American Bison Society's vision of bringing buffalo back to the west, perhaps to the Wichitas, the old warrior's eyes rimmed with tears. What Quanah had been unable to do with sheer courage and force of arms, perhaps this white man could do with his wealth, power, and laws.

Like Roosevelt, Quanah Parker was an extraordinary man who transcended his time and place. He understood that unless he and his people were able to change, they would be destroyed, and he ably led them into a changed and hostile world, profoundly transforming himself along the way. He adopted the white man's clothing, often wearing a bowler hat with his long black braids, negotiated grazing rights with Texas cattlemen, became fluent in English as well as several Indian dialects, and even became part owner of a railroad (the Quanah, Acme, and Pacific).[18]

Back in New York, meanwhile, Hornaday pored over maps of the Wichita reserve. He decided that one particularly choice spot, called "Winter Valley" because it provided rich grasses for forage and sheltered canyons for warmth in winter, would be the centerpiece of a fenced-in reserve of about 8,000 acres, or 12 square miles.[19] Hornaday also began selecting animals from the New York herd, choosing bulls and cows from four different bloodlines to avoid inbreeding and using his understanding of genetic integrity and herd dynamics to maximize the chances of reproductive success in the new herd. He had hand-fed most of these animals and grown fond of them; he even named four of them after great Indian chiefs—Lone Wolf, Blackdog, Geronimo, and, ironically, Quanah.

Eventually the executive committee of the New York Zoological Society, through the Secretary of Agriculture, offered the United States and its people a special donation. They would give the government twelve to fifteen pure-blood bison (that is, animals that had not been interbred with cattle), provided that the government supplied enough money to fence in grazing grounds in the newly created Wichita preserve. And so, in due time, it was agreed. Roosevelt was able to keep his promise to Quanah Parker, at the same time that the ancient prophecy of the buffalo's return was about to become manifest.[20]

Now it was the autumn of 1907, and Quanah Parker stood in the windswept railroad siding in Cache, Oklahoma, to witness something he could scarcely have imagined thirty years earlier. He stood there watching as wranglers offloaded the contents of the Arms Palace horse cars: the shaggy, prehistoric silhouettes of fifteen bison, nine cows and six bulls, each in its own cage like a pampered show horse, emerged from the dimness of the rail cars. An audible sigh went up from the crowd. Old warriors peered through the bars into the cages, showing their grandsons the animals that they had once hunted from horseback in a world now receding into the dimness of memory.

It was a crashing irony that these animals that were being sent back to repopulate the Great Plains from which they had vanished had been sent from, of all places, New York City, at the behest of a white man named Hornaday, of the New York Zoological Park. The whites who had nearly destroyed the buffalo were now attempting the first animal reintroduction in North American history.[21] It was an effort to turn back the bloody pages of time and achieve, to whatever extent might be possible, a kind of redemption.

Observers at the scene said the stone-faced Parker was momentarily overcome with emotion. Then he began helping the men load the caged bison onto open wagons to be transported the twelve miles to the Wichita National Forest and Game Preserve.

One big concern was an outbreak of tick-borne "Texas fever," which had devastated cattle herds in the area. So once the bison arrived at their corral at the park (where they would spend the winter before being released into the reserve in the spring), a veteran cowpuncher named Frank Rush, who'd been put in charge of the operation, had them thoroughly fumigated with tick-killing crude petroleum.[22] As a consequence, these "last representatives of a mighty race" would return to their ancestral prairie home reeking of oil and civilization.[23]

But the herd thrived under the watchful eye of the old cowboy. Less than a month after their arrival, the first calf was born. Because it came into the world on November 16, 1907, the same day the Oklahoma Territory officially became a state, the calf was named "Oklahoma." A second calf was born around the same time, and the little bull was named "Hornaday," in honor of the man who, more than any other person, was responsible for pulling the buffalo back from the brink of extinction. Hornaday, the New York Times opined in 1907, "deserves the gratitude of the Nation as the chief preserver from extinction of the American Bison."[24]

By 1919, the American Bison Society had been directly involved in creating nine different bison herds across the United States. One of its most notable accomplishments was the creation of the Montana National Bison Reserve, at the foot of the Mission Range, in western Montana. At the society's request, and with the backing of other conservation organizations, Congress was able to buy and fence in twenty-nine square miles of prime buffalo range. Hornaday spearheaded a massive national campaign to raise the $10,000 needed to buy the bison needed to seed the herd, browbeating the public with shame, coaxing them with the call of duty.

Not everyone responded to his pleas. The *Kansas City Journal* ran a snide editorial deriding Hornaday and the Bison Society as self-important buffoons, pointing out that "President Hornaday is now in the position of having a government reserve in which to place bison, but he hasn't any bison. He has appealed to the country to get him bison so he can protect them, but as yet not a single, solitary beast has been driven up to his front door. He thinks that if he had $10,000, he could buy bison, and then protect them with the money congress [*sic*] has set aside for the purpose; but this is not a cause that appeals strongly to the American public."[25]

In fact, though, it was a cause that *did* appeal to Americans, who contributed enough money for the reserve, and much more, over the ensuing years. By the end of its first decade, Professor Osborn was able to write: "The Society has accomplished the main object for which it was established ten years ago: not only is the American bison no longer in danger of extinction but it is firmly restablished in all parts of this country."[26]

The most vocal enemies of the bison, those men who had at one time sworn undying enmity toward the animals that were the primary source of material and spiritual sustenance for the savages, were now long dead. (The savages themselves were now mostly subdued and confined to reservations, so the immediate threat of war-whoops and tomahawks was receding, even as concern for the buffalo was growing.)

General William Tecumseh Sherman died in 1891, at the age of seventy-one, never having renounced or softened his views on the buffalo. Interior Secretary Columbus Delano, with his fearsome eyebrows and apocalyptic glare, was forced to resign his position in 1875 for gross mismanagement, living out his last years as a self-satisfied bank president in Ohio. General "Little Phil" Sheridan, however—who once famously commented "let them kill, skin, and sell until the buffalo is exterminated"—devoted the last days of his life to a personal crusade to save Yellowstone Park and its wildlife, chasing out unscrupulous developers and standing fast against thieves and poachers. When he died of a massive heart attack at the age of fifty-seven, Sheridan was fighting along with Hornaday on the side of the angels. Perhaps even more important, the mood of the country had begun to change, and—at the last possible moment—people began to realize the gravity of what they had very nearly lost.[27]

Although a geyser of buffalo never issued from the mouth of Mount Scott, nevertheless "a great thing had happened," historian Douglas Brinkley later wrote. The gift of bison to the people of Oklahoma, to the country, and to the world, engineered by Hornaday, enacted by Roosevelt, and blessed by Quanah Parker, "was a true token of peace, generosity, wisdom, and goodwill."[28]

CHAPTER 18

Our Vanishing Wildlife

The story of the return of the American bison from the verge of extinction was an inspiring one, certainly among the most moving and important stories in the history of American conservation. But Hornaday, who was widely credited with having been the most significant single person in that fight, was not one to rest on his laurels. In fact, he wrote, on every pioneer monument in the Great West, there should be a statue of a bronze bison or an antelope with the words "Lest we forget" engraved underneath.[1] As if any more proof were needed, the murders of game wardens Guy Bradley, Columbus McLeod, and Pressly Reeves were lasting reminders that the war for wildlife was often bitter and sometimes bloody, and the outcome was never certain.

Even so, by 1912, there had been huge and lasting battlefield victories in the war. Iowa senator John F. Lacey, an enthusiastic defender of Yellowstone National Park, had become incensed that game wardens were unable to punish poachers of the park's wildlife, and in 1894 he sponsored a bill to empower to the Department of the Interior to arrest and prosecute game-thieves in the park. (He was well acquainted with the lawlessness inside the park; his stagecoach had been robbed there in 1887.)[2] To Hornaday, it seemed incredible that this was progress—how can you have a national park if there were no real laws to protect its wildlife?—but progress it was. A few years later, in 1900, Senator Lacey became best known for the passage of the Lacey Act, which made it illegal to ship from one state to another birds killed in violation of state laws. This was the first truly effective, nationwide weapon against the plume hunters (though it was not enough to save the life of Guy Bradley). The same year, *Bird-Lore* magazine, started by Frank Chapman and later renamed *Audubon*, proposed having an annual Christmas Bird Count, to replace the shooting competitions traditionally held on that sacred day.[3]

The American public seemed to be waking from its long and deadly slumber, at long last. The National Audubon Society, born in 1886 when the crusading young editor of *Forest and Stream* magazine, George Bird Grinnell, harnessed the outrage of his readers over the feather trade, suggested a "model bird protection law" to state legislatures; and between 1895 and 1905, thirty-seven states adopted some variation of the law. Hornaday's great friend William Dutcher helped create a national alliance of state Audubon Societies, and in 1905 he became its first president. In 1911, through Dutcher's heroic and unflagging efforts, New York State—the nerve center of the global feather trade—passed the Audubon Act, more familiarly known as the Dutcher Law, prohibiting the sale of native wild birds in the state. As a result, soon after, the streets of New York began to empty of the eerie sight of exotic birds riding along as unwitting passengers on women's heads (except for feathers of farm-raised birds like pheasants and ostriches, which remained legal).[4]

But if an assault was beaten back in one place, the enemy seemed to mount another one somewhere else. In October 1910, one of Hornaday's allies in the hunting world came down to the New York Zoo to bring the director some unsettling news. At that time, a few states had laws on the books prohibiting the sale of two or three species of native game, but not one state had a comprehensive law prohibiting sale of *all* birds and game. As a consequence, "market hunting"—the grim, relentless, year-round slaughter of birds and mammals for sale to groceries and restaurants—continued unabated. And nowhere were the market hunters more indefatigable, or more vocally opposed to any attempt to regulate them, than on Long Island.

The sportsman told Hornaday that "the Long Island bunch," apparently sensing that their days might be numbered, had formed three organizations whose intent was to "wipe off our statute books all the laws for the protection of feathered game. They are going to send a man to the legislature expressly to do whatever they tell him to do about game; and they intend to make a clean sweep of all the wild life protection laws they don't like."[5]

To Hornaday, this grim news was like a bee in a bull's ear.

"Well, then, damn their souls, we will give them the fight of their lives!" the director thundered. *"We will introduce a bill to stop the sale of game, and carry the war right into the enemy's camp!"*

The old soldier sprang into action. With the blessing of Grant and Osborn, his bosses at the zoo, Hornaday turned out a blistering four-page circular meant to enrage the wildlife lovers of New York and raise money for a campaign to pass a comprehensive game law in New York State. He pointed out that New York City was not only the greatest market for ducks, geese, and shore birds that were being slaughtered along the Atlantic Coast, but it was also a "fence" for birds killed illegally in other states all across the Eastern seaboard. He mentioned the mausoleum of native birds found in one New York cold storage locker in 1902, including 8,058 snow buntings, 7,607 sandpipers, and 7,003 snipe. "I did not 'beg' for support," Hornaday wrote later. "I *demanded* it!" Contributions poured in, including gifts from plutocrats like Henry Clay Frick and George Eastman.

Once the campaign discretionary fund could pay for it, Hornaday hired a young lawyer named Lawrence Trowbridge, who drafted a bill, went up to the state capital in Albany, and began trying to enlist support among legislators. To sponsor the bill, Trowbridge and Hornaday chose Senator Howard Bayne, of Staten Island, who later confessed that at first he was "perfectly certain that [the bill] never would be passed." But the bill gained momentum, and Governor John Dix even hosted a lavish state dinner at the executive mansion in support of what was now known as the Bayne bill.

Sensing that the tide of popular opinion was beginning to turn against them, the market-gunners of Long Island sent Hornaday a proposed compromise, "to let the bill go through." But when one of the Bayne bill's supporters asked Hornaday what he thought of these proposed concessions, Hornaday bellowed, "No compromises with the enemy. *Never!* If we make any compromise now, it will be sure to rise up and plague us in the future." When various friends and supporters began to lose their nerve, claiming the bill was "too drastic," Hornaday declared that he would "go through with it if it killed me." Eventually, when the bill came up for a vote in the legislature, it passed the Assembly unanimously, and with only one dissenting vote in the Senate.

At 7:15 the next morning, in a Washington hotel room, Hornaday dashed off a letter to Josephine, addressing her as "My Dearly Beloved Empress Josephine and Queen of Hearts":

> In 57 1/2 hours I will hear the Twinkledog's honest bark bay in deepmouthed welcome as he heels it down the road to meet us! Roll Swift around, ye Wheels of Time, and bring the welcome Hour!... Yes, the Bayne bill has *passed* the Assembly and victory is ours! The hour to shout has now arrived...! I have refused to feel elated until the bill had passed both houses. Now, however, I feel *thankful* that such a sweet victory has been given us. This signal victory will lead to many others elsewhere. We will make drastic protection measures *fashionable*.[6]

The Bayne bill was a huge victory for the game birds of the eastern United States, and similar laws were quickly passed in Massachusetts and California. Still, Hornaday could not resist a certain amount of ill-tempered grousing when he recalled this fight years later. "What did I get out of it?" he wrote in *Thirty Years War for Wild Life*. "Nothing but a few brief mentions of my name by my jealous rivals far down the list of those who 'assisted in passing the Bayne law.' Not one publication (so far as I am aware) ever gave me one-half the credit for initiative and leadership to which my efforts were entitled; and that same spirit has continued right down to this day—save in the inner circle of my most devoted and generous allies."[7]

Nevertheless, he and his army of partisans continued to rack up significant victories for wildlife. The Weeks-McLean migratory bird bill was passed into federal law in 1913, after first failing to pass Congress and seeming to be almost dead. It was followed by a treaty with Canada to restrict further the hunting and sale of migratory birds. At last, a web of regulations and restrictions that would protect the wildlife of the United States from poachers, pot-hunters, and plumers was beginning to take shape. There were even a few lonely and courageous men who volunteered to serve as wardens in the forgotten places where these crimes against nature were being committed.

Yet still, everywhere Hornaday turned there seemed to be another alarming story unfolding—more dangerous, exhausting, upaid work to be done, fighting hunters, lobbyists, members of Congress, and the somnolent public to protect something that many of them might never see—a mountain sheep on a distant crag, an albatross far out at sea. The Bayne law was a great achievement, but it applied to only one state. What about all the other states?

Through all these bitter battles, some victorious and some not, "Dearest Josie" remained Hornaday's faithful companion and confidante. When they were apart, her letters arrived almost as punctually as the Sun. One day in April 1909, when he was at work in New York and Josephine and their daughter, Helen, were spending a few days at Bethany Beach, in Maryland, she wrote to him:

> Dearly Beloved,
>
> Helen suggests that I do not write you today since she is writing, but how can I allow a mail to go without writing some sort of tribute to you, my own . . . this distance makes one hopelessly helpless. . . .
>
> Last night we took a charming stroll through fragrant sighing pines, yet within sound of the booming ocean. Oh I longed for you, dear heart, and my sighs that it could not be seemed taken up and echoed by the pines. . . . Oh you must someday come here and wander hand in hand with me in these quiet, restful places. . . . No matter where I go, or what I see, there is a sense of incompleteness ever with me, but if my dear comrade were beside me, nothing more could I ask.

Hornaday was by now a respected and well-known figure, constantly in the papers, and he used his growing national reputation as a soapbox from which to preach the gospel of conservation. The downside of his prominence was that he was continually approached by people who came to him with some desperate story seeking his help to save a threatened marsh, a patch of woods, or yet another species that seemed to be under attack. Most of these worthy requests he had to turn down, simply because he was utterly consumed by all his duties, but in 1907, a gentle young watercolorist and amateur naturalist named Henry Wood Elliot came to him with a plea which Hornaday could not refuse.[8]

In 1872, at the age of twenty-six, Elliot had been sent under the auspices of the Smithsonian Institution and the U.S. government to the remote Pribilof Islands, 300 miles off the west coast of Alaska in the Bering Sea, to study the Alaskan fur seal. Elliot became the first person to study, paint—and become enchanted by—these complex and intelligent animals, whose scientific name, *Ursus marinus,* means "sea bear," and which congregated in immense rookeries on the fog-bound rocks of the Pribilofs.

Little was known about them except that they had such luxuriant pelts that hundreds of thousands of them were being killed by American and Canadian sealers every year. Elliot became a firsthand observer of the massacre, and after he enlisted Hornaday's help, the two men spent the next eight years waging what Hornaday later called a "war of the greatest bitterness ever waged in any fight over a wild animal species." The seal population plummeted from 130,000 to less than 30,000, but at the end of the day, it was Elliot, Hornaday, and the sea bears of Alaska who emerged as the winners.

One thing that became evident in this great battle royal was that, without *international* cooperation, any treaty was useless. After all, the U.S. Congress passed a law in 1898 to stop pelagic (open-sea) sealing by American sealers—but that simply left the rookeries ripe for plundering by fleets of Japanese and Russian sealers. International borders are figments of the human imagination; they mean nothing to the ancient migrations and movements of wild populations. (More modern attempts to hammer out international whaling treaties encounter the same difficulties.) It was not until 1911 that the Hay-Elliot Fur Seal Treaty was passed, between Japan, Britain, Russia, and the United States. Stopping all pelagic sealing immediately, it was the first international treaty to protect wildlife. It also put in place a complete five-year ban on *any* sealing anywhere on the islands. By 1930, there were believed to be a million fur seals on the Pribilof Islands. Although Hornaday is often credited with having saved the fur seal from extinction, in his own account of what happened he gives most of the credit to Elliot, a man with "unquenchable personal courage."[9]

Yet even so, these victories often came at such personal cost that they felt almost like defeats. "I have many ex-friends who never will forgive me for having started that fur-seal campaign," Hornaday later wrote. By now he was nearing sixty, and he didn't have the stamina for the fight that he once had.

Furthermore, it made his soul sag to come face to face with the reckless blood-lust that was so common throughout the country. For so many, it didn't matter that the fur seal would likely be wiped off the face of the Earth. That last bundle of sealskins, that last dollar, was all some people ever thought about. So long as there was profit to be had, so long as there was one last nickel to be made, every creature that walked or flew was in peril. And by some dark perversity of human nature, the rarer a species became, the closer it got to its absolute and utter end, the more coveted a trophy it became. It had very nearly happened to the buffalo, and now it had almost happened to the fur seal as well. Didn't anybody ever learn? Was there no end to the greed, stupidity, and short-sightedness of man?

It was necessary and important to fight for federal, state, and local laws to protect wildlife, but there was something else much more fundamental that seemed to be lacking in America: a sense of *moral responsibility*, and *moral outrage*, at what was happening. Wildlife did not *belong* to the hunters, who comprised only about 3 percent of the population, Hornaday argued in his books and articles. It didn't *belong* to the people who lived in rural areas, who tended to think of local birds and game as their birthright. It "belonged"—if it belonged to anyone—to all the people of the United States, and to the world, so it was a shared national responsibity, as well as a national blessing. William Temple Hornaday may not have added any new species to the incunabula of science, but he knew how to stir people's sense of ownership and outrage and, in this way, how to change the world.

In 1911, late at night, after his duties as director of the New York Zoological Park and all the rest of his work were through, William Temple Hornaday would sit down to write one of the angriest and most important books about endangered species ever written. It was to be called *Our Vanishing Wild Life*, and it would catalog, in text and photographs, the appalling condition of birds and game across the United States. Wild things of all kinds were being driven to the brink of extinction not by poachers but by the "armies of destruction"—millions of legally licensed hunters taking to the woods in a country where the hunting laws, such as they were, had essentially been written *by hunters*, to maximize the killing of game. "It is time for all men to be told in the plainest terms that there never has existed, anywhere in historic times, a volume of wild life so great that civilized man could not quickly exterminate it by his methods of destruction."[10]

Even the victories of conservationists seemed tenuous in the face of such unrelenting firepower. It was true that, by the second decade of the twentieth century, the profusion of feathered hats that had crowded the streetcars and boulevards of New York back in 1886 had now almost disappeared. But that didn't mean the feather trade was beaten—far from it, in fact. From his office in the Bronx, all Hornaday had to do was hop a streetcar over to the Manhattan clothing store of E. & S. Meyers, at 688 Broadway, and take a look in the shop window. There on display, like the raiments of angels, were 600 plumes and skins of birds-of-paradise, to be sold for millinery purposes. Birds-of-paradise were, in truth, almost too beautiful for this world. One species had a glimmering green gorget at the throat; others had spectacular explosions of yellow or crimson plumes, with iridescent green and black markings down the neck. Feathers of these birds were so coveted that, between 1904 and 1908, 155,000 carcasses were sold at auction in the London feather markets, according to one contemporary accounting.[11]

But wasn't all that illegal now? Didn't the new game laws prohibit the importation of the skins and plumage of any wild bird, for any commercial purpose whatsoever? Well, not exactly. The feather dealers had discovered a loophole. The Dutcher Law protected from the feather trade *only birds belonging to avian families native to the United States.* But all forty-three species of the bird-of-paradise were native to New Guinea or its surrounding islands. The feather trade had found a hole in the law big enough to drive a delivery truck through, and so they did.[12]

And despite the new fashion sensibilities of women in New York, Hornaday still saw carnage whenever he looked abroad. London, he wrote, was still "the head of the giant octopus" of the plume merchants, reaching its malignant tentacles out to the world's most remote places. Paris was still the manufacturing center of feather trimming and ornaments, employing thousands of people (mostly underpaid women). If the recently broadened mandate of the New York Zoological Society was the protection of "all the wild animals *of the world,*" the theater of war included Paris and London, as well as Berlin and Amsterdam, where brisk business in feathered hats had barely slackened.

As part of his research for his book, and on behalf of the New York Zoological Society, Hornaday dispatched a young ornithologist named C. William Beebe to the London feather markets in

August 1912.[13] It wasn't even necessary for Beebe to go "undercover" in the way of modern reporters; he simply studied the records of activity of the feather dealers as an ordinary businessman would. In three separate sales representing the activity of six months during the previous year, as Beebe reported, four London feather dealers sold skins and plumage representing a total of 223,490 birds. In the London Feather Sale of May 1911, for instance, the firm of Figgis & Co. reported that it had sold the skins and plumage of 362 birds-of-paradise, 384 eagles, 206 trogons, and 24,800 hummingbirds. Beebe's report included only the transactions of four firms, for half the year, so the annual total was approaching half a million birds. And that took no account of all the other London dealers, or those in Paris, Berlin, Amsterdam, or anywhere else.

William Temple Hornaday was a man whose army was always on the march, and who engaged the enemy wherever and whenever his forces seemed most likely to prevail. In January 1913, when *Our Vanishing Wild Life* was so recently published it still smelled like fresh ink, a propitious moment occurred. This time, the battle would occur in the halls of Congress. Now he had a chance to help craft far-reaching legislation that would plug the loophole in the Dutcher Law and protect *any* wild bird, from *anywhere*, from being slaughtered and imported into the United States.[14]

On January 30, when the East was still sheathed in ice and snow, Hornaday took the train down to Washington to appear before the Ways and Means Committee of the U.S. House of Representatives. For the previous month, the 69th Congress had been conducting hearings on a new tariff bill, which would rewrite the laws about products imported into, or exported out of, the United States. The House had requested Hornaday's testimony about the feather trade, and he was prepared to give them an earful.

As a kind of disquieting visual aid, Hornaday brought along with him a suitcase filled with the plumage and the skins of various exotic birds, purchased from the feather dealers. Two weeks earlier, he also had distributed to every member of Congress a freshly printed copy of *Our Vanishing Wild Life*, hoping to soften up the opposition. Even if senators refused to read the book, simply scanning the photographs—a picture of 1,600 hummingbird skins at a London auction house, on sale for two cents each; or a crumpled snowy egret, shot on her own nest as most of them were, wings splayed like a fallen angel—might have been enough to give them pause.

When Hornaday got up to speak on behalf of the New York Zoological Society on January 30, 1913, wearing his best suit and a starched shirt, he told the committee that he believed, if the current practices of the feather trade continued, at least one hundred of the most beautiful and interesting species of birds in the world would soon be exterminated. He told the gathered members of Congress that the new tariff act should prohibit the importation into the United States of *all the wild birds of the world*, not just those from families native to the United States. If Congress could succeed in doing that, the feather dealers' rape of the world's exotic birds might be stopped, or at least signficiantly slowed.

Hornaday's comments, pugnacious and vehement, were followed by those of T. Gilbert Pearson, secretary of the National Audubon Societies, a small, tidy man who gave a measured and careful presentation about declining bird populations to balance Hornaday's super-sized personality. Pearson was followed by ornithologist and lecturer Henry Oldys, whose comments were so fiercely accusatory they could have been uttered by Hornaday himself. The spirit of the age was rife with ignorance, greed, and stupidity, Oldys said, all of which combined

> to exterminate the whale, the seal, the manatee, the alligator, the American antelope, the moose, the caribou.... History will not listen to the plea, "It was not my business." I[t] will answer: "You were there and you could have prevented it; therefore, it was your business. You failed to do your duty. The only explanation is that you were corrupt, ignorant or weak.[15]

A few weeks after Hornaday's testimony, Representative Francis Burton Harrison contacted him to ask if he would draft a clause for the tariff bill that would embody his ideas about the protection of wild birds. Two days later, Hornaday sent Harrison his suggested wording:

> Provided, that the importation of aigrettes, egret plumes, or "osprey" plumes, and the feathers, quills, heads, wings, tails, skins

or parts of skins, of wild birds, either raw or manufactured, and not for scientific or educational purposes, is hereby prohibited; but this provision shall not apply to the feathers or plumes of ostriches, or to the feathers of domestic fowls of any kind.[16]

It seemed an almost airtight ban that would protect all wild birds, from anywhere, from being imported into the United States for any commercial purpose whatsoever. The clause was accepted and incorporated into the new bill, with no changes at all, and the bill passed the House on April 7, 1913.

And that's when the trouble began.

The feather millinery trade had been "caught napping" during the hearings in the House, and its lobbyists and lawyers frankly admitted it. One feather-trade lobbyist named Leo Simon told Hornaday, "You never would have got that clause through the House if I had known what was going on."[17] But now they were awake, and they were going to make sure that Hornaday and his allies did not succeed in final passage of this bill.

One of Hornaday's primary roles in the wildlife wars had always been to serve as a kind of populist rabble-rouser, a tub-thumping provocateur. That was one core purpose of his latest, angriest book. It was as much lobbed firebomb as journalistic reportage. Now he harnessed his ability to incite a riot and his own terrible rage and fear and sent out an emotional, nationwide appeal to the conscience and morality of the women of America. He and his minions sent out the word to thousands of "militant women" around the country, often those who served as presidents or chairwomen of local conservation groups, to contact their state delegations in Congress and prevail on them to fight on behalf of the birds. And the women took up the call.

The feather lobbyists responded to this with a trickier, more weasel-like approach. They didn't turn to the public at all (likely because they knew they would lose in the court of public opinion—125 newspapers in thirty-three states had come out in favor of the ban on feather imports, and only *one* spoke up in support of the feather trade). Instead, the lobbyists presented written briefs to an obscure, special subcommittee of the Senate Finance Committee, which had only three members but which also had the power to affect the outcome of the debate. The lobbyists had only three hearts they needed to change, not millions. It became clear that they might prevail after all, in spite of everything.

In a desperate, last-ditch effort, Hornaday enlisted the outrage of the general public, as he had so many times before. He drafted an indignant, three-page pamphlet that he titled, as if he were yelling the whole thing, "The Steam Roller Of The Feather Importers In The United States Senate; The Lobby Of The Feather Trade Jubilant— Thus Far; A Warning To The American People": "The two dozen or so supporting millinery houses of New York who make a specialty of wild birds' plumage and skins, are driving a steam roller through the United States Senate, flattening out all opposition to the 'feather trade,'" Hornaday began his bitter screed. "Though the hands that guide their steam roller are visible, the power that propels it is unseen and mysterious."[18]

Up until now, both houses of Congress had "patriotically responded to every reasonable appeal made to them in behalf of vanishing wildlife," he wrote. And when the House had been presented with Hornaday's proposed clause to protect wild birds in the new tariff bill, they had acted honorably—when uninfluenced by the lobbyists for the feather dealers. But when it came before the Senate, the merchants' shrewd, subterranean lobbyists had managed to sway the crucial subcommittee and circumvent the will of the people.

The choice before the American people now was stark, Hornaday bellowed in his pamphlet, in boldfaced italics: "Shall the two or three dozen New York importers of wild birds' plumage be permitted to defeat the will of two or three dozen millions of American people who abhor the traffic and desire its discontinuance?"

He sent the pamphlet out to twenty-four leaders of the conservation movement of the day, including Gilbert Pearson; Henry Oldys; Joseph Grinnell, of the California Academy of Sciences; Warren Miller, editor of *Field and Stream*; ornithologist William Brewster; and prominent women conservationists Louise Blocki, May Riley Smith, Sadie American, and Katherine Stuart. They all signed it, without making a single change. Hornaday also appended a list of the dozens of senators, both Republican and Democratic, who supported the feather ban.

When the pamphlet was printed, signed, and sent out to all the members of the U.S. Senate, Hornaday later recalled, "I quaked with fear that I would be hauled before the bar of the Senate for high treason, or at least contempt; but nothing of that kind happened." One of the subcommittee's members, Hoke Smith of Georgia, did have something to say about Hornaday and his little pamphlet, however: "I want to say for myself that, if he is no more truthful in his other publications than he was in that, the article was so utterly false, I would not care to read anything he wrote." Senator George McLean, from Connecticut, tried to soothe Smith a bit by saying that "they are zealous men, these ornithologists."[19]

When the plumage clause of the tariff bill came up for discussion in the Democratic caucus, the *Washington Post* later reported, it caused a heated argument that raged for five hours. When the caucus at last voted—deciding to throw out Hornaday's clause completely and accept the wording of the feather trade—Senators George E. Chamberlain and Harry Lane, both of Oregon, stood up to protest. They bitterly denounced the decision to essentially withdraw all protections for birds, and they announced their intention to withdraw from the caucus if the decision held. Hornaday was told later that, because "no party likes to provoke any of its important members into bolting," the decision of the caucus was then reversed, and the measure passed with Hornaday's original wording intact.

The birds had won the day.

Because of their "fearless and determined leadership in saving the feather millinery cause from annihilation," Hornaday later wrote in *Thirty Years War for Wild Life*, America owed a debt of gratitude to Senators Chamberlain and Lane, the good gentlemen from Oregon, who had staked their reputations on protecting the birds. A month later, President Woodrow Wilson signed into law paragraph 347 of the Wilson Tariff Act, broadly prohibiting the importation of plumes and skins of wild birds for any commercial purpose whatsoever.[20] For his efforts in this fight, Hornaday was awarded a silver medal from the French conservation group the Societe d'Acclimatation, and a gold one from Britain's Royal Society for the Protection of Birds.[21]

A snowy egret on her nest in the Everglades, a courting bird-of-paradise on the Aru Islands, a lyrebird cooing in the Australian outback—all could rest better now (though they did not know it) because strong new legal protections had taken effect that would help keep their human enemies at bay.

CHAPTER 19

Two Hundred Years of War

In 1926, at the age of seventy-two, William Temple Hornaday retired as director of the New York Zoological Park, after three decades of service. An adoring notice of his retirement, published in *Time* magazine, referred to him as "the presiding genius and animal-man of the Bronx." The *New York Times* observed that "if the vanishing wild life that he had labored to save could know that their great good friend was leaving a post that had given him so much authority as their foremost champion, there would be mourning in the ranges, in the high woods, and among the Sierras."[1]

But among all the many notable battles Hornaday had won, there was one he'd lost. Around the turn of the century, he'd sent letters to sixteen New York daily newspapers demanding that his place of employment be referred to as "The New York Zoological Park," and not—God forbid—"the Bronx Zoo." The latter, he sniffed, was "undignified, offensive . . . injurious . . . unnecessary, and therefore inexcusable." The only people in the city who needed to be told that the zoo was in the Bronx were "newly arrived immigrants, and the harmless imbeciles in our asylums for the insane."[2]

The papers, refusing to cooperate, gently chided the director. At a time when doggerel poetry was considered a form of journalism, one printed a ditty that began:

My name is William Hornaday–
A trifle pedagogical.

DIRECTOR I! With ALL to say!
My park is zoological.[3]

Despite his best efforts, "the Bronx Zoo" stuck. But whatever it was called, in his thirty years at its helm, Hornaday had transformed the zoo from 200 acres of woods and an idea into something truly splendid. The society's executive committee, in a letter accepting his resignation, praised Hornaday for having created "the most beautiful, the most popular, and the most widely known zoological park in the world."[4]

On his last day, Hornaday snapped closed his big rolltop desk in the zoo director's office, took the subway to 125th Street and then the train to the Anchorage, his home in Stamford, Connecticut, where the long-suffering Josephine awaited him, as always. On the occasion of their fortieth wedding anniversary, Hornaday had penned six stanzas of adoration to her, called "A Gratitude Monument," accompanied by a pencil sketch of an enormous marble tower, akin to the Washington Monument, that he wished he could build her in tribute to their years together. The last stanza read:

Each day I humbly thank the gods
For Thee, my Peerless Wife
Who forty years, through hopes and fears,
Has blessed my daily life.[5]

But his return to the arms of Josephine was hardly the final curtain call of his life. In fact, on the May afternoon he retired, he was in the vortex of so many campaigns in the war for wildlife he hardly knew which way to turn. While other septuagenarians were settling into a sweet, harmless decrepitude, Hornaday was shouting from the rootops, screaming bloody murder.

There had been great strategic victories over the years, but he never believed that he had succeeded in "winning" the fight for wildlife, or anything like it. "Anyone who thinks that the wild life of America, Europe, Africa, or India has been 'saved' is deceived," he wrote. "Today it is not necessary for anyone to write a book to prove its peril. The only real issue is, *What shall be done about it, if anything?*"[6]

Years earlier, Hornaday had realized that the task of raising funds for each of these individual wildlife campaigns was too inefficient, and too exhausting, to continue. What was needed was some permanent endowment to sustain the long-term war itself, not just each individual engagement. Having a permanent endowment would have several other tactical advantages as well. In the heat of battle, his enemies often had secretly tried to exert pressure on the Zoological Society to get him fired—in the bitter fur-seal fight, there even had been a massive "Stop Hornaday" campaign—but if his activities were privately endowed, he'd be safe from that kind of "backdoor molestation," as he called it.[7]

In 1911, Hornaday laid out a plan to create what he called the Permanent Wild Life Protection Fund, an endowment of at least $100,000 raised by appeals to the conservation-minded public. The organization would be stripped down for war, with three trustees but no president, no vice presidents, and no committees of any kind. Essentially, it would be William Temple Hornaday, fueled by donations, with "absolute freedom of action." But the fund would not merely be a vehicle for his own personal vendettas; Hornaday conceived of it as an entity that would continue the fight long after his death—in fact, for at least the next 200 years—with a succession of other brave crusaders taking the helm. On into the misty future, it was hard to say which species would be desperately imperiled, which embattled local army might need reinforcements or flanking fire, but it was certain that the side of the angels would need money, and someone like William Temple Hornaday, to lead the troops into the breach. (Although the Permanent Wild Life Protection Fund did not live much longer than Hornaday, other organizations that he helped found, such as the Wildlife Conservation Society—a successor organization to the New York Zoological Society—live on to this day.)[8]

"I would just like to know how many of my enemies have gnashed their teeth in impotent rage when they found it utterly impossible to find on this earth any man who could-and-would put a ball and chain upon me," he chortled gleefully, after the Permanent Wild Life Protection Fund had been established and had repeatedly outfoxed his foes.[9]

His enemies must have despaired, too, because Hornaday's energy, even into his eighties, was incredible. "Today, at 80, I am 'elderly' but not 'old,'" he told the *New York Times Magazine* in 1935. "My faculties are in first-class working condition, my face is unlined, my relish for food would shame a wolf. I sleep like a boy. As 'old age' goes, I will not be through even at 90."[10] During and after World War I, when he began ranting as loudly and persistently against the "Huns," the Bolsheviks, and the Socialists as he had against the enemies of wildlife, one observer noted, "Dr. Hornaday may not have won the war single-handedly, but he tried."[11]

He never stopped working, talking, lecturing, writing, or sending blistering letters-to-the-editor in local districts where he had read or heard of some environmental outrage. He never seemed to have fewer than five or six balls in the air at once. His vehemence and his vividness made it impossible to be neutral about him. Even his friends sometimes found him too much to take. George Bird Grinnell of the Audubon Society once wrote that Hornaday was "often irritating," and that he really only represented "himself and a proportion of sentimentalists of the country, most of whom are women and children." But the *Columbus Dispatch*, among his many other defenders, editorialized that Hornaday was "as agreeable a gentleman as one ever met, and so imbued with the importance of his work that he has become a sort of patron saint to nature-lovers all over the United States."[12]

Between 1913 and 1930, Hornaday and the Permanent Wild Life Protection Fund fought an astonishing series of battles in defense of wild things and wild places. He fought successfully for the passage of the Weeks-McLean Migratory Bird Law of 1913, which paved the way for a broad new federal law to protect migratory birds, the U.S. Bird Treaty Act of 1918. He fought, this time unsuccessfully, to create no-kill game sancturies within national forests, undertaking a brutal fourteen-city lecture tour to promote the idea, but at the end of the day, he was forced to taste bitter defeat. He fought for long closed seasons on mountain sheep in the Western states, as well as protection for the pronghorned antelope. He succeeded in imposing a five-year ban on hunting of the endangered prairie chicken and remnant quail in Iowa. In 1918, he helped kill the Sulzer Alaskan Game Bill, which would have opened the door to the year-round sale of moose, caribou, mountain sheep, and deer meat, allegedly "to help win the war," but really to declare a permanent open season on Alaskan big game. Later, Hornaday waded into the fight to rewrite the whole code of game laws in Alaska, arousing intense hostility in the state but ultimately succeeding. With the crusading editor of the *People's*

Home Journal magazine, Hornaday spearheaded a six-year campaign to create bird sanctuaries around the country, ultimately creating 9,066 protected reserves encompassing a total of 2.7 million acres. He fought and killed a plan to make an enormous swath of Louisiana Gulf Coast into a private shooting club for 4,000 duck hunters. Hornaday even took on fights to save endangered game and birds in South Africa and France.[13]

Long after his retirement from his official duties at the zoo, Hornaday kept up a merciless long-distance bombardment from his bunker at No. 1 Bank Street, in Stamford, Connecticut, a small rented office not far from his home. From there, he published a militant broadsheet, *The Plain Truth About Game Conservation,* with the belligerent subtitle *For The Information of Congress, The Press and the People. Take It Or Leave It!*

But Hornaday's two bitterest and most central campaigns, of which *The Plain Truth* and any number of smaller skirmishes were only a part, were the fights to reduce bag limits and to reduce the absurd lethality of automatic and pump shotguns. He believed there was no possible way that the birds and game of the United States could survive for long when—just to take one example—in 1930, there were twenty-eight states in which hunters were restricted to a daily limit of twenty-seven ducks, geese, and brant. *Twenty-seven a day!* And the new automatic shotguns—what Hornaday called "machine guns" or "slaughter guns"—were able to fire six blasts of buckshot in six seconds, without the hunter ever having to lift the weapon from his shoulder. What living thing could survive this fusillade for very long?[14]

Hornaday, of course, was well acquainted with the thrill of the hunt, and he loved the feel, the look, the engineering, the power, and even the smell of guns. He took pains to point out that there were plenty of conscientious sportsmen out there who brought a sense of ethics and decency to hunting. Some hunting clubs, such as the Boone and Crockett Club and later Ducks Unlimited, were leading conservationists; many of the higher-class hunt clubs had already foresworn the use of automatic weapons. Although he argued that longer closed seasons and lower bag limits would ultimately *increase* the amount of game available to hunters, there was no way around the awkward truth: he was trying to separate men from their guns. And in America, nothing struck a nerve like that.

And, in fact, though Hornaday fought like a demon for decades, the fight against automatic and pump guns was one that he mostly lost. The hunters argued that it didn't matter *how* game was killed, if hunters just killed to their legal limit. But Hornaday responded that these weapons promoted the maximum amount of killing, creating a new class of killer known as a "game hog," and also left appalling numbers of animals crippled or dying in the woods. "Anti-machine-gun bills" were introduced in every state legislature where Hornaday was encouraged to do so, but he almost never succeeded in getting them passed. Finally, in 1934, President Franklin Roosevelt issued a new hunting regulation that reduced the capacity of repeating shot-guns down to three shots at one blast. This was, Hornaday wrote, "tardy and imperfect fruit, much too late . . . three shots are 33 per-cent too many."[15]

In 1931, Hornaday's angry screed *Thirty Years War for Wild Life* was published. It was meant as a kind of strategic update on *Our Vanishing Wild Life*, published nineteen years earlier. The book laid out, in depressing detail, what had happened during the past two decades of war, how the enemy was currently positioned, and what Hornaday felt the most pressing tactical goals should be. Despite all the successes, the story it told was grim, and as usual, Horna-day made no particular effort to conceal his rage. "This volume is 'polite literature,'" he wrote, "but if there needs to be a next one, it is going to be so impolite as to demand judgement on all men and organizations who attempt to block the road to constructive conser-vation. . . . There will be either some sweeping reforms, or a sweeping disaster!"[16]

Just take a look at the basic math, he told his readers. In the 1931 hunting season, forty-eight huge armies, in the forty-eight states, would take to the woods and fields of the United States. These armies were immense and terrifying: the number of licensed hunt-ers amounted to nearly 6.5 million, and when added to the 1.5 mil-lion unlicensed hunters who legally hunted local game on their own land, the grand total amounted to more than 7.5 million well-armed and well-equipped gunners. This was equivalent to "*7,500 regiments of full strength, a number far exceeding all the active standing armies in the world!*" (italics in original). Compared to the time less than two decades earlier when *Our Vanishing Wild Life* was written, this represented a *400 percent increase* in the numbers of hunters taking to the field. Where did any thinking person suppose all this would eventually lead? Hornaday wanted to know. And what, if anything, was to be done about it?[17]

William Temple Hornaday intended to spend the last years of his life doing something about it, no matter what the personal cost, and no matter how many enemies he might make along the way. His foes claimed that "Hornaday wants to stop all hunting," or that "Hornaday offers bag-limits as the one cure-all and panacea for the disappearance of game." Well, he retorted, he was certainly no sentimentalist, and he certainly did not want to put a complete end to hunting. In fact, he wrote, "no other person living has published as many lists of the various causes of game disappearance, or of the different things to be done for game salvage, as W. T. Hornaday has done, from 1897 down to 1930."[18]

All he wanted to do was save the wildlife of North America, a birthright to all those who were born here and all the future generations to come. His intentions were not veiled or secretive—far from it, in fact. He'd nailed them to the door in *Our Vanishing Wild Life*, as Martin Luther had, and now, in *Thirty Years War*, he nailed them up there again, for all the world to see. They were as bold, straightforward, and plainspoken as he was:

> *Stop the sale of wild game, everywhere.*
> *Stop all shooting of birds in winter and spring.*
> *Stop the use of "pump" and "automatic" guns in hunting.*
> *Stop all shooting of shore birds, doves, robins, and squirrels as "game" and "food."*
> *Reduce all bag limits from 50 to 75 per cent.*
> *Shorten all open seasons at least 50 per cent.*
> *Stop, all over the world, the killing of birds for commercial or millinery purposes.*
> *Establish 5- or 10-year close seasons for all endangered species.*[19]

It was, in effect, a bold and ambitious battle plan to make the world safe for the wild things. To accomplish this, more close-quarters combat would be required than any one person could ever execute, even someone as tireless as Hornaday. It would take decades, or even centuries, to achieve. But it had to be done. Because through long and bitter experience, William Temple Hornaday was convinced that the enemies of wildlife had not been defeated.

They had just paused to reload.

His Indomitable Persistence

On the pale winter afternoon of January 4, 1937, an ailing, nearly crippled, eighty-three-year-old William Temple Hornaday began dictating a long letter to someone he considered an old friend, whom he nonetheless addressed with appropriate diffidence as "His Excellency, Franklin D. Roosevelt, President of the United States."[1]

That same day, a grainy black-and-white close-up of FDR graced the cover of the latest issue of *Life* magazine. The long story inside was essentially a congratulatory victory lap for Roosevelt's frenetic first term in office, describing the popular president as "a triumphant hero with a smile of silver and a voice of gold." In other news stories, the prominent modernist clergyman Harry Emerson Fosdick was quoted as predicting that "war, in time, will go the way of torture chambers, religious persecution, slavery, and a hundred other social ills that once ruled the world."[2] Meanwhile, it was reported that in Germany, a twenty-one-year-old Dutch stonemason named Marinus Van Der Lubbe was beheaded after confessing to setting a fire in the Reichstag. The executioner, wearing evening clothes and white gloves, pushed a button on the scaffold and Van Der Lubbe's head rolled into a pail of sawdust. The new German chancellor, a gloomy little man named Adolf Hitler, blamed the communists for the fire and vowed revenge.

For Hornaday, what was happening in Europe was another frightful menace about which the world needed to be warned. But by now, after forty years of fighting, Hornaday was growing weary, and his body was failing. Besides the neuritis that plagued his feet and legs, he was tormented by arthritis, by cataracts, and by ill-fitting dentures. Every day was a cavalcade of pain. Still, he longed to be back on his feet and back in the fight. He wrote to his nephew Willis:

> The doctors are completely baffled. I have been most searchingly examined by a famous nerve expert of New York who is an old friend of mine, who after he had finished his second investigation rose wearily and said to the other doctor in consultation, "There is nothing the matter with this man except those damn legs."

Above the hips, Hornaday told Willis, "I am sound as a nut."[3]

Meanwhile, although his beloved wife, Josephine, also was growing feeble with age, their devotion to each other had never faltered. In 1929, the *New York Tribune* ran a story about the Hornadays' fifty-year wedding anniversary. Two professors at Stanford had come out with a controversial study claiming that the men of America were being "feminized" by their wives, but if that was so, Hornaday said, it wasn't hurting them. "I hate domineering men and I don't admire domineering women. It should be a fifty-fifty proposition." Because of the fact that he and Josephine "scrupulously and honestly respected each other's rights," they had not had a quarrel in half a century, he said.[4]

Yet despite all the successes and accolades of his life, there were times in the previous years when Hornaday saw clearly how badly his war for wildlife was going, and he succumbed to despair. More and more, he took to referring to his life's work as "The Thankless Task."

"I am too tired to think about our wildlife protection campaign," he'd written his friend Edmund Seymour a few years earlier, "but I do know that the general situation is 90 per cent hopeless."[5]

Now, on what he knew would soon become his deathbed—his life would end here on this pillow two months later—he summoned the strength for one last appeal. This time, he wished to address "His Excellency" on behalf of all the glorious migratory waterfowl of the United States, which he desperately feared were going the way of the heath hen, the passenger pigeon, the auk, and all the other vanished species of the earth.

"Because of our long acquaintance and unbroken friendship," Hornaday began, dictating to a secretary named Betty who was seated beside the bed.[6] He hoped that President Roosevelt "would be willing to grant me a brief interview if I were well enough to stand on my feet and go to Washington to call on you in person." But this was utterly impossible, owing to the fact that he was now bedridden and "secretly and confidentially, I am thinking that the miseries I am undergoing here in my bed will finish me pretty soon by nervous exhaustion. It may easily happen that this is the last letter that you will ever receive from your long-time but faithful and sincere friend."

Then Hornaday laid out what he was after: a complete ban on all hunting of waterfowl, for three consecutive years. In a country in love with its guns, and in which duck hunters numbered in the hundreds of thousands, it was an impossibly bold request, a non-starter, ridiculous. But he didn't care. The hour was late, and the damage to waterfowl populations across the country was so severe that it would take at least three years for them to recover, if they could recover at all. "Secretly," he told the president, "I am hoping that before January goes out, you will boldly and forcefully make an announcement that there will be no open season on waterfowl. . . . I say to you in all seriousness that the only way to bring back the ducks in our country at large, and stock the sanctuaries that you have created, can be accomplished only by *three straight years* of absolute closed season."[7]

The situation had grown so dire that "in spite of a long and painful illness, I published during the last year two more warnings to the President, to Congress, the general public and all sportsmen, of the impending doom of our remainders of North American waterfowl," Hornaday wrote. But now, in his pain and isolation, he had begun to feel that all his appeals had gone unheard.

Hornaday knew well enough that Roosevelt had a long history of concern for the natural world. Like many early conservationists, he was a patrician, and as a young man, he had replanted trees on worn-out farmland at his family's Hudson River estate in Hyde Park. When he registered to vote in 1910, he'd given his profession as "tree grower," and over his lifetime, he calculated that he had grown half a million trees. He created waterfowl sanctuaries at Hyde Park and posted his land to keep birds and game safe from hunters. And he was an avid fisherman. Now Hornaday leaned heavily on these sympathies, knowing that Roosevelt would be receptive to some of what he had to say, if not all. The way forward, as Hornaday saw it, required a stark choice:

Most earnestly and respectfully I point out to you the fact that because of the multitude of curses that have been afflicting the game of the United States during the past 40 years, and the utter inability of the game-defenders to catch up with the game-killers and pass them, you now stand at the forks of a road.

For Hornaday, there was always a fork in the road, always a stark choice. His Seventh-day Adventist upbringing had imbued every human action with the imperatives of moral force. There was right and there was wrong. There was triumph or there was disaster, eternal reward or eternal damnation. Hornaday was self-righteous, he was stubborn, he was inflexible, and he might not always be right. But he was always sure. Now he tried to coax the president onto the right path, like an obstinate mule:

The right hand road . . . lead[s] to the conservation of the remnants of our waterfowl fauna. . . . The left-hand road that lies before you leads to total extinction—of not only our waterfowl, but also in equal probability, though not quite so quickly in effect, to the extinction of our faunas of upland non-migratory game birds and small mammals, and finally all of our free, wild, and killable big game animals outside of protected areas.

In conclusion, the old man thundered, summoning the old fire from his sickbed, "I am opposed to seeing the United States become a desert destitute of wild life or forests, or both. I urge you to be the master of this situation, and not the servant, or the victim of it."

He closed on a note of hopefulness. He was not alone in this fight—even though in his younger day he had sometimes felt as if he were—and neither was the president. A groundswell of rage and fear had swept through the country in previous years, leading to the creation of vast armies of conservation-minded citizens across the country. In some significant ways, the tide actually seemed to be turning in favor of the wild things. In the summer of 1935, Hornaday told Roosevelt, fully one-third of all the duck hunters in the United States—210,000 men and women in all—had chosen to hang up their guns for the season because they, too, had seen what was happening to the great migrations of waterfowl that once darkened the skies from Currituck Sound, North Carolina, to the lost lakes of

Minnesota. Flights of ducks and geese in a pale autumn sky were as stirring and majestic a thing, as *American*, as the heartland's "golden waves of grain." These reformed hunters wished to be part of the glory of the birds, not part of their annihilation. They wished to be on the side of the angels on Judgment Day. And the president could be, too.

A couple of weeks after Hornaday mailed his ten-page letter to the president, an important-looking envelope with an embossed return address marked "The White House, Washington, D.C." fell through the mail slot at 20 West North Street in Stamford, Connecticut.

"My dear Dr. Hornaday," the letter from President Roosevelt began, "it is with feelings of great regret that I read the note accompanying your letter of January fourth and learn of your suffering. I hope it may afford you some consolation to know that I have the greatest admiration for your courage and for your continued devotion in the presence of physical pain and weariness to that cause to which you have devoted your years. Since you can not give me the pleasure of an interview, you may be assured that your written statement will be carefully read and with the consideration it so eminently deserves."[8]

A few days later, from his sickbed, Hornaday dictated a letter to his grandson, Dodge. He enclosed a copy of the letter from Roosevelt. The president's letter was, Hornaday wrote, "one of the most charming and sympathetic letters that I am sure was ever sent from the White House to an old broken campaigner who wished to score once more in a public cause before closing his account."[9]

William Temple Hornaday had been unconscious for several days before he slipped away forever on March 6, 1937, in his comfortable bedroom at the place he called The Anchorage. His ever-faithful life companion, Josephine—The Empress, Her Royal Highness, My Dear Old Goose, Fairest Among 10,000—was at his side, along with their daughter, Helen.

Although President Roosevelt did not close the waterfowl hunting season for three consecutive years, or even one year, he honored Hornaday's legacy in another way. A year after the old naturalist's death, Roosevelt suggested that a mountain peak in Yellowstone National Park be named after him. Today, Mount Hornaday stands over the pristine Lamar River Valley at the northeast corner of the park, overlooking grassy uplands and cottonwood brakes, where droves of buffalo roam in the late afternoon sun much as they may have appeared to native people 10,000 years ago. It's not too far from the scene of Hornaday's "Last Buffalo Hunt" of 1886.[10] The Boy Scouts' Wildlife Protection Medal, which Hornaday created in 1915, was renamed the William T. Hornaday Award after his death, and it is still bestowed today.

Another honorific arrived unexpectedly in the mail in October 1936, just three months before Hornaday's death. George S. Meyers, a renowned ichthyologist at Stanford University (who first described the common aquarium fish called the neon tetra), wrote the old man a letter to say that, as part of his work classifying fish specimens for the National Museum, he had come across several species collected by Hornaday in Borneo fifty-nine years earlier. A couple turned out to be completely new to science, Meyers said, and one he'd officially named after Hornaday. *Polynemus hornadayi*, or "Hornaday's paradise fish," was a small, curious "threadfish" festooned with a cluster of graceful, translucent filaments attached near its pectoral fins, and which streamed gaily out behind, two and a half times longer than the fish itself. Hornaday had been twenty-three years old when he'd collected this shimmering oddity in a dip-net on the afternoon of October 2, 1877, in a muddy tributary of the Sadong River, in southwestern Sarawak, Borneo. In his letter and a scientific paper that accompanied it, Meyers told Hornaday that he'd long been familiar with *Two Years in the Jungle*, "one of the classics of zoological exploration in Asia," and that he was "exceedingly glad to be able to associate your name with at least one of the fishes you collected on your memorable trip for Ward's."[11]

Even so, despite his fifty-year strut on the national stage, and all his many accomplishments, William Temple Hornaday seems to have been largely forgotten by historians. It's fair to ask why this small, loud, imperfect man's life has slipped into obscurity. Was the Ota Benga incident so repellant that it permanently expunged all his achievements from history? Were his contributions to conservation simply eclipsed by greater men like Theodore Roosevelt, John Muir, or John Burroughs? Or is his disappearing act at least partly payback for the long enemies list he racked up during his life? In a 1971 book, Frank Graham, Jr., a chronicler of the conservation movement in America, wrote of Hornaday: "Militants seldom attract eulogists.

The directness with which [Hornaday] attacked every problem accounts for the planned obscurity into which other conservationists let his name drop immediately after his death."[12]

Yet his life *did* attract eulogists, and a good number of them at that. Several years before his death, when it was clear that the old lion was not much longer for this world, the editors of *Outdoor Life* magazine published a laudatory remembrance of him. "In the long and often weary annals of conservation progress, no man has been less bowed beneath reverses or less satisfied with success than Dr. Hornaday," the editors wrote. "Determined and intransigent, it was never his policy to go around or under an opponent; smashing straight through his opposition, he has left a long trail of personal enemies in his wake—but has never looked back. Sold out by game-hogs in high places, rebuffed by organizations purporting to have a conservation purpose, deserted even by high-principled and well-intentioned leaders who felt him too radical or truculent for his time, much of Dr. Hornaday's far-seeing effort has been single-handed. In his day of triumph, let his indomitable persistence be remembered."[13]

William Temple Hornaday's life is not simply some Gilded Age antique, as quaint and outdated as a Stanley Steamer. The war for wildlife to which he devoted his life is a battle that still rages on, with this morning's paper no doubt bringing news of some fragile species in peril, some dim fen falling to the onslaughts of human progress. Hornaday's contentious life and bloody crusades are as vivid and as relevant today—perhaps more so—than they were when he died almost eighty years ago.

But his loud, large life also changed the world for the better. Organizations that he helped build, legislation that he helped pass, and the sense of moral outrage that he helped set aflame have all made our world safer for wild things and wild places. The New York Zoological Society, where Hornaday served for thirty years, is now known as the Wildlife Conservation Society; it manages some 200 million acres of protected lands around the world, with more than 500 field conservation projects in sixty countries.[14] The bison, once a whisper away from extinction, now number about half a million in North America alone (though only about 30,000 of these are genetically pure, free-roaming animals).[15] In 2008, about 121,000 fur seal pups were born on the Pribilof Islands.[16] And the North American population of the snowy egret, once hunted to the verge of annihilation for its spectacular plumes, is now thought to number about 143,000 (though it is still considered a threatened species).[17]

George Bernard Shaw once famously remarked, "[N]othing is ever accomplished by a reasonable man." And William Temple Hornaday, whatever else he may have been, was without doubt the most unreasonable of men. Had it not been for his prophetic vision, his baleful and impolite pronouncements, and his unwillingness to sit still when he saw a crime being committed, our world would be poorer, sadder, less various, and less beautiful than it is. But were he alive today, no doubt he would tell you that his life's work is far from over. In fact, it has scarcely begun.

ACKNOWLEDGMENTS

There are a host of individuals I'd like to thank for their assistance and erudition in the preparation of this book. I owe a debt of gratitude to those who read and commented on the manuscript, including my brother Lawrence Bechtel, who's always been smarter than me; my smart and now grown-up children Adam and Lilly; my friend Jim Crawford; the apostate Dr. Steve Cory and his University of Chicago book group; and the brilliant Robert L. O'Connell. Thanks to my little "home group," Anya, Sammy, and Milo, for support and succor. I'd like to thank my agent, Don Fehr, for placing the book with Beacon Press, as well as my indefatigable editor, Alexis Rizzuto, and the rest of the staff at Beacon, who recognized the book's merit and tried to give it a fair shake in the marketplace. Two scholar-historians are owed special mention here: Gregory Dehler, of Lehigh University, who wrote a dissertation about Hornaday and a century of wildlife protection in America; and James Dolph, of the University of Massachusetts, whose dissertation focused on the part of Hornaday's life that fell in the nineteenth century. Both provided invaluable research and insight into this extraordinarily complex and interesting man. Finally, I'd like to thank the better angels of Dr. Hornaday himself, who, despite his manifest flaws, was an inspiration to me throughout the writing of this book.

NOTES

PROLOGUE: THE FEAR

1. Hornaday, *Eighty Fascinating Years*, chapter 20, page 1.
2. Hornaday, *Thirty Years War for Wild Life*, p. xi.
3. Hornaday, *Eighty Fascinating Years*, chapter 20, p. 3.
4. Ibid., p. 4.
5. Ibid., chapter 9, p. 11.
6. Ibid., chapter 20, p. 3.
7. Hornaday, *Use and Abuse of America's Natural Resources*, p. 18.
8. Hornaday, *Eighty Fascinating Years*, chapter 20, p. 1.
9. Niles Eldredge, "The Sixth Extinction," ActionBioScience.org (http://www.actionbioscience.org/).

CHAPTER 1: HIS NAME WAS DAUNTLESS

This account of "the last buffalo hunt," clearly one of the signature events of William Hornaday's life, is based largely on the three accounts he wrote of it, each with varying levels of detail and emphasis, as well as his journals from the field. He described these events in *The Extermination of the American Bison* in fairly clipped, scientific fashion; in *A Wild-Animal Round-Up* in a rollicking, popularized way (which first was published in the *Cosmopolitan Magazine* in 1887); and in his unpublished autobiography, *Eighty Fascinating Years*, a similar account filled with bitterly remembered detail and melancholy emotion.

1. Hornaday, *Extermination of the American Bison*, p. 229
2. Philadelphia Zoo website, http://www.philadelphiazoo.org.
3. Hornaday, *Extermination of the American Bison*, p. 229.

4. Hornaday, *Eighty Fascinating Years*, chapter 10, p. 4.

5. Hornaday, *Extermination of the American Bison*, p. 227.

6. Hornaday, *Eighty Fascinating Years*, chapter 10, p. 4.

7. "Sleeping car" entry, *Wikipedia*, http://en.wikipedia.org/.

8. Dolph, "Bringing Wildlife to Millions," p. 400.

9. *Harper's Weekly*, January 1869.

10. Roosevelt, *Hunting Trips of a Ranchman*, p. 244.

11. Dolph, "Bringing Wildlife to Millions," pp. 13–15.

12. Hornaday, *Eighty Fascinating Years*, chapter 2, pp. 1–2; "Behind the Scenes: King Kong," *Stereotype & Society* blog, May 27, 2007, http://stereotype andsociety.typepad.com.

13. Brinkley, *Wilderness Warrior*, p. 281.

14. *Chicago Tribune*, November 22, 1886, cited in Hornaday, *Thirty Years War for Wild Life*, p. 100.

15. *Popular Science Monthly* 37, 1890, p. 276.

16. "John James Audubon" entry in *Wikipedia*, http://en.wikipedia.org/.

17. Dolph, "Bringing Wildlife to Millions," p. 400.

18. William T. Hornaday, "Progress Report of Exploration for Buffalo," cited in Ibid., p. 398.

19. Dolph, "Bringing Wildlife to Millions," pp. 401–2.

20. "The Battle of the Little Bighorn, 1876," *Eyewitness to History* website, http://www.eyewitnesstohistory.com/.

21. *The Northern Pacific Railway, Main Street of the Northwest*, http://www .american-rails.com.

22. Taos and Santa Fe Painters website, http://www.charlesmarionrussell .com.

23. Doughty, *Feather Fashions and Bird Preservation*, p. 16.

24. Hornaday, *Our Vanishing Wild Life*, p. 247.

CHAPTER 2: A MELANCHOLY INSANITY

1. Trudeau, *Southern Storm*, p. 25.

2. Letter from Ellen Sherman to John Sherman, in Lewis, *Sherman*, p. 203.

3. Letter from William Tecumseh Sherman to the City Council of Atlanta, September 12, 1864, TeachingAmericanHistory.org.

4. "Tecumseh" article, *Encyclopedia Britannica Online*, http://www .britannica.com/.

5. Hine, *American West*, p. 127.

6. Sherman to Sheridan, May 10, 1868, in Athearn, *William Tecumseh Sherman and the Settlement of the West*, p. 197.

7. Marszalek, *Sherman*, p. 423.

8. American Indian Genocide Museum website, http://www.aigenom.com/ Delano.html.

9. Punke, *Last Stand.*

10. Grinnell, *Hunting and Conservation,* p. 219.

11. *Annual Report of the Commissioner of Indian Affairs to the Secretary for the Year 1871.*

12. "The Last Buffalo," *Harper's Weekly,* June 6, 1874.

13. Blackmore's preface, in Dodge, *Plains of the Great West and Their Inhabitants,* p. xii.

14. Rinella, *American Buffalo,* p. 158.

15. Estimate by George Catlin, cited by Rita Laws, "Native Americans and Vegetarianism," *VRG Journal,* September 1994.

16. Hornaday, *Extermination of the American Bison,* pp. 173–181.

CHAPTER 3: THE SECOND CIVIL WAR

1. Hornaday, *Eighty Fascinating Years,* chapter 10, p. 7.

2. Dolph, "Bringing Wildlife to Millions," p. 402; Drover House website, http://www.droverhouse.com.

3. "History and Genealogy," Miles City (MT) On the Web, http://milescity.com/history/.

4. Dolph, "Bringing Wildlife to Millions," p. 402.

5. Hornaday, *Eighty Fascinating Years,* chapter 10, p. 6.

6. Dolph, "Bringing Wildlife to Millions," pp. 407–10.

7. Hornaday, *Extermination of the American Bison,* p. 230.

8. Dolph, "Bringing Wildlife to Millions," pp. 414–17.

9. Ibid., 418.

10. Hornaday, *Extermination of the American Bison,* p. 230.

11. Hornaday, *Eighty Fascinating Years,* pp. 8, 9; Hornaday, *Extermination of the American Bison,* pp. 230, 231.

CHAPTER 4: SOUVENIR OF A LOST WORLD

1. Dolph, "Bringing Wildlife to Millions," p. 420; Hornaday, *Eighty Fascinating Years,* p. 10.

2. Hornaday, *Eighty Fascinating Years,* pp. 10–12; Hornaday, *Wild-Animal Round-Up,* pp. 11–14.

3. Hornaday, *Wild-Animal Round-Up,* pp. 282, 283.

4. Dolph, "Bringing Wildlife to Millions," pp. 429–31.

5. Ibid., p. 432.

CHAPTER 5: THE LAST BUFFALO HUNT

1. Hornaday, *Wild-Animal Round-Up,* p. 15.

2. Hornaday, *Eighty Fascinating Years,* chapter 10, p. 3.

3. Ibid., p. 5.

4. Hornaday, *Extermination of the American Bison,* pp. 467, 534; Hornaday,

memorandum, September 18, 1886, Official Incoming Correspondence, 1882–90, vol. H, 356, cited in Dolph, "Bringing Wildlife to Millions," p. 438.

5. Peterson, "Buffalo Hunting in Montana in 1886," pp. 2–13.

6. Hornaday, *Eighty Fascinating Years*, pp. 16, 17.

7. Hornaday, *Extermination of the American Bison*, p. 238.

8. Hornaday, *Eighty Fascinating Years*, p. 34.

9. Hornaday, *Journal of Trip No. 4*, Part II, October 20, 1886, cited in Dolph, "Bringing Wildlife to Millions," p. 447.

10. Hornaday, *Eighty Fascinating Years*, pp. 15, 16.

11. Dolph, "Bringing Wildlife to Millions," pp. 445, 446; Hornaday, *Eighty Fascinating Years*, p. 17.

12. Hornaday, Journal of Trip No. 4, Part II, October 14, 1886.

13. Hornaday, *Eighty Fascinating Years*, pp. 28–31.

14. Ibid., p. 32.

15. Ibid., p. 33.

16. "The Bad Winter," lyrics by Hermann Hagedorn; also Mitchell, "Winter of 1886–87," p. 3.

17. Garretson, *American Bison*, p. 193.

CHAPTER 6: A MYSTERIOUS STRANGER

1. Hornaday, *Extermination of the American Bison*, p. 252.

2. From Hornaday, *Two Years in the Jungle*, p. 491.

3. Bridges, *A Gathering of Animals*, p. 22.

4. "Vindication of America's Greatest," *Parks and Recreation*, February 1932; "Revolution in Taxidermy," *Commercial Advertiser* (NY), May 3, 1883.

5. This reconstruction of Hornaday's first meeting with Theodore Roosevelt is based on his account of this remarkable encounter in Hornaday, *Eighty Fascinating Years*, chapter 11, pp. 18, 19; another brief account occurs in Dolph, "Bringing Wildlife to the Millions," p. 467.

6. Hornaday, *Eighty Fascinating Years*, chapter 15, p 11.

7. Pringle, *Theodore Roosevelt*, p. 17; (nicknames) Morris, *Rise of Theodore Roosevelt*, p. 144.

8. Hornaday papers, Library of Congress, Box 1, folder marked 1909–1930.

9. Millard, *River of Doubt*, pp. 14–18.

10. TR diary entry, February 3, 1880, *American Memory*, Library of Congress website, memory.loc.gov.

11. TR diary entry, July 4, 1880, ibid.

12. Millard, *River of Doubt*, p. 17.

13. McCullough, *Mornings on Horseback*, p. 293.

14. TR diary entry, February 17, 1884, *American Memory*, Library of Congress website, memory.loc.gov.

15. Watts, *Rough Rider in the White House*.

16. "The Strenuous Life" is the name of a speech TR gave in Chicago, April 10, 1899, from Roosevelt, *The Strenuous Life*, p. 1.

17. "History," Theodore Roosevelt National Park Information Page, http://www.theodore.roosevelt.national-park.com.

18. Report of the U.S. National Museum, 1888 (Washington, D.C.: 1890), p. 60.

19. Hornaday, *Eighty Fascinating Years*, chapter 11, p. 19.

CHAPTER 7: "A NOBILITY BEYOND ALL COMPARE"

1. Dolph, "Bringing Wildlife to the Millions," p. 101.

2. Hornaday, *Extermination of the American Bison*, p. 30.

3. Ibid., pp. 215, 220, 221.

4. Ibid., p. 82.

5. Cody, *Adventures of Buffalo Bill Cody*, p. 111.

6. Hornaday, *Extermination of the American Bison*, p. 137.

7. Ibid., pp. 135–42; McHugh, *Time of the Buffalo*, pp. 258–64.

8. Rinella, *American Buffalo*, pp. 221–24.

9. Utley, *Indian Wars*, p. 144.

10. Isenberg, *Destruction of the Bison*, p. 103.

11. Hornaday, *Extermination of the American Bison*, p. 179.

12. All quotes from ibid., pp. 205–12.

13. Ibid., pp. 212, 213.

14. Hoyt-Goldsmith, *Buffalo Days*, p. 349.

15. Lott, *American Bison*, pp. 70–72.

16. Dodge, *Hunting Grounds of the Great West*, p. 116.

17. McHugh, *Time of the Buffalo*, pp. 13–17.

18. Dodge, *Hunting Grounds of the Great West*.

19. Ibid., p. 116.

20. Marder, *Indians in the Americas*, p. 6.

21. Hornaday, *Our Vanishing Wild Life*, p. x.

22. Hornaday, *Thirty Years War for Wild Life*, p. 1.

CHAPTER 8: EXPLORATIONS AND ADVENTURES
IN EQUATORIAL AFRICA

1. Dolph, "Bringing Wildlife to the Millions," p. 53; also Hornaday, *Eighty Fascinating Years*, chapter 3.

2. Dolph, "Bringing Wildlife to the Millions," p. 49.

3. Ibid., p. 54.

4. Ward, *Catalogue of Casts of Fossils*.

5. Dehler, "American Crusader," p. 38.

6. Dolph, "Bringing Wildlife to the Millions," pp. 4, 30.

7. Smith, *History of Dickinson County*, p. 378.

8. Dolph, "Bringing Wildlife to the Millions," p. 14.

9. Ibid., p. 15.

10. Ibid., p. 13.

11. Dehler, "American Crusader," p. 27.

12. Ibid., pp. 20, 29.

13. Hornaday, *Eighty Fascinating Years*, chapter 1, p. 13.

14. Ibid., chapter 2, p. 2.

15. Hornaday, *Evolution of a Zoologist*, p. 19.

16. Dehler, "American Crusader," p. 38.

17. Dolph, "Bringing Wildlife to the Millions," p. 33.

18. Hornaday, *Eighty Fascinating Years*, chapter 3, pp. 1–4.

19. Dolph, "Bringing Wildlife to the Millions," p. 39.

20. "Paul du Chaillu," *National Geographic* 14 (1903): 282–85.

21. Ibid., p. 283.

22. Du Chaillu, *Adventures in the Great Forest*, p. 53.

23. "Behind the Scenes: King Kong," *Stereotype & Society* blog, May 27, 2007, http://stereotypeandsociety.typepad.com.

24. Dolph, "Bringing Wildlife to the Millions," p. 55.

25. Hornaday, *Eighty Fascinating Years*, chapter 4, pp. 52–54.

26. Ibid., chapter 4, p. 2.

CHAPTER 9: YEARNING, TOO MUCH, FOR FAME

1. Hornaday letter to Ward, January 8, 1875, Hornaday papers, Library of Congress.

2. Hornaday, *Two Years in the Jungle*, chapter 1, p. 1.

3. Chester Jackson journal, pp. 6–7, cited in Dolph, "Bringing Wildlife to the Millions," p. 62.

4. Dehler, "American Crusader," pp. 43, 44.

5. Dolph, "Bringing Wildlife to the Millions," pp. 65, 66.

6. Hornaday, "The Crocodile in Florida," p. 320.

7. Grigg, "Morphology and Physiology of the Crocodylia," pp. 326–36.

8. *Bite Force*, Dangerous Encounters series, *National Geographic* documentary, dir. Brady Barr, 2007.

9. Dolph, "Bringing Wildlife to the Millions," p. 68.

10. Hornaday, *Hornaday's American Natural History*, p. 320; Dehler, "American Crusader," p. 45.

CHAPTER 10: THE EMPRESS JOSEPHINE

1. Dolph, "Bringing Wildlife to the Millions," p. 77.

2. Ibid., p. 79, from draft of *Eighty Fascinating Years*, Hornaday papers, Library of Congress, box 19, folder 7, pp. 2–4, and folder 9, p. 2.

3. Letter from Hornaday to Josephine Hornaday, Hornaday papers, Library of Congress, box 1, March 20, 1900.

4. Ibid., box 19, folder 9, pp. 3–4.

5. Dolph, "Bringing Wildlife to the Millions," p. 80.

6. Ibid., p. 138; Hornaday, *Two Years in the Jungle*, p. 491.

7. Chester Jackson journal, cited in Dolph, "Bringing Wildlife to the Millions," p. 82.

8. Ibid., p. 88.

9. "Canoe and Rifle on the Orinoco," *Youth's Companion* 59, March 19–April 16, 1885.

10. "Orinoco River," *New World Encyclopedia Online*, http://www.newworld encyclopedia.org/.

11. Hornaday, *Two Years in the Jungle*, p. 57.

12. Hornaday letter to Theodore Roosevelt, May 18, 1914, cited in Dehler, "American Crusader," p. 49.

13. Hornaday to Chester Jackson, December 15, 1876, cited in Dolph, "Bringing Wildlife to the Millions," p. 139.

CHAPTER II: MAN-EATERS OF THE ANIMALLAI HILLS

1. Modern atlases spell the name of the South India hills as "Anaimalai." Here, I use the spelling Hornaday used in his *Two Years in the Jungle*, "Animallai."

2. Hornaday, *Two Years in the Jungle*, p. 128; "Norfolk jacket" from photos of Hornaday dressed for hunting, in Hornaday, *Camp-Fires in the Canadian Rockies*, pp. 59, 83, 215.

3. A. J. Liebling, "The Great Gouamba," *New Yorker*, December 7, 1946, p. 88.

4. Hornaday, *Two Years in the Jungle*, p. 119.

5. Dolph, "Bringing Wildlife to the Millions," p. 139.

6. Hornaday, *Two Years in the Jungle*, p. 152.

7. Corbett, *Man-Eaters of Kumaon*, pp. 12, 16.

8. Headley, *H. M. Stanley's Wonderful Adventures*, p. 240.

9. Hornaday, *Two Years in the Jungle*, p. 174.

10. Letter dated June 25, 1877, Hornaday papers, Library of Congress, box 1, folder 1877–1900.

11. Hornaday letter to Jackson, October 18, 1877, cited in Dolph, "Bringing Wildlife to the Millions," p. 137.

12. Ibid.

13. Hornaday, *Two Years in the Jungle*, p. 474.

14. Ibid., p. 465.

15. Ibid., p. 156.

16. Dialogue section adapted from ibid.

17. Hornaday, *Two Years in the Jungle*, p. 158.

18. Dolph, "Bringing Wildlife to the Millions," pp. 183, 186.

CHAPTER 12: DARWIN'S FIRESTORM

1. *The Life and Letters of Thomas Henry Huxley*, D. Appleton & Co., 1902, vol. 1, 189.

2. Alfred Russel Wallace website, http://wallacefund.info/.

3. Barlow, *Autobiography of Charles Darwin*, p. 122.

4. Forbes, *In the Steps of the Great American Zoologist William Temple Hornaday*, p. 57.

5. Wallace website, http://wallacefund.info/.

6. Hornaday, *Two Years in the Jungle*, p. 420.

7. Ibid., p. 335.

8. Ibid.

9. Dolph, "Bringing Wildlife to the Millions," p. 237.

10. Hornaday, *Two Years in the Jungle*, p. 356.

11. Ibid., pp. 357, 465.

12. Letter to the *Literary Gazette*, October 12, 1855, in Wallace, *My Life*, p. 342.

13. Hornaday, *Two Years in the Jungle*, pp. 359–65.

14. Dialogue adapted from ibid.

15. Ibid., p. 408.

16. Dolph, "Bringing Wildlife to the Millions," p. 245.

17. Hornaday, *Two Years in the Jungle*, p. 405.

18. Ibid., p. 407.

19. Hornaday, "On the Species of Bornean Orangs, with Notes on Their Habits," pp. 438–55.

20. Twain, quoted in Sheldon, *Mark Twain*, chapter 9.

21. From foreword to Carnegie, *Autobiography of Andrew Carnegie*.

22. Carnegie, *Round the World*, p. 77.

23. *Beacon* (Boston), October 10, 1885.

24. Dehler, "American Crusader," p. 80.

25. Hornaday, *Two Years in the Jungle*, p. 488.

26. Hornaday letter to Jackson, December 2, 1879.

27. Hornaday, *Two Years in the Jungle*, dedication.

CHAPTER 13: "A THIEF IN THE NIGHT"

1. Hornaday, *Eighty Fascinating Years*, chapter 9, p. 1.

2. Kudos to Lawrence Bechtel for this insight.

3. From a 1931 letter to Rosalie Edge, quoted in Dehler, "American Crusader," p. 92.

4. Hornaday, *Eighty Fascinating Years*, chapter 9, p. 2.

5. "Spencer Fullerton Baird," *Encyclopedia Dickinsonian Online*, http://chronicles.dickinson.edu/.

6. Hornaday, *Eighty Fascinating Years*, chapter 9, p. 2.

7. Dolph, "Bringing Wildlife to the Millions," p. 570.

8. Cole, *German Carp in the United States*, pp. 543, 544; Ben Schley, "A Century of Fish Conservation" (1871–1971)," *Conservation History*, U.S. Fish & Wildlife Service, May 21, 2009.

9. Hornaday, *Eighty Fascinating Years*, chapter 9, pp. 3–5.

10. Dolph, "Bringing Wildlife to the Millions," p. 571.

11. Baker, *National Zoological Park*, p. 446.

12. Ibid., p. 575.

13. Wood, *The Origin of Public Bison Herds in the United States*, pp. 157–82; Hornaday, *Eighty Fascinating Years*, chapter 9, p. 5.

14. Neihardt, *Black Elk Speaks*, p. 33.

15. Hornaday, *Eighty Fascinating Years*, chapter 9, p. 5.

16. Ibid., chapter 9, p. 11.

17. "Samuel Pierpont Langley," *Flying Machines*, http://www.flyingmachines.org/.

18. Dehler, "American Crusader," p. 105.

19. *New York Public Opinion* op-ed, cited in *Report of the Smithsonian Institution*, 1888, p. 44.

20. Dolph, "Bringing Wildlife to the Millions," pp. 587–98.

21. Dehler, "American Crusader," p. 106.

22. Dolph, "Bringing Wildlife to the Millions," chapter 9, pp. 9–11.

23. Hornaday, *Eighty Fascinating Years*, chapter 9, p. 9.

24. Ibid., chapter 9, p. 11.

CHAPTER 14: A DREAM DEFERRED

1. Hornaday, *Eighty Fascinating Years*, chapter 9, p. 11.

2. Ibid., chapter 9, p. 12.

3. Ibid., chapter 9, p. 13.

4. Ibid., chapter 9, pp. 12–15.

5. Hornaday letter dated February 24, 1899, Hornaday papers, Library of Congress, box 1, folder 1877–1900.

6. Hornaday, *Eighty Fascinating Years*, chapter 9, p. 15.

7. Hornaday letter to Henry Fairfield Osborn, quoted in Bridges, *Gathering of Animals*, p. 24.

8. David O. Whitten, "The Depression of 1893," EH.net Encyclopedia, posted February 1, 2010, http://eh.net/encyclopedia/.

9. Dolph, "Bringing Wildlife to the Millions," p. 649.

10. Dehler, "American Crusader," p. 111.

CHAPTER 15: SCANDAL AT THE ZOO

1. "A Zoological Rivalry: The Many American Cities with Animal Collections," *New York Times*, August 30, 1896.

2. Dehler, "American Crusader," p. 117.

3. Larson, *Devil in the White City*.

4. Bridges, *Gathering of Animals*, p. 129.

5. Spiro, *Defending the Master Race*, p. 33.

6. Ibid., p. 33.

7. Rudyard Kipling, quoted in *New York Times*, May 8, 1892, cited in ibid., p. 32.

8. Dehler, "American Crusader," p. 113.

9. Larson, *Tyrannosaurus Rex*, p. 400.

10. Hornaday, *Wild-Animal Round-Up*, p. 349.

11. Dehler, "American Crusader," p. 123; Bridges, *Gathering of Animals*, p. 89.

12. Spiro, *Defending the Master Race*, p. 7.

13. Ibid., pp. 36, 37.

14. Ibid., p. 361.

15. Ibid., p. 39.

16. Hornaday, *Eighty Fascinating Years*.

17. Hornaday, *Wild-Animal Round-Up*, pp. 356–61.

18. Dehler, "American Crusader," p. 117.

19. Letter from Hornaday, October 2, 1896, Hornaday papers, Library of Congress, box 1, folder 1877–1900.

20. Letter from Hornaday about Burroughs, May 7, 1903, Hornaday papers, Library of Congress, box 1, folder 1877–1900.

21. Hornaday, *Wild-Animal Round-Up*, pp. 358–68.

22. Details of opening day from Bridges, *Gathering of Animals*, pp. 89–98.

23. Bridges, *Gathering of Animals*, p. 92.

24. Spiro, *Defending the Master Race*, p. 40.

25. Hornaday, *Wild-Animal Round-Up*, p. 354.

26. Bradford, *Ota*, pp. 4, 5.

27. Ibid., p. 12.

28. Spiro, *Defending the Master Race*, p. 49.

29. Bradford, *Ota*, 104–10.

30. Ibid., p. 120.

31. Ibid., pp. 127–35.

32. Ibid., p. 184.

33. Ibid., p. 177.

34. Ibid., pp. 172, 178.

35. Ibid., p. 177.

36. Hornaday letter to Josephine Hornaday, dated May 27, 1902, Hornaday papers, Library of Congress, box 2.

37. Ibid., pp. 177, 178; "An African Pigmy," p. 302.

38. "Bushman Shares a Cage with Bronx Park Apes," *New York Times*, September 9, 1906.

39. Bradford, *Ota*, p. 179.

40. "Man and the Monkey Show Disapproved by Clergy," *New York Times*, September 9, 1906.

41. *New York Times*, September 10, 1906.

42. Ibid.

43. Bradford, *Ota*, p. 183.

44. *New York Globe*, September 10, 1906.

45. Spiro, *Defending the Master Race*, pp. 46, 47.

46. Brinkley, *Wilderness Warrior*, p. 660.

47. Hornaday letter to Verner, in Bridges, *Gathering of Animals*, p. 227.

48. Comment by Mark Haller from *Eugenics: Hereditarian Attitudes in American Thought* (Piscataway, NJ: Rutgers University Press, 1963), quoted in Spiro, *Defending the Master Race*, p. iv.

49. Ibid., pp. 127, 130.

50. Ibid., p. 158.

51. Ibid., p. 97.

52. Hornaday, *Our Vanishing Wild Life*, p. 101.

53. Hornaday, *Wild-Animal Round-Up*, p. 27.

54. "Topic of the Times: Send Him Back to the Woods," *New York Times*, September 11, 1906.

55. *New York Evening Post*, September 10, 1906.

56. *Bridgeport (CT) Herald*, July 18, 1926; Hornaday, *Minds and Manners of Wild Animals*, p. 2.

57. *New York Times*, September 11, 1906.

58. *Bridgeport Herald*, July 18, 1926.

59. Bradford, *Ota*, p. 188.

60. Ibid., pp. 206–8.

61. Matthiesson, *African Silences*.

CHAPTER 16: THE DARK SHADOW

1. Kate Carew, "Kate Meets the 'Sultan of the Zoo,'" *New York World*, March 6, 1910.

2. Hornaday letter to Josephine Hornaday, Hornaday papers, Library of Congress, box 1, 1877–1900.

3. Jean Piper, "Zoo Man Convinced of Evolution Theory," *Brooklyn Daily Eagle*, April 5, 1925.

4. "W.T. Hornaday, 78 Today, Frets About the Rhino," *New York World-Telegram*, December 7, 1932.

5. Hornaday, *Eighty Fascinating Years*, chapter 20, p. 6.

6. Wilson, *Wilson's American Ornithology*, p. 358.

7. Hornaday, *Eighty Fascinating Years*, chapter 20, p. 6.

8. Duncan, *National Parks*, pp. 43–47.

9. Hornaday, *Eighty Fascinating Years*, chapter 20, p. 8.

10. Ibid.

11. Ibid., chapter 20, p. 5.

12. Letter from Hornaday to Charles Bessey, December 16, 1897, cited in Dehler, "American Crusader."

13. Hornaday, *Eighty Fascinating Years*, chapter 20, p. 5.

14. Ibid., chapter 20, p. 8.

15. Hornaday, *Destruction of Our Birds and Mammals*, p. 78.

16. Ibid., p. 77.

17. Hornaday, *Eighty Fascinating Years*, chapter 20, p. 9.

18. Hornaday, *Destruction of Our Birds and Mammals*, p. 81.

19. Ibid., pp. 87, 89.

20. Ibid., p. 94.

21. Ibid., pp. 87, 89.

22. Hornaday, *Our Vanishing Wild Life*, p. 226.

23. Bridges, *Gathering of Animals*, p. 272.

24. Ibid., pp. 272, 273.

25. Hornaday, "On the Destruction of Our Birds and Animals," p. 281.

26. Dehler, "American Crusader," p. 206.

27. Hornaday, *Eighty Fascinating Years*, chapter 20, p. 7.

28. Ibid, chapter 20, p. 8.

CHAPTER 17: EMPIRE OF THE BUFFALO

1. McHugh, *Time of the Buffalo*, pp. 3, 4; also Brinkley, *Wilderness Warrior*, pp. 626, 627.

2. Gwynne, *Empire of the Summer Moon*, p. 174.

3. Ibid., p. 177.

4. Ibid., p. 180.

5. Ibid., p. 264.

6. George Parker Winship, *The Coronado Expedition, 1540–1542* (Washington, D.C.: U.S. Government Printing Office, 1896) p. 581.

7. Bridges, *Gathering of Animals*, p. 332.

8. Ibid.

9. Dehler, "American Crusader," p. 197.

10. Bridges, *Gathering of Animals*, pp. 258, 259.

11. Ibid., p. 263.

12. Dehler, "American Crusader," p. 200.

13. Brinkley, *Wilderness Warrior*, p. 603.

14. *The Wichita Buffalo Range*, Tenth Annual Report of the New York Zoological Society, 1905, p. 200.

15. Erdoes, *American Indian Myths and Legends*, pp. 490, 491.

16. Brinkley, *Wilderness Warrior*, pp. 600–603.

17. Ibid., p. 581.

18. Ibid., pp. 595, 609, 611; Gwynne, *Empire of the Summer Moon*, 311.

19. Brinkley, *Wilderness Warrior*, pp. 624, 626.

20. "Wichita Mountains National Wildlife Refuge," *Encyclopedia of Oklahoma History and Culture*, http://digital.library.okstate.edu.

21. American Bison Society, http://www.americanbisonsocietyonline.org/.

22. "15 Buffalo to Go Back to the Ranges: Cowboy Rush Here to Take Part of the Zoo Back to Oklahoma," *New York Times*, October 6, 1907.

23. Dehler, "American Crusader," p. 190.

24. "Bison Preserves," *New York Times*, November 3, 1907.

25. Bridges, *Gathering of Animals*, p. 269.

26. Ibid., p. 257.

27. Duncan, *National Parks*, pp. 45–47.

28. Brinkley, *Wilderness Warrior*, p. 627.

CHAPTER 18: OUR VANISHING WILDLIFE

1. Hornaday, *Our Vanishing Wild Life*, p. 3.

2. Duncan, *National Parks*, p. 83.

3. Hornaday, *Thirty Years War for Wild Life*, p. 161.

4. Hornaday, *Our Vanishing Wild Life*, p. 114.

5. *Thirty Years War for Wild Life*, pp. 155–60; "Restricts Sale of Game: Gov. Dix Signs the Bayne Bill Protecting Native Wild Animals," *New York Times*, June 27, 1911.

6. Letter to Josephine Hornaday, dated simply "Thursday, 7:15 a.m. 1911," Hornaday papers, Library of Congress, box 1, folder 3.

7. Hornaday, *Thirty Years War for Wild Life*, p. 160.

8. *Henry Wood Elliot: Defender of the Fur Seal*, film by NOAA Ocean Media Center, 2005.

9. Hornaday, *Thirty Years War for Wild Life*, pp. 172–81.

10. Hornaday, *Our Vanishing Wild Life*, p. 5.

11. Doughty, *Feather Fashions and Bird Preservation*, p. 30.

12. Hornaday, *Our Vanishing Wild Life*, pp. 116, 117.

13. Ibid., p. 121.

14. Doughty, *Feather Fashions and Bird Preservation*, p. 128.

15. Ibid., p. 129.

16. Hornaday, *Thirty Years War for Wild Life*, p. 199.

17. Quoted in Doughty, *Feather Fashions and Bird Preservation*, p. 129.

18. Hornaday, *Steam Roller*.

19. Doughty, *Feather Fashions and Bird Preservation*, pp. 130–31.

20. Hornaday, *Thirty Years War for Wild Life*, p. 202.

21. Ibid., p. 266.

CHAPTER 19: TWO HUNDRED YEARS OF WAR

1. "Animal Man," *Time*, May 31, 1926; "Hornaday Retires as Director of Zoo," *New York Times*, May 21, 1926.

2. Bridges, *Gathering of Animals*, p. 116.

3. Ibid., pp. 116, 117.

4. Ibid., p. 410.

5. Hornaday papers, dated September 11, 1919, Library of Congress, box 1, September 1929.

6. Hornaday, *Thirty Years War for Wild Life*, p. 45.

7. Bridges, *Gathering of Animals*, p. 279.

8. Hornaday, *Eighty Fascinating Years*, chapter 20, p. 16.

9. Hornaday, *Thirty Years War for Wild Life*, p. 184.

10. *New York Times Magazine*, October 13, 1935, Hornaday papers, Library of Congress, box 101.

11. Bridges, *Gathering of Animals*, p. 287.

12. From *Columbus Dispatch*, quoted in "Alaska Big Game Endangered by Pot-Hunters and Wolves," *Literary Digest* 65 (May 8, 1920): 92.

13. Hornaday, *Thirty Years War for Wild Life*, pp. 187–91.

14. Ibid., p. 191.

15. Hornaday, *Eighty Fascinating Years*, chapter 20, p. 13.

16. Hornaday, *Thirty Years War for Wild Life*, p. xi.

17. Ibid., p. 1.

18. Ibid., p. 8.

19. Ibid., p. 8.

EPILOGUE: HIS INDOMITABLE PERSISTENCE

1. Letter to FDR, Hornaday papers, Library of Congress, Box H, correspondence 1930–1937.

2. Quotes from *Life*, January 4, 1937.

3. From a letter to Hornaday's nephew Willis, dated September 2, 1936, Hornaday papers, Library of Congress.

4. Ishbel Ross, "Hornaday Wed 50 Years; Pays Tribute to Wife," *New York Tribune*, September 12, 1929.

5. Hornaday letter to Edmund Seymour, November 11, 1932, archives of American Bison Society, box 2.

6. Dehler, "American Crusader," p. 373.

7. Letter to FDR.

8. Letter from FDR to Hornaday, Hornaday papers, Library of Congress, box H, correspondence 1930–1937.

9. Letter to Dodge, ibid.

10. "Mount Hornaday," *Wikipedia*, http://en.wikipedia.org/.

11. Hornaday papers, Library of Congress, box 10, general correspondence, Mo—My; "Ichthyology," *Journal of the Washington Academy of Sciences* 26, no. 9 (September 15, 1936): 376–77; Hornaday, *Two Years in the Jungle*, p. 386.

12. Graham, *Man's Dominion*, p. 179.

13. Hornaday, *Thirty Years War for Wild Life*, p. iv.

14. Wildlife Conservation Society website, http://www.wcs.org/.

15. "American Bison," *Wikipedia*, http://en.wikipedia.org/.

16. "NOAA Reports Northern Fur Seal Pup Estimate Decline," NOAA website, http://www.noaanews.noaa.gov/.

17. "Snowy Egret Biological Status Review Report," Florida Fish and Wildlife Conservation Commission, March 31, 2011.

BIBLIOGRAPHY

BOOKS (PUBLISHED SOURCES)

Athearn, Robert G. *William Tecumseh Sherman and the Settlement of the West.* Norman: University of Oklahoma Press, 1956.

Baker, Frank. *The National Zoological Park and Its Inhabitants.* Washington, D.C.: Smithsonian Institution Board of Regents, 1915.

Barlow, Nora, ed. *The Autobiography of Charles Darwin, 1809 – 1882.* New York: Collins, 1958.

Bradford, Phillips Verner, and Harvey Blume. *Ota: The Pygmy in the Zoo.* New York: St. Martin's Press, 1992.

Bridges, William. *A Gathering of Animals: An Unconventional History of the New York Zoological Society.* New York: Harper & Row, 1974.

Brinkley, Douglas. *The Wilderness Warrior: Theodore Roosevelt and the Crusade for America.* New York: HarperCollins, 2009.

Brown, Mark H. *The Plainsmen of the Yellowstone.* Lincoln: University of Nebraska Press, 1961.

Busch, Briton Cooper. *The War against the Seals: A History of the North American Seal Industry.* Montreal: McGill-McQueen University Press, 1983.

Carnegie, Andrew. *The Autobiography of Andrew Carnegie.* Boston: Northeastern University Press, 1986 (orig. pub. 1920).

____. *Round the World.* Teddington, UK: Echo Library, 2007 (orig. pub. 1884).

Chapman, Frank M. *Autobiography of a Bird-Lover.* New York: D. Appleton-Century Co., 1933.

Clark, Fiona. *Hats.* New York: Drama Book Publishers, 1982.

Cody, Col. William F. *The Adventures of Buffalo Bill Cody,* 1st ed. New York: Harper & Brothers, 1904.

Connell, Evan S. *Son of the Morning Star: Custer and the Little Bighorn*. New York: Harper & Row, 1984.

Corbett, Jim. *Man-Eaters of Kumaon*. Oxford, UK: Oxford University Press, 1946.

Dary, David A. *The Buffalo Book: The Full Saga of the American Animal*. Athens, OH: Swallow Press/University of Ohio Press, 1974.

Davis, Jack E. *An Everglades Providence: Marjory Stoneman Douglas and the American Environmental Century*. Athens: University of Georgia Press, 2009.

De Courtais, Georgine. *Women's Headdress and Hairstyles*. London: B. T. Batsford, Ltd., 1973.

DiSilvestro, Roger L. *Theodore Roosevelt in the Badlands*. New York: Walker & Company, 2011.

Dodge, Richard Irving. *The Hunting Grounds of the Great West: A Description of the Plains, Game and Indians of the Great North American Desert*. London: Chatto & Windus, 1877.

———. *The Plains of the Great West and Their Inhabitants* (1877). Ann Arbor, MI: Archer House, 1959.

Doughty, Robin. *Feather Fashions and Bird Preservation: A Study of Nature Protection*. Berkeley: University of California Press, 1975.

Douglas, Marjory Stoneman. *Nine Florida Stories*. Jacksonville: University of North Florida Press, 1990.

Du Chaillu, Paul B. *Adventures in the Great Forest of Equatorial Africa and the Country of the Dwarfs*. New York: Harper & Brothers, 1890.

———. *A Journey Into Ashango-Land, And Further Penetration Into Equatorial Africa*. New York: Harper & Bros., 1871.

Duncan, Dayton, and Ken Burns. *The National Parks: America's Best Idea*. New York: Alfred A. Knopf, 2009.

Dunlap, Thomas. *Saving America's Wildlife*. Princeton, NJ: Princeton University Press, 1988.

Erdoes, Richard, and Alfonzo Ortiz. *American Indian Myths and Legends*. New York: Pantheon, 1984.

Forbes, John Ripley. *William Temple Hornaday: In the Steps of the Great American Zoologist*. New York: M. Evans & Co., 1966.

Gard, Wayne. *The Great Buffalo Hunt*. New York: Alfred A. Knopf, 1960.

Garretson, Martin. *The American Bison*. New York: New York Zoological Society, 1938.

Geist, Valerius. *Buffalo Nation: History and Legend of the North American Bison*. Markham, Ont.: Fifth House, 1996.

Graham, Frank, Jr. *The Audubon Ark: A History of the National Audubon Society*. New York: Alfred A. Knopf, 1990.

——. *Man's Dominion: The Story of Conservation in America.* New York: J.B. Lippincott Co., 1971.

Grinnell, George Bird. *Hunting and Conservation.* New Haven, CT: Yale University Press, 1925.

——. *The Last of the Buffalo.* New York: Charles Scribner's & Sons, 1892.

Gwynne, S.C. *Empire of the Summer Moon: Quanah Parker and the Rise and Fall of the Comanches, the Most Powerful Indian Tribe in American History.* New York: Scribner, 2010.

Headley, Hon. J.T., and William Fletcher Johnson. *H.M. Stanley's Wonderful Adventures in Africa.* New York: Excelsior Publishing Co., 1890.

Hine, Robert V., and Faragher, John Mack. *The American West: A New Interpretive History.* New Haven, CT: Yale University Press, 2000.

Hornaday, William T. *Camp-Fires in the Canadian Rockies.* New York: Charles Scribner's Sons, 1906.

——. *Campfires on Desert and Lava.* New York: Charles Scribner's Sons, 1908.

——. *The Extermination of the American Bison* (1889). Washington, D.C.: Smithsonian Institution Press, 2000.

——. *Free Rum on the Congo, and What It Is Doing There.* Chicago: Women's Temperance Publication Association, 1887.

——. *Hornaday's American Natural History,* 15th ed. New York: Charles Scribner's Sons, 1927.

——. *The Man Who Became a Savage, A Story of Our Time.* Buffalo, NY: Peter Paul Book Company, 1896.

——. *Migratory Waterfowl Abandoned to Their Fate.* Stamford, CT: Permanent Wild Life Protection Fund, 1937.

——. *The Minds and Manners of Wild Animals: A Book of Personal Observations.* New York: Charles Scribner's Sons, 1922

——. *Our Vanishing Wild Life: Its Extermination and Preservation.* New York: New York Zoological Society, 1913.

——. *Taxidermy and Zoological Collecting.* New York: Charles Scribner's Sons, 1891.

——. *Thirty Years War for Wild Life: Gains and Losses in the Thankless Task.* New York: Charles Scribner's Sons, 1931.

——. *Two Years in the Jungle: The Experiences of a Hunter and Naturalist in India, Ceylon, the Malay Penninsula, and Borneo.* New York: Charles Scribner's Sons, 1885

——. *Use and Abuse of America's Natural Resources: Wild Life Conservation in Theory and Practice.* New Haven, CT: Yale University Press, 1914.

——. *A Wild-Animal Round-Up.* New York: Charles Scribner's Sons, 1925.

Hoyt-Goldsmith, Diane. *Buffalo Days.* New York: Holiday House, 1997.

Huxley, Thomas Henry. *The Life and Letters of Thomas Henry Huxley,* vol. 1. New York: D. Appleton & Co., 1902.

Isenberg, Andrew C. *The Destruction of the Buffalo: An Environmental History.* Cambridge, UK: Cambridge University Press, 2000.

Larson, Erik. *The Devil in the White City.* New York: Random House, 2003.

Larson, Peter L., and Kenneth Carpenter. *Tyrannosaurus Rex: The Tyrant King.* Bloomington: Indiana University Press, 2008.

Lazarus, Edward. *Black Hills White Justice: The Sioux Nation versus the United States, 1775 to the Present.* New York: HarperCollins, 1991.

Lewis, Lloyd. *Sherman, Fighting Prophet.* Lincoln: University of Nebraska Press, 1993.

Lott, Dale F. *American Bison: A Natural History.* Berkeley: University of California Press, 2002.

Marder, William. *Indians in the Americas: The Untold Story.* San Diego: Book Tree, 2005.

Marszalek, John F. *Sherman: A Soldier's Passion for Order.* New York: Free Press, 1993.

Matthiessen, Peter. *African Silences.* New York: Vintage Books, 1992.

McCullough, David. *Mornings on Horseback: The Story of an Extraordinary Family, a Vanished Way of Life, and the Unique Child Who Became Theodore Roosevelt.* New York: Simon & Schuster, 2001.

McHugh, Tom. *The Time of the Buffalo.* New York: Alfred A. Knopf, 1972.

McIver, Stuart B. *Death in the Everglades: The Murder of Guy Bradley, America's First Martyr to Environmentalism.* Gainesville: University Press of Florida, 2003.

McLynn, Frank. *Stanley: The Making of an African Explorer.* Chelsea, MI: Scarborough House, 1990.

Meine, Curt D. *Aldo Leopold: His Life and Work.* Madison: University of Wisconsin Press, 2010.

Millard, Candice. *The River of Doubt: Theodore Roosevelt's Darkest Journey.* New York: Broadway Books, 2005.

Milner, Clyde A., II, et al., eds. *The Oxford History of the American West.* New York: Oxford University Press, 1994.

Mitchell, Lee Clark. *Witnesses to a Vanishing America: The Nineteenth Century Response.* Princeton, NJ: Princeton University Press, 1966.

Morris, Edmund. *The Rise of Theodore Roosevelt.* New York: Random House, 2010.

Neihardt, John C. *Black Elk Speaks.* New York: Pocket Books, 1959.

Pringle, Henry Fowles. *Theodore Roosevelt: A Biography.* New York: Kessinger Publishing, 1931.

Punke, Michael. *Last Stand: George Bird Grinnell, the Battle to Save the Buffalo, and the Birth of the New West.* Washington, D.C.: Smithsonian Books, 2007.

Putnam, Carleton. *Theodore Roosevelt: The Formative Years, 1858–1886.* New York: Charles Scribner's Sons, 1958.

Rauzon, Mark J. *Isles of Refuge: Wildlife and History of the Northwestern Hawaiian Islands.* Honolulu: University of Hawaii Press, 2001.

Reiger, John F. *American Sportsmen and the Origins of Conservation.* Winchester, Ont.: Winchester Press, 1975.

Rinella, Steven. *American Buffalo: In Search of a Lost Icon.* New York: Spiegel & Grau, 2009.

Roe, Frank Gilbert. *The North American Buffalo: A Critical Study of the Species in Its Wild State.* Toronto: University of Toronto Press, 1951.

Roosevelt, Theodore. *The Strenuous Life: Essays and Addresses.* New York: The Century Co., 1900.

——. *Theodore Roosevelt: An Autobiography* (1913). Cambridge, Mass: Da Capo Press, 1985.

Runciman, Steven. *The White Rajahs, a History of Sarawak from 1841 to 1846.* Cambridge, UK: Cambridge University Press, 1960.

Sandoz, Marie. *The Buffalo Hunters.* Lincoln: University of Nebraska Press, 1954.

Schorger, A. W. *The Passenger Pigeon: Its Natural History and Extinction* (1955). Norman: University of Oklahoma Press, 1973.

Sheldon, Michael. *Mark Twain: Man in White: The Grand Adventure of His Final Years.* New York: Random House, 2010.

Smith, Roderick A. *A History of Dickinson County, Together with an Account of the Spirit Lake Massacre, and the Indian Troubles of the Northwestern Frontier.* Topeka, KS: Kenyon Printing & Mfg. Co., 1902.

Sommer, Charles Henry. *Quanah Parker, Last Chief of the Comanches: A Brief Sketch.* Self-published, 1945.

Spiro, Jonathan Peter. *Defending the Master Race: Conservation, Eugenics, and the Legacy of Madison Grant.* Burlington: University of Vermont Press, 2009.

Tober, James. *Who Owns the Wildlife? The Political Economy of Conservation in Nineteenth-Century America.* Westport, CT: Greenwood Press, 1981.

Trefethan, James B. *Crusade for Wildlife: Highlights In Conservation Progress.* Mechanicsburg, PA: Stackpole Co. and the Boone and Crockett Club, 1961.

Trudeau, Noah Andre. *Southern Storm: Sherman's March to the Sea.* New York: Harper Perennial, 2008.

Utley, Robert M., and Wilcomb E. Washburn. *Indian Wars.* Boston: Houghton Mifflin, 2002.

Wallace, Alfred Russel. *The Malay Archipelago.* New York: Harper and Brothers, 1869.

——. *My Life: A Record of Events and Opinions.* Vol. 1. New York: Dodd, Mead & Co., 1905.

Ward, Henry Augustus. *Catalogue of Casts of Fossils from the Principal Museums of Europe and America*. Rochester, NY: Benton & Andrews, 1866.

Watts, Sarah. *Rough Rider in the White House: Theodore Roosevelt and the Politics of Desire*. Chicago: University of Chicago Press, 2003.

Wilbanks, William. *Forgotten Heroes: Police Officers Killed in Early Florida, 1840–1925*. New York: Turner Publishing, 1998.

Wilson, Alexander. *Wilson's American Ornithology*. New York: T. L. Magagnos & Co., 1840.

ARTICLES AND DISSERTATIONS (INCLUDES UNPUBLISHED SOURCES)

Bruckner, Zoltan. "For a Balanced View of the American Indian." *Institute for Historical Review* 18, no. 2 (March/April 1999).

Coffman, Douglas. "William Hornaday's Bitter Mission: The Mysterious Journey of the Last Wild Bison." *Montana*, February 1991, pp. 58–71.

Cole, Leon J. "The German Carp in the United States." *Appendix to the Report of the Commissioner of Fisheries*, Government Printing Office, 1905.

Dehler, Gregory J. "An American Crusader: William Temple Hornaday and Wildlife Protection in America, 1840–1940." PhD diss., Lehigh University, 2001.

Dolph, James Andrew. "Bringing Wildlife to Millions: William Temple Hornaday, The Early Years: 1854–1896." PhD diss., University of Massachusetts, 1975.

Florida Fish and Wildlife Conservation Commission. *Snowy Egret Biological Status Review Report*, March 31, 2011.

Franzen, Jonathan. "Emptying the Skies." *New Yorker*, July 26, 2010.

Grigg, Gordon, and Carl Gans. "Morphology and Physiology of the Crocodylia." In *Fauna of Australia*, vol. 2A, *Amphibia and Reptilia*, chapter 40, pp. 326–36. Canberra: Australian Government Publishing Service, 1993.

Hornaday, Josephine Chamberlain. "No Shelter at Transfer Points." *New York Times*, letter to the editor, January 4, 1903.

Hornaday, W. T. "An African Pigmy." *New York Zoological Society Bulletin* 23, no. 302 (1906).

———. "The Crocodile in Florida." *American Naturalist*, September 1875.

———. "On the Destruction of Birds and Mammals." *Auk* 15 (1898): 280.

———. "The Destruction of Our Birds and Mammals: A Report on the Results of an Inquiry." *Annual Report of the New York Zoological Society* 2 (1898): 77.

———. *Eighty Fascinating Years* (unpublished autobiography). Hornaday papers, Library of Congress, 1938.

———. "The Evolution of a Zoologist." Hornaday papers, Library of Congress.

———. "The Founding of the Wichita National Bison Herd." *Bulletin of the American Bison Society* (1907): 412.

——. "On the Species of Bornean Orangs, with Notes on Their Habits." *Proceedings of the American Association for the Advancement of Science* 28 (1879): 438–55.

——. "The Steam Roller Of The Feather Importers In The United States Senate: The Lobby Of The Feather Trade Jubilant, Thus Far: A Warning To The American People." Pamphlet, 1913.

——. "Suicide of Ota Benga, the African Pygmy." *Zoological Society Bulletin* 19, no. 3 (1916): 1356.

Horowitz, Helen. "The National Zoological Park: 'City of Refuge' or Zoo?" Records of the Columbia Historical Society (Washington, D.C., 1973–74), pp. 405–29 (from a larger history of American zoos undertaken when the author was a fellow in American and cultural history at the Smithsonian Institution).

Mergen, Alexa. "From Bison to Biopark: 100 Years of the National Zoo." Friends of the National Zoo, 1989.

Meyers, George S. "A New Polynemid Fish Collected in the Sadong River, Sarawak, by Dr. William T. Hornaday." *Journal of the Washington Academy of Sciences* 26, no. 9 (September 15, 1936): 376, 377.

Mitchell, John E., and Richard H. Hart. "Winter of 1886–87: The Death Knell of Open Range." *Rangelands* 9, no. 1 (February 1987): 3–8.

Oldys, Henry. "Scarcity Forces America to Protect Its Game." *New York Times*, September 3, 1911.

Peterson, John M. "Buffalo Hunting in Montana in 1886: The Diary of W. Harvey Brown, Montana." *Journal of Western History* 31, no. 4 (Autumn 1981): 2–13.

——. "W. Harvey Brown and K.U.'s First Buffaloes." *Kansas History: A Journal of the Central Plains* 4, no. 4 (Winter 1981): 219–26.

Rauzon, Mark J. "The Diaries of Max Schlemmer from Laysan Island 1905–1907." *Journal of the Hawaiian Audubon Society* 70, no. 4 (May 2010): 25–29.

"Restricts Sale of Game: Gov. Dix Signs the Bayne Bill Protecting Native Wild Animals." *New York Times*, June 27, 1911.

Shell, Hanna Rose. "Skin Deep: Taxidermy, Embodiment, and Extinction in W. T. Hornaday's Buffalo Group." *Proceedings of the California Academy of Sciences* 55, supp. 1, no. 5 (October 18, 2004): 88–112.

Van Nostrand, Jeanne. "The Seals Are About Gone . . ." *American Heritage*, June 1963, pp. 11–19.

Wood, Judith Hebbring. "The Origin of Public Bison Herds in the United States." *Wicazo Sa Review* 15, no. 1 (Spring 2000): 157–82.

INDEX